Developmental
MANAGEMENT

ORGANIZING GENIUS

Developmental Management
General Editor: Ronnie Lessem

Charting the Corporate Mind
*Charles Hampden-Turner**

Managing in the Information Society
Yoneji Masuda

Developmental Management
Ronnie Lessem

Foundations of Business
Ivan Alexander

Greening Business
John Davis

Ford on Management
*Henry Ford**

Managing Yourself
Jagdish Parikh

Managing the Developing Organization
Bernard Lievegoed

Conceptual Toolmaking
Jerry Rhodes

Integrative Management
Pauline Graham

Total Quality Learning
Ronnie Lessem

Executive Leadership
Elliott Jaques and Stephen D. Clement

Transcultural Management
Albert Koopman

The Great European Illusion
Alain Minc

The Rise of NEC
Koji Kobayashi

Organizing Genius
Paul Thorne

European Strategic Alliances
Sabine Urban and Serge Vendemini

* For copyright reasons this edition is not available in the USA

Organizing Genius

THE PURSUIT OF CORPORATE CREATIVITY

PAUL THORNE

First published 1992

Blackwell Publishers
108 Cowley Road
Oxford   OX4 1JF
UK

238 Main Street, Suite 501
Cambridge, Massachusetts 02142
USA

British Library Cataloguing in Publication Data
A CIP catalogue record for this book is available from the British Library.

Library of Congress Cataloging-in-Publication Data
Thorne, Paul.
Organizing genius: the pursuit of corporate creativity / Paul
Thorne.
p.   cm. — (Developmental management)
Includes index.
1. Executive ability.   2. Creativity in business.   I. Title.
II. Series.
HG38.2.T49   1992
658.4'09—dc20
ISBN 0–631–16959–8

Typeset in 11 on 13pt Ehrhardt
by Hope Services (Abingdon) Ltd.
Printed in Great Britain by
T.J. Press (Padstow) Ltd, Padstow, Cornwall.
This book is printed on acid-free paper

Contents

List of Figures

Foreword

In the Beginning

With Paul Thorne's book, *Organizing Genius*, the Developmental Management series has come of age, in the process returning full circle to Great Britain. True to series form, Thorne is a practising manager, somewhat avant-garde, with a particular and in this case Anglo-Saxon axe to grind, albeit within a global context. His role has been to trace a path from the freely enterprising company to the creatively learning organization. In the 1970s the search began in earnest, certainly within Europe, for new styles of management. Rational management, both of the autocratic and of the democratic kind, had been discredited, with the result that entrepreneurs and so-called 'intrapreneurs' came to rule the roost. Tom Peters' search, and subsequent passion, for excellence[1] set the managerial mould for a good decade to follow. There was only one twist in this enterprising tale. The Japanese had been stealing a march on the Anglo-Saxons during the seventies, and their approach was anything but entrepreneurial. In other words, at the very same time as what I have termed 'primal' virtues (back to basics) were being extolled, the subtle and, in our term, 'developmental' Japanese were advancing apace.

Faced by such a paradoxical turn of events, we decided to create a series that both challenged the emerging Anglo-Saxon orthodoxy, historically and geographically, and served to renew it. Thus the first book, Ivan Alexander's *Foundations of Business*, set business within the historical context of an emergent Europe over the past few hundred years. From the outset, therefore, and long before 1992 was on the EEC horizons, we placed the European continent in a central business position. In other words, notwithstanding entrepreneurship and excellence, we felt that more was coming. Secondly, again contrary to the prevailing trend whereby American business consultants were blazing the new trails, we looked for practising businessmen – like Alexander – and managers, to set our scene.

Having laid the primarily European business foundations for the series, we looked to Japan, and thereby to futurologist Yoneji Masuda, to introduce us to *Managing in the Information Society*. After all, it was the Japanese who had been demonstrably more successful than any other country in doing just that. At the same time, and unlike Tom Peters, we felt that rational management had not yet had its day, and what better book than *Ford on Management* to remind us of that? Against the autocratic though inspirational perspective of Fordism we placed the democratic Anglo-American Charles Hampden-Turner, who had been engaged in *Charting the Corporate Mind*. My own role, then, in the context of my book *Developmental Management*, was to introduce the reader to management across the globe, feeling in my bones that its day would one day come even to southern Africa – from whence I originated. I also happened to be the only presiding academic within the series. Moreover, unlike Alexander in Switzerland, Masuda in Japan and Ford in America, I was based in England.

Enlarging the Developmental Frame

As our developmental theme was only beginning to be established, we felt it opportune, for the second group of series books, to bring the venerable Dutch management thinker Bernard Lievegoed into the fold. For in *Managing the Developing Organization*, he was setting his subject in the historically and culturally Germanic contexts of Goethe and Steiner. Needless to say, by 1990, Germany stood alongside Japan as the most eminently successful of the global economies. In fact while Japan, with its oriental culture, had taken the developmental lead from a global perspective, Germany – inheritor of Hegelian dialectics – had done so from a European point of view. Alongside Lievegoed we positioned John Davis' *Greening Business*, to provide an ecological context for the interdependent, developmental *Weltanschauung* we were following. While Jerry Rhodes' *Conceptual Toolmaking* re-rooted the series in the information age, Indian executive and management educator extraordinaire Jagdish Parikh not only broadened our oriental exposure but, in *Managing Your Self* introduced us to 'doing business in the new paradigm'.

View from the Developmental Bridge

By 1990 I was aware that our geogaphical spread was still somewhat thin. West and East seemed to predominate over North and South. For that reason we encouraged Albert Koopman, South Africa's lone business visionary, to describe his approach to *Transcultural Management*, and Elliott Jaques, who embodied the rationality of the North, to articulate his unique approach to 'requisite organization' via *Executive Leadership*. Meanwhile Pauline Graham brought her Latin passion to bear upon *Integrative Management*, being Egyptian and Spanish in her particular heritage, though operating as a manager in Britain and basing her ideas on the work of the American Mary Parker-Follet. Finally, my own book, *Total Quality Learning*, represented an attempt to bring our classical Greek heritage into the developmental fold, albeit with a strong admixture of Anglo-Indian thinking.

Redressing the Balance

By 1991, with twelve books in the series, we felt a slight unease – despite the predominance of practising managers among our authors – that theory was racing ahead of practice. Revisiting Japan, we invited NEC's chairman Koji Kobayashi to re-chart for us *The Rise of NEC*, and within Europe we published French busunessman Alain Minc's *The Great European Illusion*, thereby advancing the European economic debate beyond the EC. Finally, being well aware of the proliferation of joint ventures across the globe we invited Professor Urban of the University of Strasbourg, to write *Strategic Alliances*. It was with the advent of Paul Thorne's *Organizing Genius*, though, that I began to discern much more clearly the overall series pattern.

Re-viewing the Businessphere

Robert Reich, Professor of Government at Harvard University and author of the recently much acclaimed *Work of Nations*,[2] has argued that as we enter a combined global information age, the traditional factors of production are being transformed. Land, labour, capital and enterprise are being displaced by experimentation, abstraction, systems thinking and collaboration.

These approaches are most particularly embodied – in my own terms[3] – in the South and North, East and West, respectively. Active experimentation is characteristically Anglo-Saxon or Western; thoughtful abstraction is quintessentially European or Northern; a systemic worldview emerges most naturally out of an Eastern perspective; and a communal or collaborative one out of a Southern culture.

Charting the Corporate Mind
Conceptual Toolmaking
Executive Leadership

Abstraction

The European Illusion
Ford on Management   *Developmental Management*
Strategic Alliances
Managing the Developing Organization

Organizing Genius
Foundations of business

W   **Experimentation**   **Systems Thinking**   E

Genius
Greening Business

Total Quality Learning   *Managing Your Self*
The Rise of NEC
Managing in the Information Society

Collaboration
Integrative Management
Transcultural Management

Figure 1   The Developing Business Sphere

Organizing Genius

Paul Thorne, as a Westerner, has in fact continued on from where Adam Smith and Samuel Smiles left off. He has transformed the traditional notions of free enterprise and self-help into his contemporary idea of 'organized genius'. In that sense he is not only keeping up with the information age, but is also combining invention and entrepreneurship, design and creativity, ingenuity and genius in a unique way. Rather than separating out the process of creativity from both the creative enterprise and the organization, which is usually the case, Thorne has brought them together.

Unlike so many of our current management thinkers, who combine innovation, entrepreneurship and change in one messy melting-pot, Thorne establishes his case along two distinct continua:

- in creative attribution from Adaptor to Innovator to Prodigy to Genius;

- in creative purpose from Pure to Applied Research and Development, and from Commercial Development to Organizational Enhancement.

Moreover, starting his book in Britain, drawing on such genius as that of The Body Shop's Anita Roddick, and Virgin's Richard Branson, he continues his journey in America and then Japan, as well as into Europe. In so doing he spans individual and organization, business and environment, small-scale enterprise and multinational corporation, covering a vast expanse of ongoing experimentation. In the process he sets a path along which the faltering Anglo-Saxon economies of the 1990s would do well to follow.

The Heroic Journey

The individual path that Thorne has most closely followed, in this book, is that of Sir James Black. I first came across Black in the mid-eighties when I was doing the interviewing for my first book, *The Roots of Excellence*.[4] I can remember, to this day, sitting in the office of the deputy director of ICI Pharmaceuticals, in the north of England, accompanied also by the director of research. Before I could say a word they proclaimed, in unison, 'There's someone else who is very much part of us, and you should be able to picture him in your mind's eye. His name is Jimmy Black.'

Although Sir James had left ICI some years before, he had made such an impact on the company that his spirit had lived on, even if physically he was many miles away. Black had invented beta-blockers, the treatment for heart condition that has earned ICI millions of pounds. His impact on the pharmaceutical business has been legendary. Yet, as Thorne points out here, it is not easy to organize genius. Sir James is inevitably difficult to 'manage', as are all such creative people. Yet, unless a way can be found to do so successfully, the European business world in particular will have no future. For its greatest resource is the individual, and his or her natural inclination is to experiment. The process of abstraction, systems thinking and collaboration follow individual ingenuity in a way that generally distinguishes the Anglo-Saxons from other parts of the business world.

That being said, such individuality can also be carried to excess. Its organization is consequently a delicate task. Thorne has developed a distinctive framework for conceiving of such an endeavour, incorporating guidance, mediation, security and more give than take. In his own words:

> Managers of creative people need to believe that they are themselves creative. They have to have the capacity to admire without fear or envy. They have to be personally secure. At times, when relationships are turbulent, they become fragile. In the successful manager, this does not last long, Managers have to be able to give and take and to guide and accept each at the right time. Complete freedom kills creativity. Creative people need something to kick at, to fight for. The most important contribution a manager of creative people can make is to mediate, to champion the product of creativity. But the manager must also be the critic, must be smart enough to judge where he is championing a dog, and he must be able to say no in a way which does not create breakages.[5]

As the West evolves, then, from a world of free enterprise to the birthplace of the learning company, a means must be found of organizing individual genius. Paul Thorne has made a major contribution to such a learningful outcome, revealing its structure and function not only in Britain and America, but also, though to a lesser extext, in Germany and Japan.

Ronnie Lessem

Notes

1 Thomas J. Peters and Robert H. Waterman, *In Search of Excellence: Lessons for America's Best-Run Companies* (Harper & Row, London, 1982).
2 Robert Reich, *The Work of Nations: Preparing Ourselves for 21st-Century Capitalism* (Simon & Schuster, London, 1991).
3 Ronnie Lessem, *Global Management Principles* (Prentice Hall, 1989).
4 Ronnie Lessem, *The Roots of Excellence* (Collins Fontana, London, 1985).
5 Paul Thorne, *Organizing Genius*, p. xix.

Preface

If this were the story of one man, I would not tell it. For what is one man that he should make much of his winters even though they bend him with a heavy snow.

Black Elk

The first few years of my working life were in academic, market, motivational, operational and management research. It was as an internal consultant with EMI Electronics that I was first confronted by an organization that offered both the best and worst lessons on how to organize genius. At the company's Hayes headquarters there is a history of continuous innovation stretching back through wooden fighting planes, radio, radar, commercial analogue computers, and colour television. There were the country's experts in electronic pattern recognition and body scanning, in telemetry and many other areas which I remain unable to reveal because of the Official Secrets Act. The culture was of free-wheeling chaos. Groups of engineers and research scientists waxed and waned as their results proved competitive or offered a bellic or commercial advantage, or failed to reveal either. To an outsider, EMI's management was a magical process of seamless consensus. Dramatic movements of people and places happened without apparent warning, even over weekends.

Long-term revenue from Ministry of Defence weapons research and development work was guaranteed. Short-term cash was piling in from the sister company up the road from its immense sales of records. Those were the days of cost-plus contracts and The Beatles at their peak. From my first few weeks with EMI until today, I have been caught up with the fascination of the behaviour of the creative individual operating inside the big organization, sometimes observing dispassionately, but more often deeply involved in the battles of wits and wills which contribute most of the traffic between the two.

In 1983, I was introduced to Sir James Black at The Wellcome Foundation in Beckenham, Kent. Here was a man convinced that creativity and large organizations were intrinsically at odds, with each other. James Black has always been a man of strong views but yet always prepared to offer them up for reasoned debate. With my encouragement we applied our collective experience and understanding of organizational issues and technology to his group of 250 research and support staff who made up the Therapeutic Research Division (TRD). It was a division with a long history of relative failure, described as the most devotedly academic unit of the University of Beckenham. It was politically lively, to say the least, a place where egos and reputations were constantly at odds. Black had worked for ICI and Smith Kline. He had given birth to two of the most commercially successful drugs in history. He was high profile. The gossip said he was a bad manager. He had tried to motivate and organize the TRD into a state of grace. By the time I met him he was depressed by what had been achieved. It was still not working. We tried to put it right. We took time. We had much backing and goodwill. We very nearly made it. The radical element of the TRD team and its supporters were ultimately engrossed by organizational orthodoxy and the threat to convention.

Since the early eighties, I have spent much time and effort trying to establish how we could have made a better fist of organizing genius. Over the past three years I have sought to uncover how others succeeded, how vigorously creative people manage to reap the yield of their distinctive abilities, how organizations find, feed, support and harvest the benefits of their creative talent. I have talked to creative sufferers. I have learned from people who believe they have the secret of the successful creative organization. I have met people who have the conviction that they can manage the best out of creative talent. I have read through much of the immense literature on the theory and practice of creativity, innovation and their practical improvement. These researches of mine have not been scientifically rigorous. A search for a better answer is all I could entertain. I shall probably continue the search for years to come. In writing this book, there were issues above all which I sought to address:

- There is an immense gap between the great knowledge of those who have studied the creative individual and the creative group, on the one hand, and the practitioners who try to sustain and to manage creativity in the real world but who do it so often with such ignorance. How can this chasm be better bridged?

- There are those whose addiction to creativity cannot be suppressed. How can we help them to find a way of manipulating their organizational circumstances so as not to suffer so much for their affliction?

In *Organizing Genius*, I have tried to record some of the experiences of people who live in the fiercely competitive world of creative business and to match this with a summary of the known art and science of creativity and its management. I have not sought to question those whose creative output is not mortgaged to organizational interests, like sculptors, wordsmiths or artists.

Thus, the book is organized in three parts. In the first part, 'A Voyage of Discovery', I have tried to review the range of experiences that creative people encounter in their quest for fulfilment, using case studies of my own and from published sources. I have explored the extraordinary and frustrating world of the solo or near solo inventor, the passion of the entrepreneur, the confinement of the research scientist, and the complexity of the organization seeking to become, of itself, a creative organism.

In describing these experiences, I have tried to keep faith with the people who have helped me personally through recording their views and beliefs as expressed to me alongside the observations and conclusions for which I take full responsibility. Where these have been public figures, I have drawn extensively on already published material. Inevitably, especially in such a dynamic field, the examples date. Several of the people I met have already vanished from the positions they had. Many of the organizations referred to will have moved on in their thinking and market-places. This does not alter the relevance of the cases presented. They are there to try to offer insight to those who follow. Too often I find that people learn nothing from their own mistakes, let alone those of their predecessors.

In the second part, 'Reaching for an Understanding', I have summarized the variety of approaches that researchers and practitioners have made in exploring the nature of serious creativity and its management. In the third part, 'Searching for the Answers', I bring together many of the techniques and applications that have been used to lever more value from the creative act in the organization setting. I have tried to tell it how it is. I am not selling a particular approach, nor do I feel that I have the answers. I do believe, however, that I have caught most of the questions.

I know that there are a number of schools of thought about creativity. As I have explored these avenues over the years, I have reached some conclusions which have guided the way in which this book has evolved. To spare any reader the agony of finding halfway through, that his mind-set on creativity fundamentally disagrees with mine, let me spell these out now.

Creativity is in all of us. In most it is very underdeveloped. No-one can be creative for more than a small proportion of his day, at work or elsewhere. We all need our many habits of thought and action, and creativity threatens them.

Anyone can increase his creative output, everyone should increase his acceptance of, and search for, his own creativity and that of others. This is a changing world, becoming daily more competitive. Novelty rules, nothing lasts. We have to compete in novelty.

People have a very wide range of talents and abilities. Intelligence is not a simple matter of IQ, or of problem-solving; it is also about visualizing, kinaesthetics, music and language abilities. Any one of these, either singly or in combination, can be developed in a person by accident or design to a point where the productivity of their creativity can reach the proportion of genius.

Genius is not about public recognition, that is, fame. Genius is about taking human capacities to the level of the exceptional, and then delivering something truly unique and desirable.

There are major and minor geniuses. There are geniuses in all walks of life. Most are not happy people. The most prominent are likely to be the most difficult and different.

Personal creativity operates in cycles, and the more creative people have the greater swings in these cycles. As people get older, these cycles get dampened.

Figure 2 shows where the genius achieves and where he suffers. Those blessed (or cursed, as is often the case) with a need to create, spend much more time at the top of each of the cycles in the ring. They move from divergence (they feel different) to passion (a need to

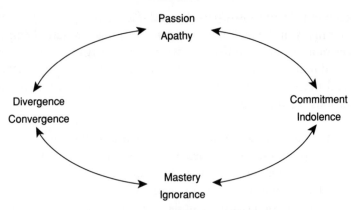

Figure 2   Personal Cycles of Creativity

prove that this difference is better not worse) to commitment (a will to reach for results come what may) and to mastery (a full command of one domain of skill or knowledge). Many times they suffer the pangs of failure and anguish, but they are driven. Most people, those who are not creative geniuses, spend much more of their time in the bottom of each cycle or moving out of the ring altogether.

All creative people, particularly those at the level of genius, are made vastly more productive by being well managed. Managing creative people is an art of a special kind. Managing the genius, of whatever level, requires a certain type of person, and calls for a certain type of behaviour. The cycles of the manager of creativity are shown in figure 3.

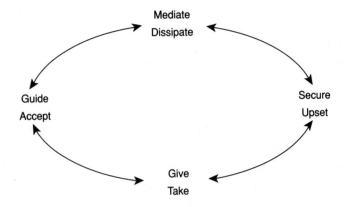

Figure 3   Cycles of Managing Creative People

Managers of creative people need to believe that they are themselves creative. They have to have the capacity to admire without fear or envy. They have to be personally secure. At times, when relationships are turbulent, they can become fragile. In the successful manager, this does not last long. Managers have to be able to give and to take and to guide and accept each at the right time. Complete freedom kills creativity. Creative people need something to kick at, to fight for. The most important contribution a manager of creative people can make is to mediate, to champion the product of their creativity. But the manager must also be the critic, must be smart enough to judge where he is championing a dog, and he must be able to say no in a way which does not create breakages. He has to dissipate.

The greatest influence on creative productivity is the culture of the world in which that creativity is sustained. Creativogenic cultures, preferably national but necessarily corporate in most cases, will induce high levels of creative outcome. Figure 4 shows how these can vary.

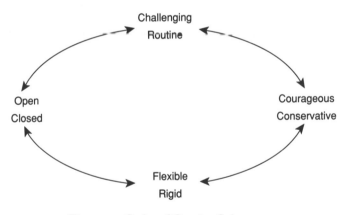

Figure 4   Cycles of Creative Culture

Cultures move through these cycles, depending on circumstances and serendipity. Creativogenic cultures aim for the top lines to be kept open, challenging, courageous and flexible, but there are times where these conditions are reversed. Perhaps the most productive culture is one in which each ring is always rotating.

Surpassing all these factors are the institutions and beliefs that bring about the culture of nations. In the West, we cannot reverse our love of individualism, we cannot relinquish our belief that our way is best. In the East, team-working is natural, competitive processes are collective. With vastly increased information, teams are needed to create, incrementalism beats breakthrough creativity, quality of education is vital. All these factors push the advantage away from the West and towards the East. Our education systems are failing us. We are smug about our position in the world.

We have to find new ways of creating a world in which our creative, eccentric, individualists can ensure our continued competitive advantage. Otherwise we will lose the economic war.

Note: Throughout the book the generic pronoun 'he' is used. This usage is not gender specific.

Acknowledgements

Creativity is one of those subject areas forbidden to the casual student of social sciences because it is so exhaustingly researched by so many people, over so many years, that literature searches can easily take up more time than is allocated for the whole project. In a sense, this happened to me. In addition to begging favours from friends and neighbours, directing and redirecting conversations with colleagues as a means to tapping the practical world, I read a lot. My shelves now contain ninety-four books which are partially or totally devoted to the subject. Academically, on the subject of the nature of creativity and creative people, I was most enlightened by Rhona Ochse's *Before the Gates of Excellence*. Already recognized for her article 'Toward the prediction and stimulation of creativity' in the South African *Journal of Psychology*, published in September 1989, this book confirmed her as a truly accomplished explorer of, and guide to the massive undergrowth of creativity research. A second major acknowledgement I owe to Robert Sternberg, through his editing of *The Nature of Creativity*. This compilation enabled me to explore different views and perspectives on the subject from a very wide range of angles and depths. It must be no coincidence that both these volumes were published by Cambridge University Press.

The third major source of published insight for me has been Peter Medawar, through the collection of some of his more remarkable essays under the title *The Threat and the Glory*. Almost all of our understanding of creativity in science seems to come from biologists, and secondarily from mathematicians, with little from most other disciplines. Medawar was one of those priceless scientists who can articulate about their science equally as well as, if not better than, they can conduct it.

There have clearly been many other sources of inspiration – papers, newspapers, *The Economist, New Scientist,* the *Sunday Times* and so on, each of which has had some influence on my thinking, and from all of which I must have plagiarized shamelessly, but unknowingly. Where the written materials and the personal contact cross, I owe an especial acknowledgement to Professor Geert Hofstede. To his highly praised book *Cultures Consequences,* he has now added *Cultures and Organizations.* These two volumes, together with all too infrequent personal discussions over the past two years, have enabled me to clarify the place that national and organization culture can truly play in the nurturing and style of organized and disorganized creative talent in the real world.

The people with whom I talked and who gave freely of their time and kindness to help me grasp the intricacies of actual creative lives, or the tortures of those who manage creative people, were many and varied. They were all people who I met with, and who had no reason to offer me help other than that I sought it. Most of them have their place in the text, but to all of the following I owe thanks:

Ken Austin, inventor extraordinaire; Helen Auty, head of Design at the Royal School of Art; Royden Axe, Design Director of Rover and Uwe Bahnsen, head of Art Centre College of Design in Switzerland and one-time head of Design at Ford gave their contrasting views; Hamish Bryce, managing director of Thorn Lighting, Alan Chalmers, Jim Coaton and Ken Scott of R&D, together with senior managers Alex Halberstadt and Richard Holdron, added to views of the under-funded, world-renowned research world provided by Ian Childs and Bruce Moffat of the BBC Research Department; David Crisp and Peter Murdoch, each of whom, in his different way, runs his own industrial design company, and a design luminary, Frank Duffy of DEGW, communicated their concerns for the world of creative design and suggested their remedies; Nigel Cutts also gave me close up insight of the ups and downs of a creative man running his own creative business; Michael Grade, Director General of Channel 4 was, like Wally Olins of Wolff-Olins, one of two people who indulged me after they had already been interviewed at some length by Winston Fletcher for his book *Creative People;* William Johnson, who features in chapter 5, leaves me with an enduring and fascinating memory of a lunch in

Knightsbridge with him and Mark Millard, which continued beyond six o'clock.

Alan Jones and Mary Del Castillo of BBC Television Design contributed to my understanding of how a particularly visually creative activity is managed within a very structured, demanding and verbally strident culture. From the advertising world, introduced to me from the inside by Trevor Chenery, who helped me throughout the years with useful hints, exhortations to keep going, and wonderful puddings for lunch at the Groucho Club, were Tony French, head of Monitor, Clive Holland of Young & Rubicam and Mike Walsh, chairman of Ogilvy & Mather in London. Through Tony French, I met Peter Wright at Lotus Cars who provided, as much as anyone, an understanding of what truly creative engineers are about.

Pippa Franklyn and John Cowland of 3M led me through the complexities of that company's long-standing commitment to creativity as a way of life. Geoffrey Guy, medical entrepreneur extraordinary, of Ethical Pharmaceutical, and an old friend, Ken Eakins, blocked any doubts that might have subverted my newly minted understanding of the true nature of effective pharmaceutical R & D. Christopher Graeme-Barber of The Technology Partnership proved that good high-growth innovative business is still possible where quality people are prepared to go for it. Each of the last three offered a coinciding case for small is beautiful, where it comes to creative output. At Edwards High Vacuum, Danny Rosenkranz, John Rimer amd Raj Rajagapol were each more than helpful in providing insight into the company and their parts in its success, aided wonderfully well by the now-retired personnel director, Frank Allen.

From further afield, I learned about the creative side of ITT from Douglas Stevenson, a stalwart of managing innovative engineers, of Apple in Silicon Valley, California; from Jean Louis Gassé, at the time I met him the about-to-be outgoing head of R & D; and last but not least, Herr Hempel of Siemens, then head of Psychological Services in Munich. Very few people whom I contacted turned me away, and I could not find the occasion to take advantage of many other offers of help I received. Incidental contacts and experiences have all clearly added to the results herein, and all of these I should acknowledge, were they not subliminal.

Two early events were more seminal than others and deserve a mention. Peter Herriot and Ian Robertson invited me to write a section on 'Selection for Creative Occupations' in *Assessment and*

Selection in Organization, published by John Wiley in 1989. Preparing this showed me just what depth of published material there was in this domain, and how extraordinarily well-written most of it is. The experience convinced me that the conventionally narrow view of creativity as something confined to a few was unhelpful, even dangerous, orthodoxy. No-one is born uncreative. In fact, it could be argued that creativity is probably the least likely attribute to be totally conditioned at birth.

The second event was working with my wife Anne, and with Dick LeHunte, head of Training at PE Inbucon, on the design of a training programme in creative thinking for Ford of Europe. This proved a very rewarding enterprise, and the favourable feedback from those attending and from tutors showed what worked and what did not work in a wide range of circumstances. It also demonstrated that even in the most organized and structured culture, there is a fierce need and a significant opportunity for people to find legitimate ways of expressing their own individual creative selves.

Finally, there are those who have made personal contributions during the writing of this book. Mark Millard worked with me closely across the whole period of research and writing, also accompanying me on many of the interviews. Neville Osrin nudged me where my momentum was being lost. Robin Currie, my recent guide to writing good English, helped reconstruct the script to make it more nearly readable. Julie Thomson, now sadly lost to us for a career teaching music, ordered the process, typed the original manuscript and made sure that meetings were attended. Denise Jay has undertaken the final arduous task of typing, retyping, revising and also putting in her bit on improved English.

Last but not least, there are two people who made this book possible: Sir James Black, who gave me the incentive, willingly or not, to have a go at putting some part of our shared exerience to good use, and whose vision and experiences have contributed so much to this text; and my wife, Anne, who has put up with this obsession for years, and even found the will to do the final proof corrections for me.

Prologue

The Dilemma

How Should a Company Chairman Handle two Prima Donna Scientists?

Enrico Rossi, chairman of Micro-electronics D'Italia (MEI), threw his arms wide and asked for heavenly guidance. 'How I envy the impresario at La Scala!' he exclaimed. 'He only has to deal with sulking tenors and raging sopranos. I am afflicted with the tantrums of scientific genius!'

His bad day had begun fifty kilometres away from corporate headquarters, at the research centre MEI had established in the Tuscan hills. Dr Marco Nardelli, MEI's director of research and development (R & D), had asked Count Giuseppe del Ponte Vecchio, who headed the Telecommunications Research Division, to come to his office and justify his request for larger financial resources.

When the count had arrived – twenty minutes late, although his own office was just down the corridor – he had sneeringly asked Nardelli whether he didn't have better things to do than fiddle about with lire like a junior accountant. Nardelli had made a dismissive gesture, whereupon the count added: 'Oh, I forgot, you are not an accountant but a glorified picture maker' – referring to the fact that Nardelli was the acknowledged world expert on the abstract subject of holographic memory. 'The only picture maker ever to have been elected to the Italian Academy of Science.'

Nardelli, normally shy and retiring, still had his pride. He had ordered the count to extinguish the cigarette he had lit (everybody knew that Nardelli hated people smoking in his office) and when the count refused, the unscientific row that resulted had lab technicians half a block away downing tools and listening intently.

Two hours later the drama shifted to Rossi's opulent office in Rome. The chairman had been forewarned by telephone that Nardelli was dashing into town in his red Ferrari. But Rossi was disconcerted when the scientist rushed in and roared: 'If you don't fire that sadistic aristocratic parvenu, then I resign. That is my final word. Either he goes or I go.' Rossi, who preferred to work quietly behind the scenes and let others have the glory, called upon his reserves of tact and diplomacy to pacify Nardelli. He could afford to lose neither of the men.

Nardelli, whom Rossi had recruited seven years ago from the prestigious University of Castiglione, where he had been senior professor of micro-electronics, had risen from a poor home by reason of academic brilliance. True, he was not a manager. True, the R & D division basically ran on autopilot, guided by numerous committees and mountains of paper. But Nardelli had been elected to the exalted post of Doyen of the Italian Academy of Science – a unique honour long coveted by the count. Although he had yet to produce a commercial product, his scientific reputation was a major asset to the company. And there was always the chance that his attempts to perfect the elusive holographic memory, an enormous breakthrough, would be crowned with success.

The count had also been recruited by Rossi. Widely regarded in the industry as the man with the golden touch, del Ponte Vecchio had, with his previous employers, been a prime mover in the development of modular public telephone switches and had pioneered the application of voice response software for telephone systems. Arrogant and irascible, universally disliked – only a few had been able to work with him without resigning – he considered that he, rather than Nardelli, was deserving of honours.

Before lunch, Rossi had succeeded in persuading Nardelli not to resign. He was simply too valuable to lose, Rossi had told him. As for the count, the managing director promised he would give that problem urgent consideration.

Rossi thought the storm had blown over, as other tempests involving the two men had abated in the past. But Nardelli drove back to the research centre, picked up the phone, and, finding that the count was absent, told the count's henchman, Luigi Como, that the game was up and his patron had better start packing his bags.

Como, who basked in the count's reflected glory and enjoyed the power the latter had given him to manage the division on a day-to-day basis, which was beneath the count's dignity, immediately contacted his boss, who had motored to Rome to attend a house-party in company time, and told him about the phone call. With the count's approval, he later wrote a withering denunciation of Nardelli, ending by threatening that he and other scientists in the division would resign if Rossi dared to threaten the count. The letter was dispatched to corporate headquarters by motorcycle messenger.

The missive arrived in Rossi's office at the same time as the count – just as the chairman was preparing to go home for what he hoped would be a quiet, trouble-free weekend. The count said he wanted Nardelli fired and himself appointed as director of R & D. After all, he argued, he was the market-oriented scientist, the man with the track record, the man who turned scientific research into new, highly saleable products. The company couldn't do without him, whereas Nardelli was a mere figurehead, a cipher whose absence from the company would hardly be noticed.

Either Rossi agreed to his suggestions, or he, Count del Ponte Vecchio, scion of a great house and one of Italy's most undervalued , under-honoured scientists, would transfer his allegiance to the American Consolidated Communications Corporation, which had offered him unlimited facilities to develop his speech-recognition software. Rossi had until Monday morning to reach a decision, said the count, storming out of the room.

Rossi did not, after all, have a quiet, untroubled weekend. He felt like a character trapped in some obscure operatic melodrama, an illusion heightened as he read the letter from Como. But Rossi didn't feel like bursting into song. He spent the whole weekend agonizing over his problem. If he fired Nardelli there was a very good chance that the board would fire him for losing Italy's most distinguished scientist. The public and academic outcry would irreparably damage MEI's good name – not to mention the hope that the holographic memory project might bear fruit. On the other hand, if he fired the count he might lose products that would guarantee MEI's future – and a third of his scientists into the bargain, if Como was to be believed. And the board would probably fire him for that, too. So what, in the absence of heavenly guidance, should he do?

This was a case study prepared by Roy Hill for *International Management* and published in December 1984. It was one of the successful 'Dilemma and Decision' series. The following answer to the dilemma was supplied by Michael Younger and Philip Middleton, who provided the material for Roy Hill to prepare this vignette.

The Decision

Free One from Management and put the Other in Quarantine

Younger: Talk about the devil and the deep blue sea, have you got any brilliant ideas how we solve this one?

Middleton: Well, I suppose commercial logic suggests Nardelli had better depart fairly speedily. As an R & D manager he's about as useful as a plate of cold spaghetti. The division's in an absolute mess, with no guidance from the top to speak of. It may be years before his beloved holographic research produces a marketable product, if at all. And really, all he wants is to write his academic papers and enjoy his scientific renown.

Y: All right, but what about the outcry when you fire a world-renowned scientist – that will cost Rossi his head, not to mention the damage to the company's reputation.

M: You obviously haven't read any Machiavelli recently. You don't *fire* him. Nardelli *retires* by mutual agreement, to pursue his research and teach, while remaining as a non-executive consultant to MEI. The size of his golden parachute is proportional to his willingness not to rock the boat.

M: After all, if ICL can get rid of Sir Michael Edwardes with scarcely a murmur from the press, I'm sure Rossi can arrange Nardelli's departure with equal diplomacy.

Y: Perhaps. But Nardelli is far too proud to go on those terms – he'd go straight to the board and create hell. And secondly, even if you get rid of Nardelli, you give over the division to the count and Como. That's like putting Nero and Caligula in charge of a convent.

M: Well, better to keep the count, and his potentially profitable products, even if it does mean a bit of temporary unrest.

Y: Temporary unrest! The count will hijack every available resource for his projects, starving all other areas of R & D funds and manpower. Since the board couldn't tell a piece of software from a piece of soft cheese, the count will be MEI's ultimate scientific arbiter, which means he does what he likes.

M: Point taken. Let's bite the bullet and fire the count, which will also get rid of Como. Rome got rid of Julius Caesar and survived.

Y: It's tempting. But then, arrogance often accompanies genius – look at Mozart. There's no way we can afford to let him go to American rivals ACC.

M: Then why don't we promote Nardelli to non-executive vice chairman and senior corporate scientist and head-hunt a good manager to run the R & D division as a nonboard general manager?

Y: That's not going to work, either. Nardelli will realize that he is being booted upstairs to get him out of the way of the count, which will hardly satisfy him. Even assuming you could persuade a good manager to put his career on the line, the count and Como would eat him for breakfast within six months. You'd be back where you started, with Rossi in a considerably weaker position, the division in chaos and morale down to zero.

Y: Let's look more closely at the personalities involved. What are their objectives and what lies behind all the sound and fury?

M: Well, take Nardelli first. He's a brilliant academic scientist with an international reputation who revels in the lionizing he receives. Perhaps his holograph research will come off, perhaps not. But it advances scientific knowledge and adds to the reputation of MEI as a pioneering force in the field.

M: Nardelli hates management, is hopeless at it, but he is liked by his people. On the other hand, as a scientist, he makes valuable contributions to other people's work as well as his own. I suppose he really just wants to be an honoured scientist without the problems of management or the continuous warfare with the count. The problem is, he is the count's boss, in theory at least.

Y: Good synopsis. If we examine the count, he's not really interested in power or money. He considers management beneath his dignity, and resents anyone trying to manage him. He's already developed two highly successful products and is looking to crown his career with speech-recognition systems that will both confirm his status as the most successful scientist of his generation and open up a market worth millions of dollars. What drives the count is the desire to prove himself the greatest, and the lust for international accolades.

M: Fine. So we've got two brilliant scientists, neither of whom is able or willing to manage. One is academically brilliant but commercially non-viable. The other is a commercial genius but impossible to manage. And they both hate each other.

Y: So the first step is to remove Nardelli from management without damaging his ego. Therefore, you keep him as director of R & D but appoint under him a general manager with a small staff, to actually get the administration into some kind of order and run the place. They do the hackwork and leave Nardelli free to make contributions and decisions on matters of science, while pursuing his research and acting as a roving ambassador for MEI. Capitalize on his strengths and remove his weaknesses.

M: As for the count, you don't leave an infectious patient wandering around. You put him in quarantine and get him out of circulation. So you build him a laboratory about fifty kilometres from Rossi and Nardelli. You give him all the resources he needs, tell him to pick a small team of scientists who want to work with him, leave him to get on with his research on his own, and ask him not come out until he has succeeded.

Y: Who does he report to?

M: Directly to Rossi. And only then if he needs more funds. The count may be arrogant, but he's realistic enough to shut down a non-viable line of research and start another. After all, it's success he craves.

PART I

A Voyage of Discovery

I

'The Yogi and the Commissar'

There are two kinds of people in this world, those who divide
everything into two groups and those who do not.

Kenneth Boulding

Creativity is an act of deviance. Creative people are deviant. Genius is
creativity at its most deviant. Most people choose to conform. The
genius seldom feels able to choose not to be creative. Most
institutions discourage deviation. Under conditions of great social
continuity, creativity is a problem, even a heresy. People in power
seek continuity. Here is the essential conflict. Institutions provide
opportunity for some people to achieve positions of power. To most,
they offer comfort and certainty. Within those institutions are the
many who conform, and only the few who contest. Under conditions
of great continuity, the natural institutional mechanisms for ensuring
conformity work. However, where there is turbulence and change,
the institution needs all of its powers to adapt; all of its capacity to
profit from deviance. Right now, from nations to families, our
institutions face turbulence. How can such institutions whose core
function is creating conformity, change focus and learn to profit from
deviance? This is the essence of organizing genius.

The dilemma of the prologue illustrates one issue of today. On the
one hand, there are a small number of people who are seen to have
the intrinsic capacity to magnify enormously the economic success of
their employing organization. On the other, there is the large majority
who are employed to provide for the continuity and predictability of
the institution as an entity. Each sees the other through the glass

darkly, shadowy, threatening, unreachable. Companies and divisions survive and even prosper despite these events. However, the nature, motivations, ambitions, and expectations of the human players in these dramas are recognizable only as cartoons. The practical focus is on the superficial, the judgemental and the need for action. Reaching for an understanding takes time, patience and human sympathy. Finding new ways of understanding the fertile ground for genius to flourish inside and amongst the organization needs understanding. Penning the creative genius in splendid isolation outside is quick, expedient and total. Most decisions about organizing genius are not human decisions, they are organizational solutions. They are about roles and responsibilities, not human gifts and frailties. Too often, they ignore the unique, complex, critical, intensely personal and potentially tragic qualities of individuals.

The interplay between the institution and its creative individuals is a drama where there is always a persecutor, a victim and a rescuer. Depending on his perceived value, the genius can be each of the first two in turn. Top managements and their consultants never play the victim. In the individualist culture of the West, the tension engendered by this drama can create genuine commercial and scientific breakthroughs. But to a very great number, it ends in heartache and lost opportunity. The tragedy of the Prologue is that it repeats endlessly wherever creativity has both a commercial value and a need for an institutional framework. More and more our world needs creative solutions, and on a bigger and bigger scale. More than ever we need to find a better way for organizations to draw out and nourish creativity from each and every individual. To do this we need to find admiration for genius, not envy, and tolerance for deviance, not suppression. We need to take the time to reach an understanding of the players in our creative dramas which is not based on squibs and parodies alone.

Left to the individual, as it so often is, creativity and innovation are matters of great emotional torment. Creative people feel obliged to fight and shout. They take Feyerbend's advice[1] as the only route to reaching fulfilment through shaking the organized tree to its roots.

> Violence is *necessary* to overcome the impediments created by a well-organized society, or by one's own modes of behaviour (perception, thought, etc.) and it is beneficial for the individual, for it releases one's energies and makes one realize the powers at ones

disposal. Free associations where everyone does what best suits their talents replace petrified institutions of the day, no function must be allowed to become fixed. Spontaneity reigns supreme in thought (perception) as well as action.

Successful organizations need to have control and continuity, but they increasingly cannot survive without a huge investment in promoting change. In the past, dramatic change has often happened by accident. So much of the history of discovery and invention has come about because of single incidents or events which were identified and put to use by individuals subsequently to the enormous commercial advantage of companies, institutions and nations. The organization created the means by which that wealth was achieved, but invariably an individual recognized the potential worth of the accident. Managing for accidents is both a contradiction in terms and a considerable expense. Managing for controlled and continuous change has become an industry. But it is a technology in its infancy.

Economic and commercial turbulence has brought with it a further and more pressing need to the institution – a need for all its members to search continually for improvements at every opportunity. Organizations are searching for ways in which each employee feels enlivened by the drive to challenge existing orders, to initiate and to support innovation, in short, to deviate. Organizing for such creativity is often like nuclear fusion: the costs of achieving it are greater than the benefits of its accomplishment. We are still searching for conditions under which all individuals feel able and willing to challenge orthodoxy without destroying establishments, and thus enable organizations to replenish the sources of today's wealth with tomorrow's.

Success and Creativity in Pharmaceutical R&D

Of all the sectors of organized life where a substantial success in managing creative genius has proved to have the most competitive advantage, the pharmaceutical industry surely has led the world over the past fifty years. Arguably it is ahead of electronics, computers and communications and certainly aerospace, if only because of the breadth of its professional span. Chemists, biochemists, biologists, pharmacologists, toxicologists, pharmacists, physicists, mathematicians and doctors of medicine of all stripes are just some of the disciplines which have been drawn into the extraordinary milieu providing for the modern pharmacy. The pharmaceutical world spends more time and intensity and attention examining its own creative soul than any other discrete industrial sub-set anywhere.

As an industry, it invests a consistently greater proportion of its revenues in R&D. Typically over 10 per cent, this is three or four times the proportion found in most high-technology producers, let alone the huge bulk of other industries, which put aside little or nothing. Every pharmaceutical conference includes at least some papers on managing for innovation. Every conference on innovation includes some papers on phamaceutical research and development. For many reasons, pharmaceutical organizations should be a fertile ground for those who are just beginning to learn how to face up to the need to organize genius.

However, examination of the viewpoints expressed in these conferences often illustrates the very dilemma which surfaced in the prologue. There are those like Dr Pedro Cuatrecasas. As president of the Pharmaceutical Research Division of Warner-Lambert Company, he gave a passionate plea for the expression of individuality at a workshop in the subject of drug discovery in 1990.[2]

> It is difficult to stress strongly enough the importance of the individual and of freedom. This needs to be reconciled with whatever actions are taken within the organization . . . Teams don't create, individuals acting independently do. Collective actions (teams, committees, task forces, etc) coordinate, compromise, legitimatize and translate into actions the creations of individuals.

He sees the contest between controlling organization and freedom-seeking individual in stark dimensions. Below is an abbreviated and edited edition of his presentation.

Opposing Values in Innovative Organizations

Precision	–	uncertainty
Order	–	disorder
Conformity	–	originality
Standardization	–	flexibility
Predictability	–	ambiguity

Authority	–	equality
Formality	–	spontaneity
Obedience	–	defiance
Secrecy	–	openness
Uniformity	–	diversity
Control	–	freedom
Rules	–	exceptions
Management	–	leadership
Quantity	–	quality

He emphasizes:

> a 'receptive' research environment goes beyond organization structure and relates to the value systems and culture that dominate the operations of the group. It is in fact more important than the structure itself, *but cannot even be cultivated unless the structural organization is able to promote it.*

At the same workshop, Desmond Fitzgerald, former General Manager, Research at ICI Pharmaceuticals, also made a plea for 'allowing individual creativity'. His review of successful 'drug hunters' showed the following characteristics[3]:

- self starters, neither seeking nor needing supervision or management.
- attitude to formal organizational needs was 'non-compliant'.
- risk-takers with dislike for the status quo, not often obvious team members.
- hold strong convictions, forcefully expressed.
- ambitious focus on their scientific pursuit not their personal careers.

Received wisdom is that even in research organizations, only one per cent of the staff are likely to be true originators. Furthermore, the identity of these people is not secret to anyone, including themselves. This point is raised time and again in different ways. As Dr Szent-gyorgi wrote in *The Lancet* thirty years ago: 'Research wants egoists, damned egoists, who seek their own pleasure and satisfaction, but find it in solving the puzzles of nature.' Professor Dr Jürgen Drews, Chairman of the Research Board of F. Hoffman-la Roche

AG, reported on an examination of five case studies relating to their discovery and development of a major drug[4]. Out of twenty individual qualities of the key scientists who championed these drugs, he asked which correlated best with eventual success? The only two were motivation and perseverance.

He concludes:

> The consequence for a research director must be to hire only scientists who are motivated, who have an idea of themselves and of their own value, and who carry what the French call the 'feu sacre'.

To have the benefit of organized genius, he argues, his organization specifically hires only those 'geniuses' whose interests and directions are congruent with theirs. The only decisions the organization has to make are first to choose the right person, and then to offer him the freedom to give of his best without impediment.

On the other side of the argument, Dr David Jack, who oversaw the most productive period ever for research and development at Glaxo, draws up this list in his presentation on the roles of Research Director[5]

1 Research policy – with other board members.
2 The definition and execution of the research programme.
3 The definition and execution of the development programme – with marketing and production colleagues.
4 The efficacy, safety, composition and quality of products.
5 The scientific and medical correctness of product literature.

Nothing comes across from this list as being about individual freedom or even warmth. His ideas on teams include the need for a clearly defined objective, an effective leader, freedom of tactics and regular access to the research director. The contrast between this formula for creativity and that of Cuatrecasas could not be greater. The reason for their different perspectives might be found in the nature of the two personalities. In his book, *The Billion Dollar Battle*, Matthew Lynn describes David Jack directly in these terms[6]:

> Jack is one of the greatest unsung heroes of European capitalism. He is not, though, a great businessman, neither is he a great financier; he is, instead, a great inventor.

He later quotes a former Glaxo board director as saying[7]:

> David Jack, to my mind, was one of the best pharmaceutical research directors there ever has been. He is not a great scientist . . . but he has this incredible ability to spot the application for something . . . (Ventolin) was a good example of his abilities, because it was right under Glaxo's noses and they hadn't spotted it.

One lesson that would be learned from these observations is that there is more than one kind of creative input even within one industry's R&D. Those searching for the one guiding principle of organizing genius could well be misled.

One of the great problems in sustaining creativity is success. Most success in the pharmaceutical research world has come from relatively small beginnings. But success can mean a very substantial payback. The temptation is to re-invest such windfall returns into large-scale organized research. Even Janssen, a phenomenally successful part of the Johnson & Johnson Group, is pressured by its success. Dr Paul Janssen never intended to make money. His research management is underpinned by two philosophies:

- build research around people.
- let research determine its own course.

To sustain these, the company insisted on only three functional levels. Now, due to growth, a research board has been created. There are now heads of heads. All of these companies forgot that it was not organized but disorganized research that provided the windfall. Organizations do not have memories. Often the prime originator of the breakthrough drug, who does have a memory, has moved on. The culture has changed. New, expensive, large laboratories get built, quickly filled with fresh young scientists. They become managed within the overall organizational ethos and objectives through the medium of an emergent Research Director. They fail to provide anything remotely close to a reasonable rate of return. Finally, doubts arise about the efficacy of the new research regime, the quality of the science and of the scientists. It happens time and again.

This was done, amongst many others, by Hoffman-La Roche with the proceeds of huge sales of Librium and Valium; by Smith-Kline with the pay-off from introducing Tagamet to the world of ulcerating stomachs; and by ICI, who built their huge facility at Alderley Edge mostly on the profits from the first effective treatment for hypertension; the beta-blocker. It will almost certainly be done again. As the person most credited with the discovery of two of these two mega-drugs, it seems Sir James Black ought to have much to say about organizing genius. And he has.

Sir James Black

Dr Black has worked for four of the world's major drug companies: ICI, Smith-Kline, Wellcome and Johnson & Johnson. The last named sponsors the Sir James Black Foundation, which he set up following his years at Wellcome. His reputation as an employee has ranged from difficult to tempestuous. He has never disguised his distaste for the frustrations, constraints and inadequacies of bureaucracy. However, each of the substantial organizations which employed him were prepared to put up with his reputation as a difficult employee to reap the riches of the products of his mind. His institutional experiences are the essence of organizing genius.

Nayak and Ketteringham included the discovery of the drug Tagamet in their research for *Breakthroughs*. While they did not manage to interview Black himself, clear signs of his impact on the organization are found in the observations they chose to publish, of Dr Paget, who was one of the first to leave ICI and join SKF Research Institute as its managing director, and of Dr Ganellin, the head chemist on Dr Black's team. Paget said[8]:

> The best research is done by people who are really committed to it, who are passionately interested in the outcome. They believe in their ideas enough to be rude to you if you don't agree with them. They'll try to argue you down if you oppose their views. They'll defend their own points of view hook and nail. It could be as frustrating as hell. When I was in charge, there were times when we were jammed up with one backlog or another, and chemists would come in and say, 'We cannot work with him (Black) any longer.' I would laugh. And then we would go on.

Dr Ganellin[9]:

> The extent of emotion was phenomenal. Feelings were running high – for many reasons. It was a very messy situation. It wasn't just

the US versus the UK. There were a lot of differences in the team on science. Some of the team didn't see the value of Black's proposal. He found people he could not get on with. He's an emotional man and he generates emotion. I suspect that that's what's required to achieve something. If you don't have emotion, you probably just don't react. Nothing happens.

Black left SKF in 1972, two years after Cimetidine, the compound presented to the public as Tagamet, had reached the end of its genuine research cycle. He became Professor of Medicinal Chemistry at University College, London.

Again, according to Nayak and Ketteringham[10], his departure was followed by a carping observation from a colleague that 'he left to attain the intellectual respect to which few industrial researchers in England ever dare aspire'. He was 'a disorderly fellow able to focus now and then on some great vision that might someday bring glory, but otherwise a sort of bumbling, blustering, lovable chap wandering quixotically among the greater institutions of British medical research – an absent-minded professor.'

In fact, Black left SKF because he believed that he could use the public visibility and intellectual freedom of the chair of medical chemistry to create the kind of productive research organization that would respond to him rather than play with him, that would not need the protection of people like his friend Bill Duncan to keep the wrath and the intrusion of the organization from him.

Academia was not the greatest of successes to Dr Black. His efforts to raise interest in research fell on deaf ears, even with the backing of his enormous achievements and productivity. He had decided to return to industry when he was offered the job of head of Therapeutic Research Division at Wellcome in Beckenham. This was a division which sought new chemical entities. It included chemistry laboratories, biochemistry, pharmacology, toxicology and drug metabolism to which he added his own experimental group. There were about 250 staff in total. Apart from the highly productive Burroughs Laboratories in North Carolina, this was the seedbed of the company's future prosperity.

It was at Wellcome that Sir James Black articulated his experiences and beliefs about the organization and management of innovative research, and put them into practice. It took several years and included more than one or two blind alleys. The effort and energy finally produced a consensus as to how to manage science in a pharmaceutical research laboratory.

His conclusions were specific to the one area of therapeutic research. He made no pretence to extend these beyond the boundaries of what he knew. However, there are lessons to be learned, so below is a summary of his thinking in 1982. It doesn't capture the elegance of his expression, but hopefully benefits from taking out the extraordinarily complex language used so easily by modern biologists.

- There is no proven route to discovery that can be specified as a set of rules. Research therefore cannot be organized through instruction.
- If luck is seen as the sole arbiter of success, then 'busyness is enough'. 'A strategy like this which *a priori* discharges obligation and responsibility is fatally flawed. Invariably these policies lead to sterility, more often than not being aborted in desperate institutional upheaval'.
- Success sought through a random sampling of an infinity of possibilities is senseless. Research policy should seek to reduce the odds against success from 'the impossible, through the unbearable, to the barely acceptable, which seems about the best anyone has achieved to date'.
- The commonest research strategy is imitation, a very successful way of reducing the odds. Such a policy is contingent upon other's successes in pursuing a less timid strategy, so does not take away the effect of the poor odds.
- Research science is open-ended. To have a research strategy, there must be constraints. These constraints are also forces – they are ideas. 'Ideas introduce constraints in proportion to their "hardness".' Hard ideas deal with real problems. 'Soft ideas come from inner voices and private wires, imagination corrupted by wishful thinking.' This is the marshmallow world that beckons and besets all of us at some time or other.
- Policy should be primarily aimed first to eliminate wishful thinking and second to seek out hard ideas. On their own, hard ideas produce nothing. The hard idea that insists 'start here' has to have come from competence, imagination and from knowledge. Its effective exploration has to follow the rigour of scientific method.

- This strategy demands a high scientific competence of each and every member of each and every team, competence which is neither questioned nor questionable by those who have no other means of judging this other than through the observations of peers.
- 'Uninhibited enthusiasm, mutual trust and the passion for winning sublimated in the goal, the hard idea, are the real time limiting factors . . .' Leaders in research have a limited capacity to generate and husband the scientific passion and creativity in others, but they have a considerable capacity to eliminate both. The leader may have to be both catalyst and standard-bearer, but they have no licence to be either dull or apathetic.

The criteria for examining any new research beginning (hard ideas) were formulated as follows:

- There must be an enthusiastic scientist prepared to champion the new work.
- There has to be a clear objective, free of wishful thinking.
- The objective entails a precise biological assay – that is, there would be no doubt what it does to living tissue.
- The objective entails an identified chemical starting-point, that is, there is a molecule of known characteristics from which there is a justifiable beginning.
- There are appropriate and available expertise and resources.
- Ultimately, the idea would be amenable to clinical evaluation; that is, that doctors would be able to test for some effect in man.

Further proposed was that all these ideas once evaluated in this way would either fail – through being wishful thinking, or because the clinical evaluation was not clearly reachable – that is, the idea was not hard enough or they could be accepted on a limited basis, to find out more about them; or, if they fulfil all of these criteria, they could be accepted into a full programme status.

The organization of the scientists was the subject of intense analysis. The conclusions could be summarized as follows:

- The process of discovery of new drugs (or any other commercially valid scientific outcome) is a highly collaborative effort between scientists of fundamentally different disciplines.

- Maintenance and progress of scientific quality requires exposure and critical appraisal from other scientists of like background and critical capacity.
- Continuous appraisal such as this enables a scientist of another discipline to have the necessary confidence in the performance of his colleagues.
- Organizational emphasis is on line management of homogeneous disciplines which creates group identity and pride and reinforces the peer evaluation process.
- Divisional structure is based upon a classic matrix which aims to distribute and balance the power between research direction and line functions while maintaining overall coordination.
- The organization enables chemists and biologists to work together in the search for new drugs and to find ways of sharing in each others' skills and experiences.

What this meant in terms of a new organization was that the dual hierarchy was introduced. Each discipline and sub-discipline had a manager as its head, a scientist of standing who also showed the skills and interest to manage the people and the resources, as well as to ensure that standards were kept consistent with best practice.

There were seven departmental heads in TRD, reporting to a general manager. Between them, they were charged with the week-to-week regulation of services, man-management, resource allocation and workload planning. Each had two or three sections reporting in to him, created to represent durable and specific scientific spires of excellence.

Within these sections were optional positions for the scientific accountability of the quality and output of the scientific research itself. The designated research scientists were charged with the requirement to develop and innovate, as well as to evaluate, influence and encourage others wherever their specialism had a contribution to make. Unlike the manager roles, section and department head, this role was deemed as optional because its efficacy depends entirely on the personal and professional quality of the incumbent. If no good candidates were available, the post was left unfilled. These scientists helped to shape and coordinate programmes and research policy; they also appraised specific programmes.

Such an organization offered no hiding-place. In its combination of guidance for selection and termination of research and the open-mesh nature of the organizational matrix, very few opportunities remained for self-serving or wishfully hopeful attitudes or people.

At a conference held in 1990[11], Trevor Jones, Director of Research, Development and Medical at Wellcome, read a paper. Early on in his delivery, he noted:

> the intellectual climate for drug discovery contains a high degree of curiosity which is both provocative and challenging, challenging not only to the individual but by the individual of his/her peers and management. It is not surprising, therefore, that at times the individuals and teams which comprise discovery research find themselves at odds with other members of their corporate community.

He credited the head of Research, Dr Salvador Moncada with these maxims regarding the process of research:

(a) Be married to success not to a particular line of research.
(b) What is the shortest route to a negative answer?

In respect of the structure of therapeutic research, he offered the following:

> Heads of Departments command both resource and the quality of their functional input to research teams. The heads of department act as an Executive Committee to the Research Director dealing with the management of resource. Each department contains a 'dual ladder' of scientists – some oriented and skilled in the management of the function and others dedicated to the pursuit of expertise in their function itself. A major factor in the efficient operation of the matrix is the emphasis on the scientific 'authority' of the individuals rather than on their functional 'power'.

The Sir James Black Foundation

Sir James Black never entirely overcame his distaste for bureaucracy. Despite his success at Wellcome, he always felt that the size of an organization inevitably defeated its creative research efficacy. Creativity is such a personal matter, that it has to be conducted between people, not units. In setting up his foundation, his view of research is clearly stated in its articles. He has forbidden his scientific establishment to grow beyond twenty people.

In what he declared to be his last interview, with Thomas Bass, reproduced in the popular science magazine, *Omni*, under the banner 'The Greatest Living Pharmacologist', Black volunteers no mention of his time with The Wellcome Foundation. For the record, asked whether he did have a violent row with ICI prior to leaving, he replied: 'That is absolutely not true! There is a gossip machine out there generating all kinds of myths. I left because I lose interest in a project as it goes from R to D.'

Would he have stayed if ICI had offered to fund the research that Smith Kline subsequently did? 'How can I know? I tried to fly the idea. I don't throw tantrums about it when I'm in a company, I hustle for my point of view. But I think that's always been accepted, and my behaviour has never been destructive or threatened the integrity of the company.'

He has learned from his experiences in industry[12]:

> R & D are totally different. The development process responds to hierarchical management, to whipping, kicking and pushing. But it's inconceivable that you can make research go that way. Research has to be constrained and channelled. But the more you try to make it efficient, the more inefficient it will become. You'll kill the goose. The R man, like me, would be crazy to run a big corporation. That's why my present passion is to split R from D. R is an activity for small groups. People have room to express themselves but not wander or get lost.'

At his foundation, all work that is not basic research has to be contracted out. To Sir James, for research at least, small was not only beautiful, it was constitutional. The foundation has almost been a real-time experiment in leaderless groups. The thinking that seemed so revolutionary to TRD and Wellcome in 1982 is accepted, understood and operated as routine at his foundation. The disciplines of science are rigorously maintained. The atmosphere is informal. Conflicts arise, and are addressed. There are two factors that create real problems within this small group. First, there have been scientists who have not been the best at their subject. In such an open environment they can quickly feel threatened, and become insecure and defensive. Second, the scientists are all very much younger than Sir James. There is a missing generation.

There is so much to learn and that is hourly being added to knowledge about life sciences, that Black's team is in constant risk of rediscovering the already discovered. Such a group needs a scientist that such very bright and testing people will work with and respect, yet who is also experienced enough to recognize where their enthusiasm for the chase can lead them down cul-de-sacs which have already been explored. Additionally, such a person needs to have a sufficiently broad perspective to be able to cover the width of disciplines in the way that James Black has. They need a minder. Even in a small group, highly selected and very focused, there is a clear need for structure and hierarchy, of a specific kind.

Conclusion

Pharmaceutical R&D is a world of intense focus on creativity as an industry. It has wealth. It has history. It has spectacular success and spectacular failure. For fifty years there has been much thinking and exploration of how creativity can be enhanced and genius organized and marshalled to produce continuity of commercial success. By and large, the effort has produced strikingly little. The arguments continue, the mistakes repeated. The conferences go on, and still ask the same unanswered questions:

- How can you manage to maintain a balance in short-, mid- and long-term research?
- How do you stop a research project when you know it is not showing progress?
- How can you find or train people who are simultaneously creative researchers, good managers of people and good administrators?
- How can we find or develop the old research leaders we used to know, the ones whom everyone looked up to?
- Are champions good for progressing research, or is there always a serious risk that they hang on to, and continue to promote, what has already exhausted its value?
- How do you measure the performance of the creative researcher, and monitor the status of a truly innovative research programme?

Many of these questions have been answered by someone somewhere. Sir James Black has come nearest to answering all of them for himself and for his team. For example, he concluded that to achieve a balance in the R & D portfolio, it was necessary always to emphasize, seek out and support the long term. The short term will invariably arise and interfere. It has its own vitality and unlike the long term, needs no life-support system. But do not plan it in detail, because long-term programmed research will drive out creative insight. Just make sure the long term tops each and every agenda.

Such a proposal naturally creates another potential for conflict between the individual and the organization, most of which have commercial pressures of a totally different timescale than R&D can sustain, even at its quickest. Creative organizations are not comfortable places in which to work. People have to perform. No one can hide. The organization of the future has much to learn if it is to use its best creative talent. But equally, that creative talent must find better ways of making its organizations work. The answers must be found. The players each have their responsibilities.

As the actor Simon Callow, once put it: 'It is not enough to have talent, you have to have a talent for having talent.'

Notes

1 Paul Feyerabend, *Against Method*, (Verso, London, 1978), p. 187.
2 In Stuart R. Walker (ed.) *Creating the Right Environment for Drug Discovery* (Quay Publishing Lancaster 1991), p. 54, 57, 60.
3 Ibid. p. 41.
4 Dr Jürgen Drews, World Pharmaceuticals Conference (March 1990) Financial Times Conferences, London.
5 Ibid. Walker, p. 70.
6 Matthew Lynn, *The Billion Dollar Battle* (Heinemann, London, 1991) p. 176.
7 Ibid., p. 152.
8 P. R. Nayak & John M. Ketteringham, *Breakthroughs!* (Rawson Associates, New York, 1986).
9 Ibid.
10 Ibid., p. 117.
11 IBC International Conference 'Success and Creativity in Pharmaceutical R & D' – 30 April 1990, The Royal College of Surgeons.
12 Sir James Black interview by Thomas Bass entitled 'The Greatest Living Pharmacologist', *OMNI*, November 1990.

2

Inventors

My brain, it work along 'appily without me.

Philippe Starck

Whatever their education or occupation, almost all creative people see themselves as professionals. To be creative, it is necessary to have mastered the domain, the field of knowledge or endeavour, in and around which their creativity is to be targeted. In most cases, it is also important that near mastery is to have been achieved in other, not necessarily related, domains. The more proficient creative talent will probably have shown some early evidence of psychoneurosis, but will have been given the opportunity to put a consequentially and abnormally strong motivation to positive use. The lesson of chapter 1 is that the contest of wills between the genius and the organization is too often resolved to the satisfaction of neither.

At MEI SpA, in the Prologue, each side concluded that the contest was unresolvable. Many creative people feel this way. Some keep well away from organizations, some set up their own. Sometimes organizations will back individuals or small groups of creative people and agree to an arm's-length relationship. In this chapter, we look at some examples of how self-consciously creative individuals, not always geniuses, have found their solutions to the conundrum: organization or genius. The creatively driven individual is seldom an obvious socialite, and often seems to be relatively uncaring about his fellow men, and even a little arrogant, although is seldom without charm. These people may well be naturally caring and sociable but the drive to create often consumes all other desires in the quest for expression. This alarms other people and organizations who can, and will, compromise in the interests of stability and consistency.

Most inventors will point to the frequency with which significant changes and new products have been brought into organizations from the outside – and how hard it has been for such innovation to be accepted. Ron Hickman[1] took his prototype of WORKMATE in vain to six major British manufacturers. They all said it had no potential. For four years, before Black and Decker, he made and sold it himself. One study of twentieth-century inventions[2] showed that only about one-third have their origin in industrial research laboratories – more than half came from individuals, either working independently or in a university.

From the point of view of the self-consciously creative professional, the organization represents a succession of compromises. Sometimes the creative individual can accept these; sometimes, in such domains as nuclear physics, he has no choice but to do so. But for others, it is all too much. In organizationally crowded circumstances, the creative person can find a place to work on his own, or he can seek a close relationship with an organizational resource, be it man, machine, or idea, which gives him freedom and in addition offers him some leverage. Or he can set up his own company, and acquire the baggage of an organization which, at least at the outset, can be designed to his own specification. All of these are possible routes for the artistically creative. They are much more difficult for their scientific brothers.

Most organizations wish to reap the benefit of creative innovation. But the typical firm would fear for its fundamental stability and the consistency of its direction and purpose if it were to provide in its house the natural bedding of the maverick.

In this chapter, four different outcomes of creative people and organizations finding their compromises are examined through case studies.

The Inventor in his Shed

As has been illustrated by many studies, the genius is often the product of a socialization process which is outside the sphere of normal custom. The combination of a focused fascination for a narrow range of interests, and a restricted emotional environment, often produces a child who feels different, but who also needs to demonstrate that this difference has to be worked on to prove its value. Having established this feeling of difference, of being an outsider, it becomes very important to the individual to show that this difference is the result of his superiority, not his inferiority. Most inventors are outsiders. They are people who have become obsessed with cracking a problem. Their education is often unconventional.

Their achievements are seldom a complete reflection of their talents or accomplishments. Such people become soloists. They are usually late developers. They almost always suffer the indignity of being undervalued. Where fields of knowledge are fresh and changing, old knowledge and old technology well learned can be an obstacle. Fresh minds can succeed even without formal education. Formal education may even be an impediment in electronics. Many an accomplished thermionic valve man struggled through transistors only to be beaten by integrated circuits and the silicon chip.

The case of Kenneth Austin

Ken Austin was born in Lancashire in 1957. He did not like being a child. He had three younger sisters. From the age of two he developed an interest in electronics. He started taking things apart from this early age. From the age of nine, he designed circuits. He never finished them or put them to the test. 'What would happen if they did not work?' he fretted.

Austin left school at sixteen. He hated school with a passion. He hated being told what to do. He hated being lodged in an environment where he felt weak and out of control of the events around him. He learned very little beyond the basics. He was shy, inarticulate and withdrawn. No one told him *why* he should learn the two-times-table, or how to write well. '. . . if they had explained it to me logically, I would have done it,' he insists.

After school, Austin went to the local technical college and studied mechanical engineering to the City and Guilds standard. His first job was as a motorcycle mechanic. He loved it, and took a great deal of pride in his work. He worked through his tea breaks. His biggest pleasure was when people came to him in great surprise and asked, 'Ken, how did you do this?'

He went on to work for a motor-trader, in the service department. His director encouraged him to get serious about his career: 'The job has to be number one – it pays for everything else.' Again he worked hard. He became foreman. He became service and parts manager. But the further up he went in the business, the more he was presented with the problems of people. He was an introvert. He needed to keep away from people. Also, he felt the clock was ticking. His time was running out. It was time to move on.

While he was employed at the garage, his interest in computing and electronics deepened. He felt he had a lot of creative ideas, about new uses for micro-processors, new designs. He got into cryptogenics, coding machines, through his interest in electronics. He formed his own company called Advanced Electronics when he was twenty-five. He designed application-specific integrated circuits (ASICs), circuits which were created to manage a prescribed set of data in unique ways. He took these as far as he could at home, but was limited by facilities to take them far enough for his own satisfaction.

Eventually he went to Plessey and talked to their people in Encryption. They made him feel embarrassed about his lack of education, and he concluded that they did not take him seriously. This started him thinking about ways of getting accepted. He thought a lot about an Open University course but concluded, 'Seven years, for what? Just to prove I am as good as them. There must be other ways.' After a few days, he decided that even three years' time-out doing a full time degree would be a waste of his time. All he wanted was the intellectual pedigree – he already had the knowledge. So he approached MENSA, took their tests of intellectual power, and passed their standard. He went back to Plessey, more confident. Plessey were not in MENSA. Austin was. So both they and he started to believe in him. He stopped being so shy and introverted. He decided that if he was going to do what he had to do, he would have to change the way he was. And he did. He discovered that you can change *how* you feel if you really want to.

In 1986, he was introduced to Geoff Iley, at the time on the main board of Pilkington. Through Rainforth Venture Capital, Pilkington's venture fund, the two men set up Pilkington Micro-electronics. The basis of this company – the dynamically programmable logic device (DPLD) – was Austin's invention.

Plessey have taken up a licence to manufacture DPLD. This chip carries up to 10,000 integrated circuits, any of which can be reprogrammed while the chip is working. It can be used to call up circuits as required, or repair them by substituting unused for faulty ones. The dynamism makes each of three circuits the equivalent value of ten especially designed ones, with the additional versatility that their reconfiguration can be done at long range. The DPLD is patented, and Austin believes that it could become an international semi-conductor standard. The idea for the DPLD, he says, came to him in an instant. He started thinking about the possibility of the DPLD because of the intrinsic repetition of the ASIC design and the frustration of designing individual ASICs each time a new application arose.

By 1990 he was close to satisfying a driving motivation: the necessary financial security to do what he wants to do in the long term without having to worry about money. He has a minority interest in Advanced Electronics, and in Pilkington Micro-electronics. The people employed in these companies are few. All are software or hardware engineers. They take Austin's designs and assess how viable they are. They make them work. Now and then, they expect him to turn up and solve problems.

He used to build, to use his hands. Now he thinks in terms of properties or functions. He questions at the extremes: thought experiments. He thinks in terms of diagrams, not words. Everything has a picture. He has added the skill of presentation. 'You're the guy who invented it, you sell it.' He feels that there are many people who have good ideas, but do not have the vision or the drive to make them happen.

He is not an employee. He is a contracted consultant. He says he would die if he was an employee. His hobby is thinking. His belief is in himself. His message: Get a vision of all the ingredients, have the total picture in mind before showing it to the world, never go in half-baked. Credibility is as precious as gold. The hardest thing for an inventor to be is critical of his own product. Question everything.

The Case of Willy Johnson

Willy Johnson is an enthusiast. He ran his own company called Scientific Applied Research plc., set up to market inventions for a time based in mansion offices in Knightsbridge. He has patented the flying frog, a personal hydrofoil: 'Some people say it looks like me, squat and misshapen. I'm inclined to agree.' He has begun to research the possibility of using ivory nuts, a forest crop, as a substitute for now illegal ivory. It could be a cure for deforestation and elephant extinction in one fell swoop.

Johnson has registered the name Swallet for another idea he came up with. It is the first innovation in wallets for five hundred years. He has made it rigid and robust, not soft, and has included a combination lock and alarm. He called it Swallet in honour of Swatch, which the Swiss used successfully to introduce a new concept in watches some years back. He went to the manufacturers of Swatch in Switzerland and offered them his invention. They turned it down and threatened to take him to court. On the public stage, he comes across as intense, likeable, and surreal. He sees himself, and is seen, as a character.

Willy was brought up in the middle-class English home counties. An only child, he tried to please his father through his creativity and originality, a striving which has never ceased. The people who brought him up, including two 'lovely old ladies', always encouraged him to have his own ideas. To copy was a sin. Derivation, yes, inspiration from another, yes, but never copy. At school he was predisposed to the arts, from his first day preferring English and history to science. He also enjoyed handicrafts until one day he read his school report, 'William pulls his wool too tight.' So he stopped. He was an undersized youth, and something of a loner. He was the object of jokes. He went to university to read English and history. He was sent down before completing his first year, but insists, 'I didn't do anything terribly naughty.'

He was sent forms for National Service. He did not fill them in. Nonetheless he was drafted. The two lovely old ladies 'packed him off to war' in suit and hat, with a silk dressing gown in his luggage. Arriving at the railway station in a first-class compartment he was assumed to be an officer, and was escorted to his quarters by a corporal who carried his bags. Willy thought the army a charming and civil place. Until the corporal realized his mistake. At kitting out, Willy requested to be issued with boots, one of which was size seven and the other size eight. He always had a problem with his feet. His silk dressing gown attracted some close attention and with it some ridicule.

He was quickly nicknamed Misfuck, which he truly enjoyed as being so much more original than bastard. On day two he was nearly trampled to death in the rush for breakfast. He went back to bed. Caught and questioned, he simply observed that he had to keep warm. He found he had none of the mechanisms that help others to cope in an environment so rich in seemingly arbitrary rules. He had no way of understanding what was wanted of him, or of adapting to army life. After only five days, his corps commander arranged his discharge on medical grounds.

Johnson then went to South Africa, to work for De Beers. He made a series of blunders, gaffes and mistakes, culminating in a crashed jeep. This resulted in 'the best sacking I ever had. My boss was terribly sweet about it, he said to me, "Billy you're a nice lad and I'm sure you have much to offer, but diamonds are not really your métier are they?"'.

At a London publishing house he worked for a gay of considerable instability and cussedness. 'Nothing I could do ever pleased him, so one day I did something rather wicked.' His boss was 'delighted' to find, plastered across the company noticeboard Willy's Shakespearean tribute to him:

> A bum! A bum!
> The boss doth come

'I couldn't very well stay after that, could I?'

A few other experiences convinced him. There was no other option. 'I'm not really an inventor,' he says. 'Invention found me, because I was unemployable.'

So he started out in the world of inventing, on his own. He got involved in making up toys and games. He sold his inventions to companies. He borrowed money from banks and from private sources to keep going. It was a great struggle at times, but he eked out a bare living.

At a time when glue sniffing and solvent abuse hit the newsstands Johnson worked on a solvent-free 'Tippex'-type product for W. H. Smith. He developed a white, solid, transfer type strip for use in schools and classrooms. For Adidas he developed the 'micro-pacer', a computer in a shoe. The pacer was used in jogging shoes to calculate speeds and distances.

He also developed a 'ski meter' along similar principles, tried to patent it, but was out-manoeuvred by the big guns. Out of these experiences was conceived the idea that became his company, SAR. From acquaintances and friends he put together a board of people with stature and a wide range of contacts. All were people he could trust.

SAR revolved around Johnson's individual inventiveness which was based upon a love of the novel, a desire to improve the lot of the world ('Very important to make lighter bricks so that women can be bricklayers') and a commercial eye. With his board he was able to meet clients and university research dons on a scale he had not experienced before. Whether inventions sprang from his imagination or whether they were bespoke, Willy found that the key to success was marketability. There was nothing to be gained by inventing things which did not have an obvious market. He believes the starting point of successful innovation is an acute and considered knowledge of the market.

He has found the input and experience of academics invaluable in his research and development. They have been quick and keen to help – and, one senses, less concerned than he about exactly what it is they get out of the help they give him.

His approach to the process of innovation appears innate and obsessive. Willy lived for a time in a converted church, has a daughter called Tranquillity, Quilly for short, 'an ugly little thing, for now'. He has given up reading novels ('they reduce creative thought') and speaks with colour, conviction and style. He sees the world in a different way than most. That is his métier.

He once went to a psychiatrist, who said, 'you seem to be getting increasingly anxious, Mr Johnson'. Johnson replied, 'I am indeed, I've no idea how I'm going to pay your bill.' He added, 'It was amazing how quickly, having said that, he seemed to think I was getting better!' It has taken him five years to develop an egg-enveloping package that tells you when the egg is cooked and then doubles as an eggcup. He repaid the company which invested in the product only to find that it had not been perfected. He has learned to be cautious and defensive because so often he has found others taking advantage of him. However, he tries to maintain an honour in his conduct. SAR has sponsored young inventors and he was keen always to give them a quality of service few companies had ever given him. His 'deals' are based upon commercial sense – not commercial greed. While not a scientist, he relates well to those who are. His lack of formal training is an asset in part – he refuses to accept conventional wisdom.

Johnson's most exciting, and potentially most profound, piece of invention may prove to be a new style of televising on to a flat screen – one that will redefine the rules about screen design and use. Typically, the breakthrough came from a well-remembered half comment by a 'screen expert' coupled to a discussion about another discovery in a quite different scientific arena. It was then that the notion suddenly slid into place.

Two of his more recent inventions include one serious and one comic:

Fire Hoods Johnson obtained R & D support from a major petrochemical manufacturer by convincing them they were in the 'fire business'. Again he stood convention on its head. 'It's far easier to design a fire hood that suffocates people than one which saves their lives. It can take forty minutes to get someone out of a burning building . . . the real killer is not suffocation – it's blindness. Once the fumes get in your eyes you can't see and your chances of escape are dramatically reduced.'

Tantrums These are light plastic replica bricks for use to vent anger and frustration. They can be hurled at the TV without doing damage. The slogan? 'Throw a Tantrum!'

Johnson spent £70,000 to register the name 'Tikkaways', which he sees as the next McDonald's. He plays in an open field, realizing that his most precious gift is his next idea. Everything else can be contracted out.

Willy Johnson naturally does not support the conventional wisdom he sees offered by, and to, those who operate in big-business R & D. He feels the need for freedom. He sees himself as having gifts that cannot be taught. He regards himself as a creative opportunist who knows that attention to detail, hard work and persistence are all he needs apart from himself. His lack of convention extends to all aspects of his life. He is indeed unemployable.

The Case of Nigel Cutts

Nigel Cutts was born the middle child of an ambitious mother and a semi-professional father, a Yorkshireman, in 1944. He went to the local grammar school, and scraped through five O-levels. His sole interest was art. He would have spent all day in the art room if he could. He went further in engineering drawing, in art and in history of art.

He wanted to be an architect. He studied first at Leeds, then at Kingston College of Art where he gained proficiency at ballroom dancing and water-skiing. After a few years working with interior designers on hotel, cinema and office interiors, he decided to set up in practice on his own at the age of thirty-three. It was not an easy start, but in the early eighties business began to pick up.

After only a few years, he and his partner parted company and Cutts found himself to be the main creative designer as well as being the salesman. Now came the time for growth. His base was in London, his clients were amongst the many who moved into offices in London. He offered services all the way from design to installation, from private homes to whole office blocks. He grew. He lured draughtsmen and designers. He moved to larger premises. He started to think about expansion. He took on a marketing manager, a design head, draughtsmen and researchers. By the late 1980s, he was employing nearly forty people, making money. He could have had a Porsche, his accountant said, but he felt this was too pretentious, instead he went for a Jaguar Special.

In 1987, he looked at his five-year growth. Projected forward, it would take his company to over a hundred people. He needed to think of structure. Could he manage? How should he proceed into this unknown territory? He was being tempted by offers from bigger designers to take over his company. His greatest weakness was that he was still the only man in his company who could come up with fresh, original, creative solutions. All the others depended on his gifts.

By 1989, the company was gone. His capacity to manage, to hold on to clients, to get new ones, to add value and to find people who could provide him with the help he needed ran out of steam and the company backed one bad project. It was enough. The process of collapse was quick, if not entirely clean. This particular creative designer ceased to trade.

Cutts & Co vanished because it was too small to afford the specialist management needed to grow to a stable size. It was undercapitalized and too dependent upon a very few clients. Most importantly, it was a creative designer's extension of himself. Cutts is a determined man, who had learned his trade and had the courage to pit his wits in competition with others having much greater financial backing and employing more people with flair. His was the downside of creative independence.

Design companies have been a cottage industry for years. Both contractors and designers have been happy to acknowledge that the designer needs smallness, freedom and intimacy, whereas the customer needs resources, market volume and cost commitment. The relationship is distant and occasional.

Change will come. Some design companies are already becoming significant players, and could well survive the loss of their founder by more than a few years. But it is a dangerous route. It is too easy to grow beyond the size that the available financial and business acumen can sustain. For every successful company managed with financial competence, there are ten which overreach their own abilities in stretching for new markets for their undoubted creativity. It is a business built on reputation and referral, a very personal framework.

If it is so risky, why is there a continual replacement of those who leave the field of small innovative companies with those just starting up, full of enthusiasm and optimism?

Brian Larcombe, a director of 3i, the UK's largest venture capital company, was quoted in the *Financial Times* on 20 March 1990 as saying that more and more companies are looking at 'promoting entrepreneurship' by corporate restructuring. Referring to the fictional wheeler-dealer, he says:

> 3i has identified a new kind of hidden entrepreneur, not a whizz-kid or an Arthur Daley, but a trained professional manager who wants independence. In a recent survey, it found that 13 per cent of senior UK directors were actively contemplating what it calls 'breakouts' – either buyouts or setting up their own company. Of the advantages of going it alone, 93 per cent cited job satisfaction and making money, and 83 per cent freedom from bureaucracy.'

It seems that the larger organizations have yet to learn from experience how to get the best out of their creative people through providing them with the freedom they seek.

The Case of Lotus Engineering

Lotus Engineering was set up by Colin Chapman. It is a company of six hundred people who develop new systems and new engineering solutions all round the world. Colin was a hard driving, creative engineer. He could quickly tell the difference between a real technical problem and technical incompetence. If the problem was real, he might put the whole company behind solving it. If the latter, he was not a man to suffer fools.

Chapman put his organization together in a way that maintained great flexibility. He liked people. He was a structural engineer, concerned with suspensions, not engines. He was always harder on people who were in the same specialism as himself than on those outside it. He could always smell out where the problems were. He always seemed to ask the right questions. He was a perfectionist, acutely conscious of the details.

He ran the originally small engineering team himself. The racing team was separately organized. In his team there was a high rate of burnout. It was an exhausting environment. Chapman would push people to the limit of their ability. Some, a few, thrived, many more gave up trying to live with the pace.

Chapman died in 1983. His widow kept the racing team, but the rest of the organization struggled on financially, with a variety of owners, until it was bought by General Motors.

The principals who stayed on after Chapman's death remained determined to maintain and improve on the style he had developed. If necessary, they will fight for it. GM have left them alone. They certainly recognize that this is a tender flower.

General Motors need Lotus. In the view of Peter Wright, for some time managing director of Lotus Engineering, GM has the creativity sanitized out of it. In his view, legislation and product liabilities impede and ultimately anaesthetize creativity. Major manufacturers simply cannot afford it. The importance of racing cars is that they give the engineering group opportunities to innovate.

Peter Wright again:

Take suspension. The ground effect on a racing car can produce a force on the suspension of three to five times the mass of the car. We had two options – to develop a dual suspension or develop an active suspension. We find that having our engineers solve problems of this complexity and uniqueness makes it easier for them to solve the 'usual' ones. It's the same with involvement in Sunraycer (a solar-powered car) or Voyager (a plane to fly round the world without refuelling). These kind of projects help us attract good engineers and develop their problem-solving skills. It also means that we realize we have to accept peoples' mistakes if they're trying to innovate.

At Lotus Engineering there's very little pure research. It is about applying technology. They act as a link between those conducting pure research and the car manufacturing industry. They are consultants to car producers throughout the world. They particularly need engineers who can see the car as a whole, and buy in specialists when the need arises. All engineers are taught how to drive the car very fast. Consequently the company employs many ex-racing people. They also have a network of contacts in universities and research establishments.

Their closest competitor is Porsche, whose production is several times that of Lotus. Both try to produce highly efficient, integrated, and well-handling road cars. Ferrari, on the other hand, tend to produce racing cars to be driven on the road.

People enjoy working at Lotus. Fifty out of the six hundred employed in 1990 could be called creative originators. These people can be difficult to manage and find it hard to integrate. Peter Wright tries to give them as much freedom as possible:

> We have to identify their good points, accept their bad points and limit the damage as much as possible. Often we have to train them to improve their communications skills. Their written is usually worse than their spoken. (They also enjoy a good fight.) The creative people have to be able to imbue the finishers (who take concepts through to implementation) with their sense of vision. That is why communication is so important. Creative people can also be great salesmen – they just have to obey one rule: 'If it's profitable you can do it, but only if you can get the customer to agree to the cost.'

Creative people are enthusiasts, they know where the opportunities are. They do not join companies like Lotus for a career, but for the experience, for interest, for intrinsic rewards. Notably, where these individuals leave and clearly take their secrets with them to competitors, these secrets stay with them and are not shared with their new employers. Their understanding of the value of intellectual property is acute. They honour it and its ownership. Those who leave Lotus often quickly want to come back. They miss the edge it gave to their working life.

Conclusions

There are individuals who are creative, who trade on that creativity as individuals. They are often people whose very individuality has excluded them from the normal experiences of growing-up. As they have aged, they have created their own defences. They have learned to accept and sometimes to love their own differences. The alternative would be to despise these, and that is the start of neurosis. They have found strength in their gifts, and have worked to develop them.

To put these gifts to productive use, creative individuals have to find the means to extend their power and opportunity. They have to find other people who have the resources they need and to deal with them. This can be a very painful and initially humiliating experience. Often advantage is taken, and the sole innovator has to learn street wisdom the hard way. It is easier for them now than it has been in the past: the design world has facilities which are up for sale. There are small companies and institutions which will deal with creative people, on the basis of trade, of joint venture, or sharing gains. They can offer research laboratories, test beds, pilot manufactures. The task becomes one of networking.

In other cases, organizations are set up by creative people sometimes in their own image, sometimes conventionally. Such organizations exist as an expression and extension of these creative entrepreneurs, as in the case of Cutts & Co. They are seldom financially successful over the long haul. They are often violent places in which to work. They are never peaceful working environments.

The greatest problem facing the founder is how to build a creative organization when creative people are so relatively keen on autonomy. How do you achieve a group when its members like working on their own? Creative people tend not to gather together. They see differences more than commonalities. They are seldom good at small-talk.

It is a hard task to find enough people who will recognize and respond to a founder's leadership. So the creative founder tends to take too much on himself. The business suffers. He suffers. His business becomes a trap from which he can escape only by death or bankruptcy.

For the people who are the subject of this chapter, such practical matters are irrelevant. They have to do what they do. They have no choice. It is the others who have to choose. How can organizations profit from the driven inventor and the independent and uncompromising creative genius?

Notes

1 Walter Goldsmith, WORKMATE (J. Chartered Institute of Patent Agents, July, 1982).
2 J. Jewkes, D. Sawers, and R. Stillerman, *The Sources of Invention*, 2nd Ed. (Macmillan, New York, 1969).

3

Creativity for Sale

Find me a pot noodle!! Bring the excitement back! Make me money where no money existed, make an old man happy!!

Ben Elton, *Gasping*

There are some kinds of creativity that people traditionally only want now and then. They could not justify having access to it on a day-to-day basis. Moreover, this is creativity provided by people who are perhaps a little too scary for organizations to believe that they can handle. They are people who not only will not conform, but who rebelliously and profoundly object to conformity. They are necessary, but they are dangerous. So institutions are set up to provide their services while insulating clients from their excesses. Structures are convened to mediate between these creatives and their customers. This is creativity packaged for sale.

The evidence grows that for people who have a restless inner need to create, organizations represent a considerable barrier, both physical and psychological. It is for this reason that other organizations have come into being to sell innovation, market creativity, and provide commercial venues for creative passion to be exploited. How do they manage to organize their genius?

Advertisers, designers, architects, media folk, storytellers, picture painters and many others offer their creativity to commercial buyers. In terms of pure volume of business, advertising is probably the biggest of these. It is certainly the one with the highest profile. But only a small minority of advertising revenue is spent on creative output as such, whereas in design studios this is a significant component of the budget. Advertising agencies exist wherever there is a more or less mature economy. Their numbers often astonish: 10,000 in the US, 3000 in Japan, over 2000 in France. There are 1400 in Brazil. Most are small. The largest employ over 5000 people. They come and go. They change names at a bewildering rate. They pay their senior people very considerable wages. They communicate an image of great zeal, gloss and mystique. Usually they keep their genuinely creative people well out of the way. Few clients are allowed near these denizens.

Designers are not so flash or so flush. Many design consultancies grew at a great rate over the 1980s, but some of those which grew most quickly have not survived into the 1990s. People like Rodney Fitch, Michael Peters, and Pentagram have been, or remain, higher profile than the many smaller designers, but possibly at some cost in both financial and non-financial stress. The essential issue of all sellers of the creative process is managing the value-to-effort relationship. Most creative ideas seem to arrive without strain. Perhaps the most creative solution to a client's problem takes only a fraction of a second to reach. Yet it may be an idea that is worth millions of pounds.

How does the seller charge for this so small effort? How can he persuade the buyer to measure the validity of the fee against the yield that is produced, rather than the apparent ease of its inception? The most common answer is to surround the creative core with an edifice of supporting services and expressive gadgetry. The corporate imagers hire management consultants, company and market researchers and clinical psychologists. They add a deeper understanding of the nature of the client's real business, and so help the creative image designer to get closer to perfection. This increases the cost base. Therefore, it justifies the higher revenue. More importantly, it creates the feeling of value for money.

All advertisers have their planning departments. These are the analysts, supporters, gatherers of information, pre-digesters of views, who shape the environment and provide the nourishment from which the creative departments can produce their added value.

The relationships between agencies and clients are often uneasy. There are great culture gaps. Values clash over a whole range of positions. It is the same clash that attends every interface between the non-creative and the creative units, but when it is admixed with commercial contracting, it is surrounded by yet more ritual and insecurity. Most big companies have their own architectural, advertising, design and promotional departments. These usually include people accustomed to the culture of the creative agencies: poachers turned gamekeepers. Many companies have considerable experience of working with them, especially those companies which deal in commodities like baked beans that depend upon advertising volume, and novel forms of presentation. Even these companies are often restless at this interface. There is a fear, a deep insecurity attached to the relationship. Beauty contests are frequent. A big feature of agency costs is the constant competition for business, old and new. Marriage brokers are common.

The easy answer is often the one taken. The purchaser goes the conservative route and chooses the biggest supplier of creativity, the one with the name, the supplier that seems to have most in common with the purchaser. It is ironic that this almost certainly produces the least creative value for both sides.

The World of the 'Creative'

The noun 'creative' is accepted terminology in the advertising world, referring principally to the copywriter, but also applied to the film-makers, art directors and other visualizers who help to transport his message.

Eric Clark, in his book *The Want Makers*, offers some telling insights into this world.

> The creatives are often regarded even by their fellow advertising men as strange creatures. All agencies give them some latitude. An (anonymous) agency Chairman told *Campaign*, 'They are like babies, all totally naïve. They have to be because they are talking to other babies (the rest of the creative department) about what is essentially trivia. Can you imagine anyone remotely adult composing, "Hey, Tosh, Gotta Toshiba?" '[1]

The creative is given a strategy. He is asked to learn in depth what the product is, who is buying it, and why. Clark goes on:

> What creatives do at that stage is read, interview, talk, think. They become experts on subjects for brief periods. David Abbott has written sixty print ads for Sainsbury, the British grocery supermarket chain.

'For two weeks', he told me, 'I am an expert on cheese or pink champagne. I write the advert, and move on to the next thing.' Like many creative men, he likes 'the fact that it is a comparatively short attention span'. Neil Patterson, as creative director of TBWA in London, 'piled into medical toolshops and libraries', visited hospitals and special units to research anorexia for nursing recruitment ads – 'I even took an anorexic to lunch!'[2]

Some of the more famous creative outputs were the result of advertising people exploring the problems of the product. Clark quotes Obie Winters in the 1930s as having to deal with the falling demand of a horse lineament called Absorbine. Testing for alternative uses, he discovered that it cured ringworm in feet. His creativity was not just this discovery. In targeting the product to a new public, he invented 'athlete's foot' as the name of the ailment, thereby apparently tapping a whole new field of acceptable disease.

Claude Hopkins noticed that grains of wheat and rice were steamed to explode in containers that looked like cannons. He immediately coined the phrase 'Food shot from guns', a phrase some thought to be 'the idea of an imbecile'. But it worked, and is still used in advertising puffed wheat.

A last example from Eric Clark is of a creative team struggling for months in trying to find a means of getting across Volkswagen's winter reliability. Finally they decided that a snowplough driver would be a good spokesman. It was a further week after that when one of the team said aloud 'How does the snowplough driver get to his snowplough?' This line is one of the all-time greats in the annals of advertising.

Creatives in advertising can come from all sources. There are always far more people seeking to join the creative side of advertising than there are positions to fill. Once in, very few leave easily. They get trapped by the glamour and by the rewards of success. Unlike most other creative people, they do not need to know a great deal about the domain in which they seek to be creative. In fact, knowing too much can be a real inhibitor. It becomes almost obligatory to keep them from becoming 'street-wise'. Tony French, managing director of Monitor Advertising sees it thus:

Creatives are simple, child like people. They need simple messages. They have no patience. But they are not always genuine. Creative directors do put on an act. Our financial director said of one of ours, 'See how bloody cogent and analytical he is when he wants more money'.

Mike Walsh, at the time of interview, the chairman of Ogilvy & Mather in London, believes that:

> The best kind of creative people can deliver any time. They will always come up with a good idea. But these are very rare people. More often people are truly creative in patches, then go quiet for a time, sometimes as long as four or five years.

Very little science is used in selecting people for the creative positions in advertising agencies. Tony French, again:

> People never ask others when hiring 'creatives'. They are known to move about, with folders full of beautiful ads, but nobody makes reference checks to seek how much of these was theirs to claim. I once rang a previous employer of a secretary I hired to ask about something that worried me about her. The man at the other end said I was the first person whom he had ever heard make such an enquiry about anyone.

The consistent view in the industry is that creativity is not a measurable factor that can be used in selection. Only previous creativity predicts future creativity. This begs the question of how previous creativity can be demonstrated. So much clearly depends upon the competence of the previous employer's management. So much comes from the contributions of peers. Circumstances can deprive the best potential creator of opportunities to make a significant mark on the industry as a whole.

Getting the best out of the creative department is another area of great concern and theory. Tony French is more cynical than most when he says: 'There's not much creative thought left in advertising; they're all thieves of each other's ideas and of their own past successes.' There clearly has to be a cocoon and a structure. Mike Walsh believes that:

> The best creative works come from a tight *disciplined* brief. Asking a creative to 'just come up with something good' or 'any wacky thought will do' gives no focus – the way this focus is given has to be creative as

well. The old research department has now grown into today's planners – who are articulate at translating consumer attitudes and needs into a meaningful message to impact on creatives – using pictures and analogies to communicate.

Clive Holland, a long-time top management survivor at the London office of Young & Rubicam, supports this.

> The planning people are key. They work with the client, develop the brief, produce a creative strategy on one piece of paper. Then they go to the creative people and work things through. If they're good, it will work. If not, they're shunned. The planner is the expert on the consumer. He knows everything about the people who might buy the product. He brings out the ideas, it's easier for him to say no to the ideas that are no good. The client saying 'it stinks' is a killer. Planners know how to say the same thing without the same result.

Managing these people does seem to occupy the minds of many. As with other creative people, the hardest part is saying no. Mike Walsh sees this as an especial part of the skill of management: through conversation, through an open reception and discussion of their ideas, you have to get the creative people themselves to recognize that there is something wrong with their idea, and to understand what needs correction.

Some of the research people can be as creative, or perhaps as unorthodox, as the creative themselves. Most advertisements are aimed sub-cortically. They are not intended to inform. Their purpose is to influence. The most heavily advertised products are those which differ least from their competitors. The success of the advertisement is brought about by creating a mood, a sense of goodness about the product, a means by which a positive feeling is generated.

Research is therefore not only about discovering purchase behaviour and influence, but also about trying to look into the general unconscious. Some researchers uncover these hidden persuadables through attempting to by-pass the conscious censors. They induce the creators to mimic, to dramatize, to illustrate or even to model (for example in clay) the products in symbolic terms. They try thus to reach for the form of communication, via the creative, that seriously addresses the underlying subconscious decision-influencing mechanisms of the consumer.

Designers

People who design products, graphics, offices, buildings, interiors and the like are altogether a more serious and less extravagant group of people. There is no tradition of high pay in the field of design. Advertising takes its expense account from the salesman, the flamboyant, the risky, the young. Design is closer to manufacturing. Something ultimately has to be built from their ideas beyond castles in the air. Design does not have the perishability imposed by an advertising schedule. Most people who go into design as a profession believe they are creative. Except where they are architects, they come from art schools rather than universities. By and large, graphic skills are undervalued when compared to the literal or the numeric.

Peter Murdoch is a designer. He was not happy at school, a common characteristic of creative individuals. His rebellion stays with him. He may well have an artistic gene. His mother and both his daughters are exceptionally good artists. He started out determined not to conform. He would not join societies where conformity was the price to be paid for membership.

He went to Kingston Art School and to the Royal College of Art. Early on he found he was good with his hands, and enjoyed crafting. Over the years this has developed. In middle life one of his interests is making furniture from trees, going through all the stages of cutting, planking, weathering, sanding and polishing. He won the RCA Silver Medal and a scholarship to the United States as a result of inventing a fully functional chair made exclusively of paper. In two years he had raised the money and was in business making and selling this revolutionary chair. He became a full-time salesman, of which role he very quickly tired. He formed a design business in New York and got out of the chair production business. He and his partner bought air tickets on impulse and left New York. They went to Mexico where his partner knew an architect on the Olympic Games committee. They found that the Mexicans had a time problem. They also had an identity problem. They were copying the Japanese, who were the organizers of the previous Olympics. The Mexicans were also dominated by Spanish design concepts. They needed help. Murdoch set up a parallel office.

The authorities gave him and his partner six weeks to come up with a new identity for the Mexican Olympics. They were put together with several cultural professionals, including Mathias Goeritz. They did it. They found the identity through searching the Mexican culture, not the Spanish one. This image created its own power. Despite considerable political pressure they stayed on in Mexico and successfully tackled all the design issues for the 1968 Olympic Games. Murdoch left as the Games began, two years after his arrival in Mexico. Since then, he has built up a design practice outside the orthodox design world, working, amongst many other companies, for McDonald's, Sunseeker Boats, Swift Caravans and Venesta, designing and developing environments and products as well as inventions for which he registers his own patents. He moves his small practice often, because he adamantly refuses to pay rents for buildings which he believes do not justify them. Latterly in Tooley Street, near London Bridge, his design studios are far from the West End luxuries of the advertising world's front offices.

Murdoch, like most genuinely creative people, is very self-conscious about his own creativity. He senses he has many more ideas at the ready than ever come to the surface. Faced with a design issue, he will always deliver a multitude of possible outcomes. Superficially, he is a modest, conventional man, quietly spoken; not obviously fluent, but quietly considered. He sees his creativity as a 'stewpot facility', an informal, never-ceasing churning of ideas and resolutions.

> Basically men need repetition to create comfort and relaxation. As they get older, more and more they say 'time flies'. This seems so because we become more set in our ways. To stay creative, to stop consciousness and conservatism from controlling you, you have to constantly break up routines, walk different routes, catch different trains. Keep yourself detached and free from the addiction of routine. To me, keeping creativity alive is a matter of pride. I feel like Dolores Ibárruri, 'la Passionaria', who said: 'It is better to die on your feet than to live on your knees'.

Murdoch suffers, like many others in this field, from the lack of competent, devoted and understanding sponsors. People like him need patrons. The design business cannot support the lookers-after, the planners, the research departments that provide support to the otherwise exposed egos of the advertising world. There are rare cases, like Fitch or Wolff-Olins, where the critical mass of public acceptance is reached, and they have become part of the Establishment. Demand forces up perceived value.

A company in demand from the orthodox majority can afford to build the barricades of supporting activities. Few of these add to net creativity, but most of them justify a fee structure and show the growth which is comfortably self sustaining, at least for a time. For the Peter Murdochs, the proud outsiders, such a path is not an option. However, he grates vigorously at the sense of his own under-utilization.

> The Government should have a trade war ministry. Great Britain has not yet registered that we are not in peacetime. I am in that war, and am more than ready to play my part, but I am just not being used properly.

The problem exists at the interface with the potential customer. People such as Murdoch are too small to be noticed. They are also too many to be searched among. He says:

> The whole industry has been hijacked by people who have created an ethic by which success is judged by size and by turnover. The ethics of design are now compromised by the needs for short-term results. We need a new approach for the nineties. No more architects who cannot draw. Industry is being conned because they are buying insurance, not results.

He is angry, because he knows what he can do, and he knows what needs to be done. But he cannot keep his identity and pride as well as break through to his market. The distance between the buyer and the seller is too great. It needs intermediaries who can interpret the needs of one, and explain the virtues and the fit of the other.

Murdoch is not alone in this view. David Crisp is another of the two-hundred-plus product designers in London in a similar situation: a creative individual who runs his own company, but always at the commercial margins. In more than twenty years working as a designer, Crisp has met only four 'product champions' within British industry who have fought for, and carried through, development in their companies. In his view, expressed in *Design* magazine in March 1988, 'Management has been desultory. We criticize the design of our products in the UK but it is not due to a lack of engineers or designers, it is that management is so very conservative.' He finds that he has to seize the initiative and carry the risk himself past the design stage, in order to patent, develop and take the product beyond prototype. His final comment was: 'Designers want two things in life, they want recognition for what they have done and they want paying for it. That is all they want, but too often, they don't get either.'

Product design is an area where creativity is at its most exposed. There are always at least two customers: the client and the ultimate user. They may well be in conflict, as was the case with the Ford Sierra. The creative designer cannot be so creative as to miss connecting with the capabilities and tastes of the end-user but he first has to satisfy the expressed needs of his client. So he has to be a man of the people, as well as a man not of the people. And he has to be accepted at three levels: by his peers (from whom he needs recognition), his clients (who must pay his fees and must return for more), and his user (who must buy the new product preferentially to the old). It is hardly surprising that many designers go wrong. Furthermore, creative design is very often the most constrained of creative venturing. An ashtray has very limited features. The human body varies within some tight parameters. Fashions are beyond the influence of all but a very few. Finally, most designers are holistic and pictorial thinkers, whereas most of their customers are verbal and segmented.

At its most demanding is design that is housed within a giant manufacturing company. Rodney Axe has spent a lifetime of design in motor manufacturing, with Rootes, Chrysler in the USA and, for most of the 1980s, with Rover. Uwe Bahnsen was chief of design in Ford of Europe over this same critical period, and now heads up a rapidly growing and successful design college in Switzerland. Each of these two have had to stand in their corner, and defend ideas at a high level of abstraction. Each has had to be the vehicle for risk, for change, for redirection of investment where most of those around have favoured conservatism.

In the United States, Axe pushed for the mini-van people carrier, for off-the-road vehicles, against resistance by marketing, which saw no precedence, no active market. Six years later, most of the profit in Chrysler came from sales of vehicles like the Voyager.

Uwe Bahnsen was in the middle of the fight for survival that faced Ford in the early 1980s. He was one of the people who stood up for the Sierra design as a great symbol of public confidence which was to change the world's view of the failing company of the early 1980s.

The prominence and opportunities afforded design operations in these companies depend very largely on the inclination of the chief executives. People like Sir William Lyons and Lord Austin were design people, who communicated a sense of personal philosophy into their organizations and their public. Axe's concern now is that insufficient time is taken in thinking through the company philosophy, and, subsequently, the design philosophy. Designers need a focus but not a straitjacket.

For example, if Rover could define Britishness in its culture and its product, a Britishness which was good, like Rolls-Royce is and like Jaguar was, then creative designers could work from a meaningful concept to a practical product. Axe saw Gerald Egan, the then chief executive of Jaguar, as wrong in his belief that the essence of the Jaguar car was encapsulated in the XJ6. Who knows how much of the company's rise and fall over the past twenty years was attributable to some highly subjective design decisions unaided by truly creative thinking?

Designers very often agree amongst themselves what is good in design terms, but Axe and Bahnsen believe that creative designers show themselves as such very readily. The pressures on design are almost all from the organization. Products are often cancelled for political or investment reasons after many man-years of effort. Lack of vision in marketing is also a frustration. Particularly in such a high-investment-risk area of business, there is often a feeling that the best ideas will always end up looking much like all the others. A daily problem faced by those who manage designers is the finding of people who have a wide range of different skills and who will also be able to work together; hiring those who will work with marketing, engineering and production with equal effect, and who will renew their enthusiasm daily, and not worry about their creativity running out before they are fifty. Both Axe and Bahnsen have left their respective giant corporations. Both have moved to much smaller environments which give them the freedom that they previously had to fight for and earn.

Donald Norman wrote of the field in *The Design of Everyday Things*. Two rules stand out in his recommendations:

Make sure that (1) the user can figure out what to do, and (2) the user can tell what is going on.

Design should make use of the natural properties of people and of the world. It should exploit natural relationships and natural constraints.

As much as possible, it should operate without instructions and labels. Any necessary instruction or training should be needed only once; with each explanation the person should be able to say, 'of course', or 'yes, I see' . . . If the explanation leads a person to think or say, 'How am I going to remember that?' the design has failed.[3]

In essence, there is a paradox relating to the creative designer. He has to use his unorthodox, pattern-breaking, inventive skills to create objects which are instantly accepted and usable by those who have none of these qualities.

Image-makers

There are a number of organizations which operate exclusively to present others in ways which will increase some aspect of their commercial success. This is true fashion business, often based upon some tenuous premises. Wolff-Olins is one such image-maker. A company called Imagination is another. Gary Withers, its founder, creates events. His company has two hundred staff – architects, writers, technicians and producers. Barely more than ten years old, its turnover exceeds £40 million. It puts on product launches, extravaganzas and light shows, and designs public interiors, all on a big scale. Withers is reported to have shown entrepreneurial flair at the age of eight, running a blackberry-picking business from the family garage. He went to St Martin's School of Art. His first job was to be in charge of the exhibition unit of an advertising agency.

Withers is quoted in *Business*, August 1990, as saying:

> Selling extravert ideas to conservative clients is far from easy. 'Large corporations in particular want to play it safe. They're trapped by the fact that they never tried something before,' he says, 'now, because of our track record, we're beginning to attract clients with vision because they see we have vision ourselves.'

Later on, however, he adds that the company is often called in by up-and-coming young managers, 'looking for a battering ram to help demolish boardroom conservatism'.

A particular advantage that might be underplayed is that Withers' organization is able to point to the Ford Motor Company as a long-term and loyal client of ten years and more standing. The clients themselves understand the requirements demanded by such a role. Ford say: 'We have turned down stuff that was either too big for our budget or just light years ahead of its time.' A British Telecom spokesman offered: 'Gary has great talent, but it has to be harnessed in the right way. I wouldn't let him loose without a tight budget.'

Withers' approach contrasts with the conclusion reached by David Bernstein in his book *Company Image and Reality*, where his complaint is that corporate communications are intrinsically dull. As he puts it in 'Bernstein's Law': 'Product advertising takes minor differences and maximises them, whereas Corporate advertising takes major differences and minimises them.'[4] He goes on:

> Corporate advertising which takes as its raw material a company of diverse human beings and diverse activities in diverse locations and even diverse products and markets, more often than not succeeds in summing it up in a phrase of numbing ordinariness and parading a virtue to which all businesses lay claim.'[5]

Companies are all green, but also all sensibly economic. They must be big and old enough to be trusted with your money, but small enough to respond quickly and with goodwill both to your complaint and to your specific need. They must be good employers, but not if it costs so much as to make them expensive to their customer, or unrewarding to their shareholder.

Essentially most owners of a corporate image do not want to be seen to be different, just good. Whatever the differences they show that might please one part of their public, these will be sure to provoke an adverse reaction elsewhere. Advertising is not an easy field in which to be creative.

The Creative Architect

Very little formal research has been published about the qualities and origins of those who are traded for their creative art. Most of the evidence there is comes from biographies of the famous, or beliefs expressed by the successful, rather than from any truly experienced investigation. One of the few studies seriously undertaken on creativity in a specific occupation was that completed on architects by Donald MacKinnon. MacKinnon has been one of the two or three leading lights in creativity research over the past thirty years.

In choosing architects for his study, MacKinnon supported the commonly held distinction between the artistic creativity of poets, novelists and essayists, and scientific creativity. Artistic creativity he saw as a relatively unconstrained expression of the creator's inner need, thus externalizing something of himself to the public. He saw the product of scientific creativity (industrial research, physical science, engineering) as unrelated to the creator as a person, but operating on an aspect of his environment to produce an original outcome. He wrote:

> The domains of creative striving in which the practitioner must be both artist and scientist were represented in our researches by mathematicians and architects. Mathematicians contribute to science, yet in a very real sense their important creative efforts are as much as anything else personal cosmologies in which they express themselves as does an artist in his creations. So, too, in architecture, creative products are both an expression of the architect and thus a very personal product, and at the same time an impersonal meeting of their demands of an external problem.[6]

This latter expression could well describe the condition of all those who trade in their creativity: designers, copywriters, script-writers and film producers. All have to put themselves up for sale as people, yet always within the boundaries of need imposed by others.

In his research, MacKinnon asked five professors of architecture each to nominate the forty most creative architects in the USA. They produced eighty-six names between them, only thirteen of which were nominated by all. However, there were forty architects for whom at least two professors offered their endorsement. Before drawing up a final list MacKinnon considered comments about their work in eleven American architectural journals, and from the architects themselves. Two other samples of architects not seen as creative were listed. These provided controls against which to contrast what other distinguishing marks the creative architects had.

The results can be summarized as follows. Creative architects:

- were more inclined to have a good opinion of themselves;
- more often described themselves as inventive, determined, independent, individualistic, enthusiastic and industrious;
- less often described themselves as responsible, sincere, reliable, dependable, clear thinking, tolerant and understanding;

- did not differ much in respect of their view of their weaknesses. All described their desires for self-improvement as concerning personal attractiveness, self-confidence, maturity, intellectual competence, higher energy levels and better social relations;
- showed the only difference in their needs for personal improvement as that they more often sought greater sensitivity. The less creative wanted *both* to be more original *and* more self-controlled;
- in measured personality scales, rated as having a much higher femininity;
- showed a clear preference for the complex and the asymmetrical;
- on the Myers-Brigg Type Indicator, came out as 100 per cent Intuitive. The general population estimate is 25 per cent Intuitive. Being Intuitive means habitually looking for implications and consequences of experiences rather than taking them as they come;
- on the Myers-Briggs were also much more Perceptive (open to experience and happy with ambiguity) than Judging (concerned for control and the regulation of experience);
- more often believed, in common with creative scientists, that it is not sufficient that problems be solved, but that the solutions must also be elegant. They sought both truth and beauty;
- in word association tests, produced rare mental associations. This was one of the best predictions of rated creativity, especially the frequency with which they offered answers normally given by no more than 1–10 per cent of the population.

In respect of the early life of the creative architects, MacKinnon offered observations both less specific and with less confidence. The main ones were:

- In youth, creative architects were offered by their parents both great freedom to make their own decisions and support for them whatever the outcome. At the same time there was often a formality and distance between child and parent.
- Mothers especially, but fathers too of creative architects, were models of autonomous achievement.
- In pre-adult life, the more creative often experienced much more movement and diversity of cultural exposure. Some of this

turbulence could well have led to a dislocation of social growth, producing shyness and isolation.

- Creatives showed an early interest in art and drawing. This was not induced by any pressure to follow any vocation. The interest came from within, not without.
- They were unwilling to accept anything at face value from their tutors, showing 'profound scepticism' in school. 'One of the most rebellious, but as it turned out, one of the most creative, was advised by the Dean of his school to quit because he had no talent'.

This research has been detailed at length here because of its relevance to the sale of creativity as a business.

Most architects in the UK are clearly no more creative than most veterinary surgeons. They tend to be at the conservative end of creative commerce. The bulk of designers are nearer to the inventive writers in terms of their strong need for self-expression. However, the problem for the would-be-creative architects is no different than for the others. If the patronage is only available from the orthodox sponsor, then the creative talent has no significant or commercially viable outlet for the pressures within him. In that event, to make a living, either he has to suppress his creativity and suffer the yoke of oppressive convention or he has to be very lucky.

Succeeding in the Market for Creativity

The lessons for success seem simple to enumerate, but are harder to put into practice. Most people who expect to trade in their creativity are obliged to be entrepreneurial in some sense. This means that they have to sell themselves to their market. Creative people are not often good salesmen, which is one reason why there are so many agencies who do sound business being the creative individual's entrepreneurial arm. As has been pointed out many times, creative people are not always the easiest employees. They will tend to go their own way wherever they can. This presents the second problem they will encounter, which is that the more successful they become, the more they will need to have help and, in consequence, the more they will need to become organization men. If, like Gary Withers or Philippe Starck, the high-profile and highly successful French designer, they happen to be larger-than-life characters, or, like Wolff-Olins or J. Walter Thompson, they now have a market position and image within the trade, they might well attract people of similar creative talent to join them. For the most part, however, each member of staff that they take on will weaken the very creativity that produced the opportunity to expand, both because it asks of them that they manage as well as service their clients, and because creative people do not make good or willing employees.

There are several ways of solving these kinds of problems. In advertising, people get paid well provided they produce. The creatives are given licence to dress and behave how they will, but are constrained by the limitations of appropriate corporate-like behaviour to ply their trade within clearly confined boundaries. In the world of the arts, music, and theatre, there are several strata of intermediaries who manage the interfaces between the artist and his market. In the fields of architecture and design in general, organization structures are kept very flat. More often, with growth, these structures become more like grapes on the vine than pyramids in the desert, each keeping its close boundaries, equal status, but feeding off the collective source. Grapes are prone to fall off especially when ripe, and seed themselves elsewhere. Partners fall out at such regular intervals in these creative businesses, it is as well for the occasional client always to check before making a personal visit.

To succeed, the creative supplier must not be so outrageously different to his client that it causes him anxiety, but he must be sufficiently different to communicate the prospect of genuine creative added value.

So much of the image of creativity and of organizations is put across by the buildings that these companies occupy. They are never conventional. From Wally Olins' airy open-plan, converted factory near Euston through Withers' high perch furnished with a grand piano, to Peter Murdoch's converted warehouse near London Bridge station, all of the premises have this air of difference, of glamour, or of unconventionality. The biggest problem these traders in creativity can have is too much success. The second biggest problem is too little. It is a very exposed occupation. It should be no surprise that the image-makers give themselves so many prizes each year for excellence, or that the occasions on which these prizes are given out are so well attended and public, or that the judges of those who get these prizes are always from their own number. In no other field of endeavour do so many get together so often to judge, award and congratulate each other for their own excellence.

Conclusion

Despite its significance to the commercial world, little published evidence exists about the nature, the qualities and the effective management of the creative individual in design and advertising. David Ogilvy, *éminence grise* and arch-publicist of the world of advertising, is one of the very few people who have ever tried to explain how creatives are recognizable by some aspect of their behaviour other than their acclaimed products. Searchers after truth within the domain of the creative world are often kept at arm's length by their minders, the management, the account directors, and the planners. The industry trades in mystique, but has to deliver results. It is a sensitive and fragile body.

In contrast to the client organizations served by the design industry, the advertising world is atomistic, labile and volatile. People come and go, form and re-form, acquire and divest at great speed and with little evident long-term purpose. Organizations are small and flat. If they get large, they tend to reconfigure naturally into sub-units. As often, they expire. It is a very personal business. For all this, however, it is a successful business, and has proven that profit can be made from creative people. Despite the clear message that so much more could be done, there are lessons to be learned.

First, the creative individual who is trading his creativity values it more than he shows. It seems so easy, yet he is offering a mixture of his own identity while accepting the commercial and practical constraints of his brief. In doing this, he does not have the mask, the reinforcement of a position and a role that protect most people in the organizational world from personal pain.

While it seems easy, and appears to take little effort or time, there is a cost to the individual resulting from offering up his ideas for public scrutiny. The skills of managing such a process demand intermediaries.

There are people who can face the client, and interpret his needs through conventional intercourse, and then, with equal facility engage the creative in constructive production. This is quite a skill. The successful interpreter has to have the capability to say no without inhibiting. He must package information yet keep an open mind. He needs to manage to very tight deadlines, yet without putting undue pressure on the creative process.

Even in the business of creativity, there are relatively few powerfully creative people. Most are provisioners. They provide work, manage relationships, give support, and simply add numbers. The truly creative in this business can provide the novel, the unexpected, even the breakthrough with speed and ease. The biggest challenge their organizations and clients face is to agree the value of these ideas and then to manage them.

Notes

1 Eric Clark, *The Want Makers* (Jonathan Clowes Ltd, London, 1988), p. 53.
2 See note 1 above.
3 Donald A. Norman, *The Design of Everyday Things* (Doubleday, New York, 1988), p. 188.
4 David Bernstein, *Company Image and Reality: A Critique of Corporate Communications* (Holt, Rinehart & Winston, Eastbourne, Sussex, 1984 and 1986), p. 185.
5 See note 4 above.
6 Donald W. McKinnon, 'The Nature and Nurture of Creative Talent', *American Psychologist*, 17 (1962), pp. 484–95

4

Entrepreneurs

When the most famous creators and leaders are under scrutiny, the distinction between creativity and leadership vanishes, because creativity becomes a variety of leadership.

P. K. Simonton

There are people of genius who express this through commerce. Some have a natural ability to conclude a deal, others find that their charm and energy brings people together to reach for a common and collective purpose. Organizations grow up around these entrepreneurs, almost in spite of them. They take on their character, become extensions of their personality. Such people seen by orthodox executives as odd fellows, untrained and unsophisticated in the ways of managing. However, not all is as it seems.

The mind of the executive has received numerous studies over the years. These studies have moved from the prescriptive to the empirical with an accompanying change in their true value. The evidence of Kotter on general managers[1] showed clearly that, far from the ordered, planful decision-making and delegating of objectives that the classical writers of the past had propounded, most managers, especially general managers, spent most of their time and effort nudging, positioning, influencing incrementally, the efforts and outcomes of others. They operated within the boundaries enforced by the formally structured and acculturated world of which they were a part.

They had to deal with creating better focus in a world seen only as a blurred picture. They had to create certainty where there was no reason to believe that this could exist. They had to manage time when there was never enough, to move across areas of expertise where they were often ill-equipped to make an informed comment. Above all, they had to create and maintain relationships with a wide range of people, mastering a multiplicity of networks.

Complex commercial actions could be sustained only through playing harmonies on the positions, needs and commitments of these many people in their many places. Unless this web of relationships is in place, few commercial initiatives are possible. Robert Sternberg has extended thinking about what he called 'executive intelligence' in his book *The Triarchic Mind*. He refers to the work of Isenberg as emphasizing opportunistic thinking which is:

- responding to opportunities, including the suddenly unexpected ones;
- developing ideas and judgements on the run, before there is the full evidence on which to base a sound decision;
- reaching conclusions from readily available information, with only minimal search for more;
- consistently applying the same opportunistic search and conclusive style to all aspects of behaviour.[2]

All recent researchers and writers focus on the integrative aspects of executive thought processes and the willingness and preparedness to make a decision when conditions determine it to be necessary. At their best, there is little doubt that the executive thinking processes in the commercial world have much in common with creative thought in any other domain.

Perfect information is always far from available. Therefore, when judgements have to be made, they are often obliged to be intuitive. Working hypotheses are the nutrition of good executives, sustaining them as they seek to suspend final judgement until necessarily obliged to close off options. The same feature is true of the best scientific thinking, which recognizes that the truth of any scientific proposition can never be completely demonstrated. However, as elsewhere, there are grades of success. If genius is to be recognized by its rarity, then commercial genius would be highly visible. Fortunately there is evidence to help understand what differentiates the workaday from the maestro.

Biographies of high-profile business people have become a popular growth market in the past few years. Iacocca, Victor Kiam, John

Harvey-Jones and so on have all explained their success to the waiting public. The essential problem for those wishing to learn from these treatises is, of course, their specificity.

The 'excellence' books of the 1980s, and their subsequent take-up by many organizations seeking direction, suffered greatly from the fact that so many of the companies which showed up well in the original analysis turned out to be less than excellent only a few years later. Each business age creates its own heroes, and the qualities of each of these heroes would appear to depend on the characteristics of the age.

The other issue which has to be the concern of those seeking to learn the secrets of the commercially creative success stories is that the people presenting them are not just the people writing the scripts, but are also possibly as much part of the problem as part of the solution. Widely as Harvey-Jones has been admired as a man, as a symbol of ICI's turnaround in the 1980s, and as a television character, very few ICI employees of that time would ever endorse him as the prime driver in the actual strategic shift and reconstruction of the company. This was a board accomplishment.

As with all evidence in creative achievement, there are few pure examples of specific people who can clearly be shown as able to take full responsibility for the productive excellence of organizations, even over a short period of time. In researching the world of commerce for evidence of genius, as measured by outcomes of merit and standing rather than simply business growth or cost reduction based upon momentary fashions, it is noticeable how rare this is. In the following chapter, four cases are summarized, three of which feature people who have grown organizations from scratch over a decade or more, where their success is proven, and their philosophies are unchanged by the experience. Richard Branson, Alan Sugar and Anita Roddick. The fourth case is of an organization which has survived many crises over many years and, with its identity intact, has come to be a world leader in some vital niches of the engineering world: Edwards High Vacuum.

Branson and Virgin

Richard Branson owns Virgin. Branson is Virgin. When the company went public in 1987, he retained 55 per cent of the shares. He raised

£21 million from the issue. At the end of its first year of trading as a
public company (and its last, since Branson almost immediately
bought it back) it turned over £250 million at better than 10 per cent
profit.

Branson started the company little more than fifteen years earlier,
because he found discount record selling a profitable way of funding
his foundering magazine *Student*. Mick Brown in *Richard Branson:
The Inside Story* explained the opportunity as arising because record
retailers in Britain feared the possibility of price-wars, as had
happened in America, and had tacitly maintained a cartel to keep
prices fixed. He goes on:

> In fact, to the occupants of Albion Street [where *Student* was
> produced] record prices were quite obviously a 'rip-off'. There were
> thousands of young people, readers of *Student*, who would jump at the
> chance of buying rock music cheaply.[3]

Branson knew nothing about music himself, but there were enough
people in Albion Street who did, and the magazine provided a perfect
medium for advertising.

> The name for the new enterprise also came out of an evening of
> communal joking and suggestions – Student Records? Slipped Disc?
> Then Virgin – because, as Branson and the myth would enforce, 'We
> were novices in business.' But also, as somebody pointed out, and the
> night dissolved in laughter, because Virgins were the one thing, apart
> from money, in short supply at Albion Street.[4]

Branson then moved out of the magazine world that had launched
his commercial career. He went into direct retailing, opening a shop
in Oxford Street because the 1971 postal strike left his mail order
business immobile. He set up more and more shops because he had
to generate cash or else go under. He survived a criminal charge of
tax evasion by the Customs & Excise, having his financial embarrassment at the costs of his indiscretion rescued by his parents'
generosity.

Branson went into record production as a leap in the dark, buying a
house in Oxford to provide a base for a recording studio with money
he could not afford. He got lucky through sponsoring the unlikely
success of Mike Oldfield's very unconventional record 'Tubular
Bells' as he set up his own record company. By the time he was thirty,

Branson and his company had one of the top three record-shop chains in Britain, a music publishing company, a book publishing division, a small film company, a tiny island in the Virgin Island group, a nightclub and a number of state-of-the-art recording studios. In 1980 came the recession that nearly bankrupted many of the older, wiser and better-financed companies around the world. Branson's reaction to this was to agree to cut-backs, but only as a springboard to further expansion – expansion such as buying more nightclubs – against the advice of anyone he cared to ask. Virgin came out of the recession rocketed by the successes of such recording stars as Phil Collins, Human League and Culture Club.

Branson subsequently went into film production, started an airline, and manufactured contraceptives. The airline was the strangest of his ventures. He took up where Freddie Laker had been forced to leave the field, the bridge being provided by an eccentric lawyer called Randolph Fields who initiated the complex procedures for reintroducing an independent cut-price transatlantic service from a UK base, and took this to Branson.

Branson talked to Laker, and learned some good lessons. International air travel is a fiercely competitive business; some might say violently and unpleasantly so. Small-time upstart companies are allowed, but, as Laker Airlines and People's Express found, try to get big and you get hurt. Branson went in small, cleverly covered his downside risk through some very vigorous negotiations with suppliers of aircraft, money, and insurance against risks of adversity in both, and, when his turn quickly came to face the same price war that had brought down Laker, he showed a smart turn of speed in getting big political forces to aid his case, and survives, at least at the time of writing.

Richard Branson is an entrepreneur who made serious business in several commercial worlds of which he had no genuine experience or insight. He had no taste for what would sell musically. He had no experience of retailing, he certainly had no idea how to run an airline, or make a movie. Yet he succeeded in making money in each of these ventures. Those who have interviewed him report a man who conveys little of the stylish, dynamic, articulate, free-flowing rhetoric they would expect. He has little small talk, and seems very ordinary in his interaction with people. He does show enthusiasm, and, more so on the telephone, a persuasive line of argument, but he does not project the man who has done what he has done.

It seems that Branson's secret is partly luck and partly trust, but each is mixed with an enormous amount of energy, a 'can do' approach to everything, a low boredom threshold, and the capacity to get other people to do things for him that they would not do for themselves. He will focus on a business need for as long as it takes him to feel safe enough to move on. This makes him an essential deal-maker, an opportunist, and an extemporizer. He has managed to build a big business because he is prepared to trust others to get on with their assignments without interference, a trust based on relatively little track record. He is not an easy man to get on with. He is a practical joker, and his personal morality is not without its flaw. Brown cites:

> . . . the Richard Branson that, when playing wicket-keeper in a company cricket match, would tie cotton around the bails and then 'when the batsman has been in long enough' yank them off with a roar of laughter all the more resounding for the look of fury on the fallguy's face. Revenge was seldom, if ever, the motive in these pranks. It was Branson, the eternal child, wielding a pin at the balloon of grown-up dignity.[5]

So here again is the child, the experimenter, the manipulator, the unpredictable source of creative energy.

The Body Shop

Anita Roddick invented The Body Shop in 1976 and opened for business in No. 22 Kensington Gardens, Brighton, Sussex. She started with a £4000 loan from her local bank. It took two visits and was raised only because she offered the assets of her existing business, a restaurant and a hotel as collateral. In the foreword to a business profile written by Gilly McKay and Alison Corke, Anita Roddick wrote:

> The Body Shop produces products that cleanse, polish and protect the skin and hair. How we produce them and how we market them is what is interesting about us. We are innovative, we are passionate, and we care. We are innovative in our formulations; we are passionate about environmental issues; we care about retailing. The image, goals and values of our company are as important as our product. What is our

mission statement? It's easy–we will go diametrically in the opposite direction to the cosmetic industry.[6]

In April 1984, The Body Shop went public. Twenty per cent of the equity was sold – for £1 million. In the subsequent two years the price multiplied twelve-fold. By that time, The Body Shop had franchised two hundred shops around the world and had a turnover around £10 million, with more than 10 per cent profit.

Anita Roddick was born in 1944 of Italian immigrants in Littlehampton in Sussex. Her parents ran a café modelled on the American soda fountain, seating a hundred. She learned early the work ethic and the service ideal. Her parents wanted her to be a professional. She wanted to act. She became a teacher, but a very dramatic one. Full of wanderlust, she travelled all over the world on and off, until she met Gordon Roddick, another world traveller but this time an agriculturist turned poet, and quickly had two children by him.

In her travels, her curiosity took her to the villages of Polynesia where she made the discovery that beautiful skins could well owe their texture to the liberal application of cocoa butter. Back in Littlehampton the Roddicks started a hotel and a restaurant, but, exhausted by the long hours of trying to make these work out and concerned for the needs of her children because of her long absences, Anita decided that a shop would better suit their needs.

McKay and Corke report that:

> Most of the original features of The Body Shop were born of necessity and Anita's inventive mind overcoming obstacles. The characteristic green paintwork of the shop evolved from having to paint the ceiling green as it was the only colour that would hide the damp patches. The larch-lap garden fencing was put up to hide the wet walls – the water dripped down behind. The problem of how to fill a shop with just twenty-five products was overcome by selling five-sizes of every product, and any spaces left over were filled by green plants.[7]

The character, the naturalistic green colour of the shop, the wide range of sizes, the recycling of packaging each came about for practical reasons, but each ultimately provided a great value to the business. Anita Roddick chose the name 'Body Shop', because she remembered seeing it on a sign in American garages, and how much it had appealed to her. Franchising was not commonplace when she and her husband expanded the business in earnest. It came to pass for The Body Shop because they could not afford to expand as much as they wished through borrowing money to provide the leverage.

For all this, there is a consistency throughout the development of The Body Shop, and it is clearly the extension of Anita Roddick's personal values. She has made most of the marketing and product decisions herself, and she has been right much more often than any of her competitors could have expected.

Her husband represents that breed of people without whom the active opportunities of such people as Anita Roddick would produce little of any enduring value. He is seen as follows:

> Gordon Roddick is, in many ways, the antithesis of Anita. Where her presence speeds up any operation, invigorates and possibly intimidates people, Gordon's presence is relaxed, easy, and reassuring. One doubts if he would be the chairman of a multi-million pound international business if it were not for the determination and ambition of his wife. He would probably still be writing poetry and short stories and travelling round the world with a billy-can clanking from his backpack. Where Anita talks nineteen to the dozen, never finishing a topic before she has leapt to the next idea, often leaving out the interlinking points, Gordon speaks in more considered tones, interrupted at intervals by a stammer. He talks considerable sense and is very often the voice of reason in the face of Anita'a boundless and somewhat reckless enthusiasm. One close friend remarked, 'The only person in the whole world who can change Anita's mind is Gordon.'[8]

The Body Shop has a place in *The 100 Best Companies to Work for in the UK*, published in 1989. It was recommended for its willingness to back energy, loyalty and commitment ahead of education or experience. Clearly ideas for improving the business are 'eagerly sought'. There is a strong emphasis on training, and the evangelical attitude persists across the company at all levels. Its market profile remains high. Its managing director continues to be vocal and active across a wide public stage.

The Shadow

The need for the trusted tidier is absolute in these opportunistic entrepreneurs. If they are to make their impact, they need the reassurance that someone is willing to take up the controlling and regulation aspects of the business. Everywhere there is a recognized, prominently successful commercial 'genius', there will be a shadow. Almost all entrepreneurial failures are brought about by poor financial management, or by the entrepreneur overpowering his shadow, and in the process losing his balance, then his perspective, and finally his business.

Richard Branson had his equivalent counterpoint in his old schoolfriend Nik Powell. Powell joined him on the magazine, left apparently because he did not care for the interpersonal competition, but was induced to return by Branson in 1971 by a persuasive tongue, a share offer and the big job.

Mick Brown again provides the background:

> The relationship just picked up exactly where it had left off. 'Richard going out and splattering the world with ideas, and Nik coming along behind him tidying up, budgeting them and holding them together,' as Mundy Ellis (Branson's girlfriend at the time) put it. . . . 'But it was not without tears. Just as their childhood friendship in Shamley Green had been marked with spats of temper and fisticuffs, so the business partnership thrived as much on tension as friendship.' [9]
> But whatever the tensions between them, it was clear to both that they needed each other, even loved each other as only old friends can . . . Through stoicism, methodical attention to detail and the occasional display of belligerence, Nik dealt with recalcitrant shop managers, local authority planning regulations and the chores of stock-taking, grumbling for a while but bearing the brunt of the jobs Branson had no time for. [10]

It was Branson's character that prevailed, despite the efforts of his colleagues. Throughout the history of the company to date, it has been very clear that his iconoclasm, energy, his fast-dealing style, and his personal control over the funding of the enterprise have had a consistent imprint on everything that it has achieved. One of Brown's few comments on the nature of the organization itself reinforces this:

> [In the early eighties] Out of the apparent random chaos of the Virgin organization, a business philosophy – almost an entrepreneurial blueprint – could be discerned. By situating each company in its own – albeit small and determinedly unglamorous premises – overheads were kept to a minimum, but more important, a familial atmosphere was

created among staff. As the record company had grown, it too had been broken down into smaller units: Din Disc had been a model for two more affiliated labels, 10 and Siren.[11]

The greater the number of small companies you have, Branson reasoned, the greater the number of people to whom you can give responsibility, 'encouraging entrepreneurship', as he put it, under the umbrella of Virgin.'

Despite this easy-going philosophy, not all of Branson's initiatives succeeded. Sometimes he tried things that failed. He failed in ventures in retailing clothes, a serious venture into magazine publishing with *Events*, a catering operation called Top Nosh, and an air-conditioning servicing business. He could yet fail if he puts too many of his eggs into the one basket and is obliged to go for size.

Alan Sugar

There have been many false trails laid for the hero-hunters of the 1980s. Many have been elevated by the protracted boom of the decade. Of these, a number were examined to find the sources of their potency and the results used to point out eternal verities, only to find that the hero had feet of clay when the economic boom ceased to be sustained. One of the survivors in the UK, to place alongside Branson, is Alan Sugar. Fortunately, he too has been the subject of a published biography.

Compared to Branson, he is a rough and ready individual. Born in the Jewish East End of London in 1947 as the fourth child of a semi-skilled garment worker living in a council flat, he certainly had none of Branson's favoured heritage. Alan was brought up much as an only child, being a good deal younger than his nearest sibling. The evidence of his biographer, David Thomas shows him as a somewhat solitary child, certainly no joiner, a slight boy growing up in a rough neighbourhood, and demonstrating a very early fondness both for trade and for finance.

He made money at a very young age, and he saved money without effort. A clue as to why he had the genius to become a star in the UK business scene where thousands of more, or equally, able and financially motivated youths languish in obscurity, lies in the following comment from Thomas:

By the time he left school, Sugar had already discovered an urge to trade and sell that ran deeper than a simple wish for money. He was later to compare this instinct with other people's gift for music. 'I seriously believe I've got an inborn talent,' he explained. 'I've got an inbuilt aptitude for trading and dealing and scenting the way the wind is blowing'.[12]

Sugar left school at the age of sixteen, with some O-levels. Science and mathematics were the subjects at which he felt most able, but with no one in his family committed to longer-term education, or with any experience to offer on how to be an entrepreneur, he joined the civil service.

Like Branson, Sugar's expertise was in turning the talents and knowledge of others to commercial advantage. In Sugar's case, it happened that his first partner in business, Malcolm Cross, was a television engineer. This led him into commercial paths which laid the foundation for his business empire. At twenty-one he married and founded Amstrad, Alan M. Sugar Trading.

Once into the business, he became totally caught up in it – living, thinking, dreaming little else. He took up the manufacturing of audio equipment, gradually adding to the range and to his success. From then on, the formula worked for Sugar on a larger and larger scale. Principally he sold packages that looked more expensive than they were, and which did a whole job, like the Tower system or the word processor, without fuss. When Sugar entered the computer market, he knew no more about computers than he had about television. To him, business opportunity was about people's needs and profitable sales.

Sugar continues to dominate his company in a very personal way. He also makes sure that the people he needs to work for Amstrad get rich through shared ownership. He has been able to keep this dominance partly through limiting suppliers and customers to those he can keep in touch with. As he grew, so he added joint venture partners like Weinstock of GEC, STC and Rupert Murdoch. This delayed the inevitable, but not for long. Alan Sugar met the killer of entrepreneurial flair and organizational flexibility: size. His biographer, Thomas, draws the parallel with Apple – the $1-billion-turnover barrier. Apple's solution to the problem of size was to hire John Sculley, and ultimately to lose Steve Jobs. Sugar was more of a businessman than was Jobs. He cut costs and dropped product lines.

Then he hired two professionals, in finance and manufacturing, and in the process created an additional layer to help him ride the $ billion tiger.

Whatever happens to Amstrad there is little doubt that Alan Sugar will be a subject of deep analysis and reflection for students of business for many years to come.

The Entrepreneur

The Shorter Oxford English Dictionary essentially lists two definitions of entrepreneur: 'One who gets up entertainments', and 'A contractor acting as intermediary between capital and labour'. The latter definition was introduced in 1885 and has not been updated since.

Much has been written about the traditional entrepreneur, often with very little recognition of his true state of mind. Some time ago, Michael Dixon in the London *Financial Times* quoted Swiss industrialist Stephan Schmidheiny as saying that the entrepreneur is an artist, a sportsman, an inventor, a politician (in the sense of an influential communicator), an orchestra conductor and a father, noting that he is still only human. This presentation of the entrepreneur as an altruistic, creative leader, offering the security of success and growth to all who follow, produced a considerable reaction from Dixon himself, little of it in agreement with Schmidheiny.

Entrepreneurs are seldom the willing subjects of psychological analysis. It is often suggested that dark and secret wells of past pains drive them to succeed where others falter; that to talk about these private trials openly is too much for them to bear. On the other hand, as Peter Drucker has pointed out, all entrepreneurs have an infinite ego and an unfailing willingness to discuss their business interests to the point of exhaustion.

The successful entrepreneur is a person dominated by single mindedness. He has a few things to do, one or two goals to reach, a target to mark, which together exclude all others. He is hooked on practical achievement, gets high on ownership and can often become overdosed on materialism. To an outsider, which to most entrepreneurs means everyone else, this can make him seem greedy, amoral, and brutish. The success of many entrepreneurs is often pinned down, as with Branson and Roddick, to strokes of great good fortune. Many of the successful entrepreneurs in the public eye did have a sizeable piece of good fortune near the start of their empire-building. But, conversely, many entrepreneurs have suffered substantially from bad luck also. Unlike most, however, misfortune does not change their basic need to go for it.

To be successful, the entrepreneur needs very few attributes other than single-mindedness. Of these, the two most important are the instinct of a trader and the charm of a sorcerer. The one enduring memory shared by most who have experienced the charm of entrepreneurs is their capacity to make people feel they are the most important in the world, yet a day later, or even an hour later, these same people feel just as intensely that they are of no consequence at all. The timing, concentration and attentiveness of the entrepreneur when there is something someone has that he needs, is exquisite. His indifference is chilling.

Few accomplished modern entrepreneurs have not been traders. Manufacturing is complex, risky, heavyweight and slow. The trader moves fast, relies on his wit, depends on no one except those he owns, those who love him, and those who live in fear of him. Where successful manufacturing entrepreneurs are to be found, more often than not their strengths are in marketing, and their manufacture is soon subcontracted.

For the entrepreneur, this passion for trading is endemic. He does deals everywhere. Deals are done for what they achieve for him. He does not make fixed promises. He makes term promises, which, like term insurance, once out of time leave no trace. When the business gets bigger, he does deals with his employees in the same way.

The entrepreneur only delegates when he is drawn to a new horizon. Then it is done with great suddenness. He/she manipulates people, including his wife and family/her husband and family (there appears to be no gender difference in this respect, except that the woman feels more guilty about doing it) as a matter of habit.

In his book *Profile of the Entrepreneur* Alan Bartlett's characterizations of an entrepreneur include:

> He is self-centred, self-opinionated and self-contained. He usually has a chip on his shoulder and an inferiority complex with regard to social forces and education. He does not need others. He welcomes their confirmation, but he does not mourn their absence. He is consistently inconsistent . . . will be extremely generous one day, then endeavour to . . . reduce the cost of his generosity the next . . . more

often than not the benefit promised is never enjoyed. He is generously selfish. He is an actor of consummate skill . . . and is an able dissembler.[13]

From such an analysis of the person, it follows that people working for entrepreneurs have to put up with some difficult behaviour. Bartlett again:

> . . . he keeps all around him in a constant state of uncertainty and lacking in individual confidence. The nature of the entrepreneur is to discourage criticism and brook no interference. Since he is successful, there appear to be no rational grounds for adverse comment, and his attitude and appearance would deter a *kamikaze* pilot, let alone an executive dependent upon his boss for his standard of living . . .
>
> A strong entrepreneur surrounds himself with competent specialists but prefers compliant management. To a very great extent, initiative is to be discouraged. The entrepreneur does not seek advice in the normal sense. He searches for information from which he can select that which he believes he needs.[14]

The conclusion that has to be drawn from these observations is that those people who wish to remain in the employment of an entrepreneur, need either to be so reactively devious or sycophantically submissive that their own thoughts and views only surface where they match those of the founder. Alternatively, they must be so devoted and in so awe of the entrepreneurial charisma that every crumb from the founder's table is as a banquet to others.

For those who fit neither of these categories well, life is more difficult. The benefit they receive from working in the entrepreneurial organization is the chance to be excited and enhanced by its growth and vigour, to have their smaller talents amplified by its momentum. In such an environment, the possibilities seem boundless, powers of action quick and certain, and their compensation both varied and direct.

As the entrepreneur's company grows, so the seeds of its eventual failure often begin to find fertile ground. The more successful the entrepreneur, the more convinced he becomes of his own infallibility, the more unwilling he is to listen to criticism, and the less he understands the conditions necessary for his company's continuing success.

Commercial Genius in the Mature Company

The fourth case history is of an organization which has sustained a high level of loyalty and affection in the hearts and minds of its employees over many years, a great proportion of which were difficult and arduous. Over a period of sixty years, a sense of the identity of the organization was sustained in the minds of its employees, irrespective of its changing financial success or ownership.

It is an innovatory organization, not because of its position of market dominance or its leadership, although good leadership can quickly and clearly bring out the best in it in any company. It is innovatory because of its heart, because it attracts and fascinates innovators, and because, by and large, it has given them their head.

The Story of Edwards

Edwards High Vacuum International was started in 1919 by Frederick D. Edwards, who had been a lecturer in physics and electrical engineering, at what was then Northampton Polytechnic and is now the City University. There is an annual Edwards Memorial Lecture at this university on the subject of advances in vacuum and associated technology. One reason why Edwards started the company was because he was made redundant. At the time, his father ran his own business making laboratory furniture. Soon after Frederick D. opened his first premises in Allendale Road, Camberwell (with his wife and savings of twenty pounds), Frederick's brother became the third partner in the business. The original capital of the company was £470. Frederick's contribution came through importing vacuum pumps from Germany, the USA and France, then selling them to research laboratories in England. At the time, laboratories were almost the sole customers of vacuum equipment, with the electric lamp and radio-valve industry yet to come.

Edwards began making vacuum pumps in South-east London in the late twenties and thirties. Throughout this period, there were constant liquidity problems, sometimes needing voluntary and enforced wage reductions as a means to continued survival. Every few years, the company moved on to new premises, never investing in freeholds. As a privately owned partnership, raising money for investment always proved hard. It was not until 1939 that F. D. Edwards & Company (London) Ltd was formed. Frederick Edwards was a philanthropist, a socialist turned businessman, who believed passionately in the responsibility that people had for themselves and each other. The company was paternalist in a lasting way.

In an interview published in *Scope* in 1954, Edwards was quoted as saying:

> 'I happen to possess a very calm disposition and to be able to take any sort of troubles that come without getting rattled. In a small business that has to build up from small beginnings, a lot of troubles arise, and where the existence of a firm hangs on a very slender thread, as ours did for twenty years, this personality has been a great asset.'

At the onset of the Second World War, manufacturing started in earnest. Vacuum pumps were a strategically important product. Atomic energy research needed vacuum. The optics for submarine periscopes were almost useless without the enhancing properties of vacuum-assisted coating. Imports from Germany ceased. The Government started funding research within the company. Most important of all, the Atomic Energy Authority (under its cover name, T.I.) provided Edwards & Co. with its first technical director, the exceptional Arthur Stephen Barratt. A scientist turned businessman, Barratt was a shrewd judge of people and opportunities, with a great command of language. It was Barratt who had most influence upon the post-war growth of Edwards as ever-increasing uses for vacuum technology began to emerge.

Over the two decades of the fifties and sixties, more and more applications for vacuum came onstream. Freeze-drying of blood plasma was an early one. Because Italians at the time did not seem to respect patents on foreign pharmaceutical products, Edwards bought SAS Getters in Milan to provide freeze drying for pharmaceutical products made locally. Then the electronics world came into its own; the manufacture of radio valves needed vacuum pumps; television tubes had vacuums; Mullards required a hundred vacuum pumps per line in their early high-volume factories. Capacitors needed plastic coating which was thinner and more effective when deposited under vacuum. Large telescopes, such as at Greenwich, needed thin film.

And so it went on. For each of these applications, thanks largely to Barratt's technical charisma, Edwards was in the forefront. The salesman's job was essentially about telling customers how long they would have to wait to get their supplies.

In 1954, Edwards became a public limited company, and moved to purpose-built premises on eleven acres at Crawley, supported by the Crawley New Town initiative, and rented a factory which remained rented until it was bought in 1983. At this time, sales turnover was over £500,000, capital value estimated as £300,000, and 30 per cent of sales were export. In the City, it was a glamour stock. Employees were lent money at low interest to buy stock. Many made the kind of capital gains at a rate which occurred again only in the few pre-crash years before October 1987.

The size and complexity of the company had begun to outgrow the experience and capability of its management to direct it. Gradually, it was taken over by union organization. Frederick Edwards was getting old, and needed a successor.

With the onset of the sixties came a depression in Edwards' fortunes which lasted until the early eighties. The company became financially very shaky. Industrial relations disintegrated with increased restrictive practices and heavy increases in unit wage costs. There were riots on the shop floor at Crawley. Things were getting out of hand. Finally the managing director decided he must break up the domination of the shop floor and eighty people were made redundant. There followed from August 1962 to March 1963 what was, at the time, the longest continuous strike in UK industrial history. Eventually broken up, it created much bitterness and division within the company. For years thereafter, the company stuttered along, living a hand-to-mouth existence, yet for all that still keeping a fine product reputation intact.

The company lost its credit rating, and its price and status on the stock market took a huge dive. About the same time, in March 1966, Frederick Edwards died. On his deathbed, Edwards said, 'Keep my company British.'

When three or four potential purchasers of the company appeared, the company was in a poor state to resist their offers. Mindful of Edwards' last wishes, however, when the American company Varian came forward as the strongest contender, twelve senior managers took a stand. They said they would all resign if the company were taken over by a foreign buyer. Faced with a meeting with the Varian president, the twelve agreed to resist passively, to ask unpleasant questions and never to smile. At the end of the meeting, at which they maintained this reaction to a man and to the letter, the Varian representative felt the strength of their resolve so keenly that he said, 'Now I know why you guys won the Battle of Britain.'

This news hit the press. A *Financial Times* leader noted that for the first time in history, employees had defeated a bid. By this time, the British Government had taken an interest in Edwards and were involved in finding UK purchasers. There were two far-from-eager runners, EMI and BOC. After many months of negotiations, the BOC technical director pushed that bit harder for BOC. Aided and abetted by the Treasury with a £2 million low interest loan, BOC finally bought Edwards in 1968.

At this point Edwards made a new start on the difficult process of weaning the company away from its old philosophy of making anything to do with a vacuum. 'You the customer call the tune, Edwards will do it' was a common expression of the sales-led company. The new managing director promoted the alternative view of 'Let's do well what we *can* do well'. His decision to invest in a fundamental redesign of the company's entire range of primary pumps was a courageous break from past behaviour and served to dramatize his determination to focus the effort.

During the period 1977–80, the pumps were designed to be rugged and vibration-free. The low-vibration characteristics were an extension of the 'clean-room heritage' from the early years of the company's experience. The combination proved an important advance over competitors' models. However, the company was still struggling. The modest profits of the mid-1970s disappeared and losses started mounting. By the time Danny Rosenkranz took over as managing director in early 1983, the number of people employed by Edwards was down to 725 in the United Kingdom, the lowest for twenty years.

One of the most vital events of these times, and pivotal to the success of Edwards in supplying the world semiconductor manufacturing market, was the dramatic change in manufacturing performance. Down in Sussex, the instruction was: increase production capacity by 50 per cent. It is only to be speculated that 25 per cent did not seem to be enough, and a hundred per cent would have caused disbelief. The target set was certainly too round a figure to have been calculated, and the new market was far from predictable.

It was an expression of confidence in the new, tough, direct-drive vibration-free pump, but more than that, it was an expression of faith. In Shoreham, factory manager John Rimer and his newly appointed production systems man Dr 'Raj' Rajagapol took it very seriously. In the process, they produced a minor epic that eventually doubled the output, factory size, and workforce at the Shoreham plant during three short years of a general recession (1981–3) with an investment of £5 million.

Rimer and 'Raj' were, and are, intellectually complementary. Raj is a professional engineer with a specialism in statistics. He is rational, analytical, very bright and sharply focused. If he has a fault, it is that he can become too focused in his determination to reach the right answer. John Rimer is more rambling, more intuitive. He wanders around a subject, looks at it from all sides, tries to reach a feel for a problem. He comes to odd conclusions, and seems always significantly under-focused. But he gets results. His forte is getting results. Between them, arguing, discussing, researching and trying again, Rimer and Raj achieved one of the more famous results in British manufacturing in the past generation. They turned a conventional manufacturing operation into a high-technology, cellular system, upgrading the personnel, the systems, and the volume at the same time as vastly reducing the stock and work-in-progress costs. This was done, including moving premises, without any loss of production. At times, staff would arrive for work not knowing where their machine might be. Newly skilled people were required to train newly appointed hires while maintaining these high volumes.

How was this possible? Essentially, the two managers with the idea and the ownership of the problem were given their head. They were trusted and, between them, they offered both the creative new ideas and the evaluative practical assessment, each respecting the worth of the other. Since 1983 sales have increased three-fold and profits more than eleven-fold. Demand has grown strongly. Pump capacity has doubled, and manufacturing facilities have been added for the expanded product range. Product lead-times have been considerably reduced as a result of more efficient production. The sales department has lost its preoccupation with volume; it is now more concerned with satisfying all a customer's vacuum needs, while at the same time ensuring that returns are satisfactory.

Demand in the semiconductor industry boomed. Cost systems were much improved. Armed with better market knowledge and increased capacity, Edwards was perfectly poised to exploit the buoyancy of the market for semiconductors.

Edwards also reacted more quickly than its competitors to the enormous potential in the Japanese market, the largest and fastest-growing in the world. In 1983 it was the only foreign vacuum company to have significant representation in Japan. Some of Edwards' best sales professionals moved to Japan to develop its market position. The number of layers of management was reduced, and managers were given more accountability. Younger managers were encouraged through promotion, and where necessary skills were brought in from outside.

Rosenkranz initiated a regular programme of six-monthly presentations on all three UK sites, to keep employees briefed on the company's strategy and its progress. There was a greater climate of openness and cooperation throughout the company. It was considered that recruiting good quality people was crucial; during the period 1980–1986 over £5 million was spent on recruitment and relocation (equal to the total expenditure on new plant and equipment). Substantial amounts of money were also spent on retraining and management development.

For all the company's difficulties over the years, the people who work at Edwards do not like to leave. Even some who had announced their intention to stay only for a couple of years as a career move are still there several years later. Throughout the company, the combination of such a wide range of complex products with a never-ending growth in their application creates a perpetually refreshing level of interest which both fascinates and rewards employees. This leads to a form of corporate addiction. It is locally called 'vacuumitis'. This disease has been known to be terminal.

Edwards & Co. has been the subject of a London Business School case study. Rosenkranz has been interviewed and featured in the *Financial Times*. But the hero of the story is the company itself. By most commercial standards it is not the greatest success, but it is in a line of business where there are no advantages to be had other than the quality and commitment of the people who work there. It cannot stop innovating, or it will die. It might die even if it continues to innovate, because the world stage in which it competes is always a hard one in which to stay ahead.

Conclusion

Commercial genius seems to be about a style of thinking, a considerable commitment to a goal. It is a willingness to back judgements even without clear supporting evidence, or even the level of knowledge that could truly assess the evidence available. It has a strong capacity to engender loyalty and support in others, especially people who are temperamentally very different. Above all, it depends upon great opportunism.

The person of commercial genius is not as educated as some types of genius. In a sense, formal education offers little advantage. He does know the important people in his own domain. And he does keep in touch. He will not know everything that goes on, but will place trust in others. He will communicate easily and frequently. Short of a piece of data, or of an opinion, he will always know who to ask.

The novelty and originality of commercial genius is apparent not in its substance but in its outcome. Jan Carlzon was famous for his impact on the failing Scandinavian Airlines, fluently illustrated in his subsequent biography, *Moments of Truth*. He points up the difference:

> Literally hundreds of people have since told me, 'There was nothing new about that. We've been saying for years that you should lower prices. It's obvious that you could attract more customers if you cut prices in half.' Since the idea was simple and obvious . . . [15]

But only Carlzon did it. And only he took an even greater chance with SAS. He says the decision was based on intuition. He went on to say:

> Unfortunately, many corporate executives are noticeably lacking in intuition, courage, and conviction. The hierarchical company is traditionally headed by people highly skilled in economics, finance, or other technical expertise. These people may be extremely bright, but they are often disastrous decision-makers and implementers. They find ten solutions to every problem, and just as they are about to decide which one to try, they discover five more. In the meantime, opportunities have passed them by.
>
> They are faced with entirely new problems and must start the process all over again. Sometimes I suspect they think up new alternatives in order to avoid taking the crucial leap . . .
>
> To the rational observer, investing an additional $50 million in improvements at a time when SAS was losing $20 million a year might have appeared reckless. Indeed, it would have been just that had the improvements not been integrated into an overall business strategy. [16]

So the consistent indicator of commercial genius at work is not the content of the innovation, but the act of being innovative. Edwards was the only company which had invested in a major and very risky restructuring of its manufacturing capacity, changing method, technology and location all at the same time, with no margin for error, in the episode now referred to as the Shoreham Miracle.

Branson backed the record industry when it was in depression. Roddick backed her values with everything she had and without the evidence that there was a market, or that, even if she created one, it would not be easily taken from her by any of a number of successful competitive organizations.

As has already been pointed out, the value of genius can only be measured after the event. This does not mean we should not try to learn the lessons that the entrepreneurs have offered.

Notes

1 J. P. Kotter, *The General Managers* (Free Press, New York, 1982).
2 Robert J. Sternberg, *The Triarchic Mind: A New Theory of Human Intelligence* (Viking Penguin, New York, 1988), p. 210.
3 Mick Brown, *Richard Branson: The Inside Story* (Penguin Books Ltd, London, 1988), p. 53.
4 See note 3 above.
5 Brown, *Richard Branson*, p. 137.
6 Gilly McKay and Alison Corke, *The Body Shop: Franchising a Philosophy* (Pan Books, London, 1986), p. 6.
7 Ibid., p. 23.
8 Ibid., p. 98.
9 Brown, *Richard Branson*, pp. 62–3.
10 Ibid., p. 67.
11 Ibid., p. 137.
12 David Thomas, *Alan Sugar* (Random Century, London, 1990), p. 29.
13 Alan F. Bartlett, *Profile of the Entrepreneur or Machiavellian Management* (Ashford Press Publishing, Hampshire, UK, 1991 and 1988), pp. 12–13.
14 Ibid., pp. 10–11.
15 Jan Carlzon, *Moments of Truth* (Harper & Row, New York, 1987), p. 76.
16 Ibid., p. 77.

5

The Creative Reservation

Berenger: That seems clear enough, but it doesn't answer the question.

Logician: (with a knowledgeable smile) Obviously, my dear sir, but now the problem is correctly posed.

Ionesco, *Rhinoceros*

Many organizations have need for creative input on a permanent basis. They need new products, new directions, creative solutions. They therefore set up R & D groups. Most of this work has to be done within teams. It has to be supplied by a large investment in capital equipment. It is usually done by scientists. Not all scientists are creative, but enough of them are to make an organization employing them as creatives treat them as very different kinds of people to the rest.

Science is often seen as the world of the boffin, either a backroom boffin or a mad boffin; even, at times, the mad backroom boffin. Scientists are people in white coats in laboratories, never having quite outgrown their schooldays. They are regarded as people whose analytical skills and prosaic temperaments discount them from the possibility of creative thought. There are exceptions, like Einstein and Newton, who stepped outside the humdrum, and were larger than life. But otherwise the picture stays – of rather intense, almost suffering people, introverted, serious and boring. They speak in a language known only to themselves, excluding the passer-by with written and spoken symbols that set them apart, even from each other.

Inside the laboratory, these scientists divide amongst themselves.

Physical chemists, who make intricate measurements and work in deep mathematical formulations, see the organic chemists as mathematics-blind pot-boilers who do little more than guess at what they are preparing as they shake their fiery little tubes for days on end.

There are the divisions between the empiricists and the theorists. The first, often experimenters, need the feeling of the laboratory bench, the sense of getting their hands around an experiment. The second group, often more mathematically oriented, deal more in symbols, and in such abstractions that there is often no way of telling, unless by another such specialist, whether their thinking is sane or pure indulgence. These are the people of Dean Swift's Grand Academy of Lagado, in Laputa:

> The first man I met was of very meagre aspect, with sooty hands and face, his hair and beard long, ragged and singed in several places. His clothes, shirt and skin were all the same colour. He had been eight years upon a project for extracting the sunbeams out of cucumbers, which were to be put in vials hermetically sealed, and let out to warm the air in raw inclement summers.
>
> He told me he did not doubt in eight years more he should be able to supply the Governor's garden with sunshine at a reasonable rate; but he complained that his stock was low, and entreated me to give him something as an encouragement to ingenuity, especially since this has been a very dear season for cucumbers. I made him a small present, for my lord had furnished me with money on purpose, because he knew their practice of begging from all who go to see them.[1]

In reality, being creative in a scientific arena has to be a more demanding task than in most other areas of endeavour, if only because of the time it takes to master the vast accumulated knowledge base of each scientific discipline. A medicinal chemist working in a pharmaceutical laboratory would have had a first degree, then a Ph.D. and around two years' 'post-doc' experience before he would be considered as employable in a commercial environment. It would then take another three years of laboratory experience before that person could raise an original issue with an authority which would make others listen to him. By this time, he is already nearly thirty. It is a long haul, and a long wait for the scientist to find out whether he has it in him.

Most of the insightful writings about how scientists think and create have been written by biologists and mathematicians. Reading their views constantly leads the observer to note just how human they are. Even the most famous echo the words of Shylock:

> If you prick us, do we not bleed?
> if you tickle us, do we not laugh?
> if you poison us, do we not die?
> and if you wrong us, shall we not revenge?[2]

Peter Medawar was a biologist who had a talent for more than science. He also had a talent for communicating what a scientist was. In considering creativity in science, he wrote:

> . . . That because imaginative writing is the only form of creative activity most people know, even educated laymen have no idea of the width of the gap between conception and execution in science. A writer who hits on a good idea – or even a composer who thinks of or, like Sullivan, overhears a good tune – can take up pencil and paper and write it down;
>
> He does not have to sue for bench space in a laboratory or send in five copies of an application explaining what his poem is going to be about, how many sheets of paper it will occupy, what imagery it is going to be clothed in; or how mankind will benefit from its completion. But when a scientist has an idea he has merely reached the beginning of a long hard haul which will certainly involve an appeal for funds which he may easily not get. He cannot simply walk into his laboratory with a purposeful and dedicated look on his face and execute the idea he has in mind.[3]

Jacques Hadamard also wrote of this:

> The psychologist Souriau has noticed, there is, between the artistic domain and the scientific one, the difference that art enjoys a greater freedom, since the artist is governed only by his own fantasy, so that works of art are truly inventions. Beethoven's symphonies and even Racine's tragedy are inventions. The scientist behaves quite otherwise and his work properly concerns discoveries. As my master, Hermite, told me: 'We are rather servants than masters in Mathematics. Although the truth is not yet known to us, it preexists and inescapably imposes on us the path we must follow under penalty of going astray.'[4]

The essential constraints on creativity in science are about cost and opportunity on the one hand, and the management of information on the other. If it is true that creativity comes from the novel restructuring of existing elements from within the two separate domains of knowledge, this means that original science has to stem from scientists of two separate disciplines coming together, sharing their knowledge, and, as one, making a new synergy. Indeed this is how scientific discoveries often do get made. Rarely is it any longer possible for one scientist alone to emerge with something totally new. It is now a matter of organizing genius.

Scientists Together

Very few scientific research establishments have comprehensive strategies. Many of their organizations have evolved from a university department. Almost all have taken their staff from academia in one way or another. Perhaps it is less so now than once was the case, but academics are more inclined to follow their own interests than most other people in the employed classes.

J. D. Fitzgerald of ICI wrote of the issues of scientists in industry in 1982:

> Coming from academic life, a scientist will have grown up in an atmosphere of rigorous scientific methodology applied to issues of his own choice and studied for their own intrinsic interests, with little time constraint . . . Such persons tend to be logical, critical, opinionated, clannish, and do not suffer fools gladly.
>
> This pattern of behaviour, which intuitively rebels against conformity, makes it difficult for a scientist to accept the traditional behavioural patterns encountered in business organizations . . . The innovative scientist may have some of the following characteristics: he tends not to be mainstream, is noncompliant, brittle, has a strong ego, and is a risk-taker. He has a high need for achievement and tends to be a loner. Furthermore, he has irreverence for the status quo and he has less to lose by change than colleagues running an established business operation.[5]

An organization grown by people who follow their own interests is likely to be very atomistic. It is naïve to assume that commercial scientific laboratories escape from the tendentious political wrangling that permeates other organizations. If anything it is more violent and vitriolic here than anywhere else. An example of some personal notes taken in an interview with a senior chemist, talking about his colleagues (names changed), will confirm the point:

> Peter is more a manager than a scientist. He is a mechanical person, who is as cold as a fish. A very political animal – people don't like him and don't want to work with him. Tony regards him as a bully and thinks him unscrupulous. He is slick and methodical in organization, and he is bright. Tony has tried to work on him to find his better side but is beginning to give up. He was brought in by Professor Adams, who was an arrogant reformist who came into industry to get away from serendipity. He was a powerful dictator who ruled with a rod of iron, and who was generally feared until he fell out with his boss, got his wings clipped, and retired early.

Such people are not the easiest of individuals to get to pull together, and it should come as no surprise that this has rarely been achieved. The scholastic image of science is of objectivity and correctness, of truth and reason. It follows that the scientist is an honourable clean-cut rationalist. Much more often, as with the daily news, the darker side of the scientist is made public rather than the lighter.

Peer comparison is much easier in science than in most other creative domains. The scientist's consumer more often than not is another scientist. An artist, a musician, a designer, or a writer, on the other hand, can be scorned by his peers and yet have a devoted public. The barrier between such creators and their ultimate consumer is quite small: a publisher has to be convinced, or a gallery, to provide a place to hang the artistry. The scientist has to contend with a panoply of examiners, endless scientific panels on professional journals and the huge accumulation of directly comparable published work. The scientific meta-literature is full of internal jealousies and bitter rows. Just a sample will illustrate the competitive works of science.

Robert Oppenheimer was a physicist. He is perceived as the man who made the hydrogen bomb. Ed Regis summarizes Oppenheimer in *Who Got Einstein's Office*.

> But he was also a poet and a writer of short stories. He was writing poems by the age of ten and twelve, and later he had one published. He studied philosophy, literature, languages. He knew eight languages and used to read Plato's dialogues in the original Greek, and the Bhagavad Gita, the ancient Hindu epic, in Sanskrit.[6]

He was a chemist turned physicist, his own man, and not one to mince words; his views of one establishment: 'Princeton is a mad house: its a solipsistic luminaries shining in separate and helpless desolation.'[7]

Such people bump into the scientific establishment's 'careerists' with a noisy clamour. Robert Milliken, another physicist, was a lesser luminary. 'Milliken loathed Oppenheimer . . . and harassed him maliciously.' Ultimately many more turned against him ostensibly because of his political views.

Milliken, in his turn, was not accorded all of the respect he might have expected, as a man who spent years determined to prove Einstein wrong, and himself received a Nobel Prize that some thought he did not deserve. On a fence near a partially completed building near Caltech, the American educational establishment where he was a director, a poster declared: JESUS SAVES. Under this a local artist added: BUT MILLIKEN GETS THE CREDIT.

In most laboratories, such dramas are enacted almost daily, although not always at this exalted level. Again, it is hard for the traditional organization man not to think of the analogy with the junior school playground.

The common image of the scientist as the honest searcher after truth is one that many find hard to break. This is despite the numerous mistaken and fraudulent claims that have been publicized over the years. Some of these misrepresentations were accidental. Gregor Mendel was famous as a father of genetics. He reported perfect results in his experiments on plant breeding. R. A. Fisher, years later, showed clearly that statistically these results could not have occurred, there had to be some error. They were too perfect. As Medawar put it:

> The explanation could be as simple as that Mendel was a nice chap whom his gardeners wanted very much to please, by telling him the answers they suspected he would dearly like to hear: moreover as Mendel was an abbé, his assistants may have felt there was an element of heresy in securing results other than those the Reverend Father was convinced were true.[8]

So the scientist is human, and if he is creative, he is just as likely to show all of the frailties that beset others who burn with the need to originate and innovate in other fields. Again Medawar has said it best:

I once put the matter thus:

Scientists are people of very dissimilar temperaments doing very different things in very different ways. Among scientists are collectors, classifiers and compulsive tidiers-up; many are detectives by temperament and many are explorers. Some are artists and others are artisans. There are poet-scientists, and even a few mystics.

If only I had thought to add '. . . and just a few crooks', then I should have drawn a clear distinction between the scientific profession and the pursuit of mercantile business, politics, or the law, professions of which the practitioners are inflexibly upright all the time.[9]

How do organizations get the yield of scientists, when the latter are commited to their science more than to the organization's needs, and to their own ego needs ahead of their science? How can an organization harness the output of people who need to publish, who need to exchange privileged data, to go to conferences to talk and to listen to people like themselves. It is a difficult business, uneasily done. It needs a consistent, clear strategy, and practices which create no favourites or favours.

Unlike designers, artists, copywriters, media producers (even those of the latter still working in the BBC) and the like, scientists expect to have careers. This is partly due to the one-time employment of large numbers in government research establishments, and partly because they so often join large organizations like oil companies, utilities, and pharmaceutical manufacturers, which have (or have had) a culture of careerism, and sell hard to new graduates the prospect of advancement and growth in status and income. Like all opportunities, however, careerism in science has its problems, and, as usual, the problems exist not for the elite, but for the lower flier.

Young scientists bring with them an assumed contemporaneity, a freshness of thinking, an energy and an ambition mixed with the latest perspective. As they age, scientists, especially mathematicians, are assumed to decline. As creative people they are expected to be past their best by the time they reach forty. Beyond this age, unless they have shown some special rare scientific quality urgently sought after within their organization, or have learned and proven themselves able as managers or leaders of other scientists, they quickly become an embarrassment. Most organizations have great difficulty, and, to be honest, pay very little attention to sorting out which scientist falls into which category. The difficult decisions that need to be made often get postponed or reframed so as to be more easily soluble. One way of avoiding the issue is to create a hierarchy of positions, and thus replicate the bureaucracy of the parent organization. This means that a young, ambitious scientist is required to report to a person, who reports to another person, neither of whom add much to his scientific productivity. Furthermore, all the evidence, and common sense, says that steeply structured hierarchies are the quickest way of eliminating creative output.

In the past, commercial organizations kept their scientists apart from the rest of their business. They isolated their careers. They let them follow their own interests. As the number and variety of scientific people and disciplines have grown, so have the problems of productivity, of coherence, and of strategic management. Not all of these problems have been overcome, or even approached. Where they have been, there have been successes, but often at considerable cost. Very few of those organizations that employ scientists of genius, or even those with some creative potential, yet understand how to get the best from them. These scientists do not need complete freedom. Even the very best of them need structure.

Scientists at Work

Britain is notable for its tradition of scientific endeavour. It also has an unenviable reputation for neither resourcing nor recognizing scientific excellence. It is sadly often the case that where there is most inventiveness in the creative output of R & D in the UK, there are also to be found the worst conditions. Take, for example: the case of Thorn Lighting.

The Case of Thorn Lighting R & D

In 1928 an Austrian who had been a sales representative in the UK for an Austrian lamp company set up the Electric Lamp Service Company. Jules Thorn started manufacturing electric lamps in 1933, in direct competition to the then cartel. In 1948 he negotiated a licence from Sylvania Electrics Products of the USA to make fluorescent lamps. As the company prospered, it also became a leading light, so to speak, in the business, thus making the purchase of innovation from others less likely and the need to initiate innovation from its own resources more important.

With the merger of Thorn Lighting and AEI's lighting division in the fifties, and the subsequent additions in 1968, Thorn Lighting acquired a sizeable collection of researchers and developers. The two operations were quite different, with AEI very strong technically, whereas in Thorn it had to work by Monday. At the end of 1979, Thorn and EMI became Thorn-EMI. With EMI came the Central Research Laboratories (CRL), a considerable electronic research venture in West London.

Thorn Lighting suffered its first fundamental commercial setback in 1981. It lost money for the first time, and made two thousand redundancies. At that time, there were two major research and engineering centres, employing over three hundred people. Four years later, in Leicester and Enfield, more than half the staff were over fifty with more than twenty years of service. Because of their age, accrued benefits, and the absence of any alternative similar employment, these people have had little chance to find anything to look forward to in their future work.

To these centres of technology were added about 25 per cent of the effort from CRL, but with the market down, and the company struggling, quality research was not a priority. The marketeers in the mainstream wanted new products. They pulled them through from R & D unfinished. They presented them to manufacturing, which could not make them. In such situations everyone starts to blame everyone else. The process, in the words of Ken Scott, the ex-technical director needed: 'a coating of rationalization'.

Today's marketeers want the answers tomorrow. Researchers need time, and developers need assurance. The organization was reconfigured and R & D became part of newly formed business units. This created a new distress for research and development. In breaking continuity across the existing R & D divisions their essential synergy was lost. Market logic does not always match developmental logic.

The research programmes had ranged from such factors as sick buildings, and seasonal affective disorder, to the impact of lighting on both. Basic research looked into opto-electronic materials: how to use electronics to put power straight into the glass envelope. Revenue was being sought by R & D from directly selling their intellectual property outside the holding company. Investigations were being made into a whole range of features that affected fixtures, fittings, applications, and their commercial consequences. The problem was, within a declining business of such maturity and complexity, that the R & D function, far from being a reservation, became its own tiny mainstream, and its relationship with the manufacturing and selling company became both tenuous and adversarial. Thorn-EMI have tried to sell the whole business, unsuccessfully, with consequential cost-cutting and more to come. It is an organization which can only die slowly, by dismemberment and ultimately from malnutrition.

Picture outer Leicester, where what is left of the folk memories of a seventy-year history of research and development into lighting echo down the corridors on the first floor of an archaic building. One corridor is called Harley Street because of the number of doctors in residence. They are doctors of physics, of chemistry, of electronics, and of mathematics. The ceilings are high, the ambience gloomy and unwelcoming. At the far end of the corridor are the deep thinkers, the physicists, the mathematicians. Nearer the entrance, where the managers sit, are those looking at applications, greater efficiencies, longer-lasting light sources, and colour effects. Physically it is not a place to inspire. Yet it is the place where Maurice Cayless was the first to explain the workings of the fluorescent light. It was here, in 1970 that Jim Coaton and others found a revolutionary new way to extend the life and performance of tungsten halogen lamps to a practical level, using bromophosphonitrile.

Around the right-angled bend in the corridor, there is a widening. Three old chairs, a battered filing cabinet and a low table support an electric kettle and some cups. This is the meeting area for the professional innovators. This is where the score or so of those scientists, some world-renowned, have their private meeting place, encouraging them to share thoughts while passing coffee-time together. At eye level, in the window, there is a mock bird's-nest, made recently with freshly laid, but ersatz, straw. In this nest are two light bulbs, the larger of the two presumably the cuckoo. To acquire this little, scruffy token to interdisciplinary ideational sharing, Alan Chalmers, as the laboratory head, had to fight tooth and nail. He had to put up with the complaints of featherbedding and special privilege which issued from those others on the site who show no taste for the values, culture or research output of this tiny group.

As a business, Thorn Lighting became too small to survive in the rapid globalization of such commodities. Only through research and innovation, at all levels in the organization, could it have hoped to retain its identity, to grow, or even to survive. Yet research seemed to be seen as an overhead, uncalled for, unsought and unloved. These people were different. But not that different. The difference is both valid and valuable. In a changing world, it is conformity to present expectations and values which will bring down the very continuity it seeks to sustain. This light sources (bulbs and tubes) business was sold to GTE in 1990. Let us hope that Harley Street survives to enjoy a more propitious future.

This example is not atypical of R & D in financial or marketing-dominated organizational settings. There is no go-between. The cultures are too far apart to create sound communication channels. They are both misunderstood and undervalued by the operating businesses and are left to grow old with neither a sense of purpose nor a prospect of renewal. Inside these organizational units, especially where they are merged units, with long histories, and a diverse culture, there is a battle for funds, for ascendancy and for focus. The climate can range from anger to despair, but mostly it is despair. Most R & D people know of examples where a project completed means that its champion no longer has a job, and where, with a great new innovative product in the final stages of development, the team that started it are let go altogether.

BBC Engineering Research

The BBC is probably the largest single organization in general broadcasting in the world. An income of over £1 billion is matched by a diverse but highly qualified staff of over 25,000. It is a very public body, very much in the public limelight both for what it does and what it does not do. Originally set up as a vehicle for British radio manufacturers to provide what would now be called 'software' services and thus encourage the market interest in their products, it has now outlasted almost all the indigenous manufacturers of nearly every kind of broadcast-signal-receiving equipment. It alone represents land-based technology of broadcasting in the UK. No one could describe the business of broadcasting as low on innovation or change over the past forty years.

The BBC produces a very large annual report which details accomplishments across the whole range of activities from News and Current Affairs to Enterprises, whose task it is to make commercial profit from the BBC's properties. The Engineering Research Department comes under the jurisdiction of the Engineering Directorate. It is housed in a 150-year-old mansion in Surrey, in the country but within the M25 boundary. In 1990, it had a staff of over two hundred, half of whom were qualified engineers, physicists, mathemeticians and technicians. In the BBC's annual report, it seldom rates more than three column inches.

Bruce Moffat has the responsibility of running a department which is seen in some aspects of its research as a world leader, and which includes some of the world experts in broadcasting technology. His job requires more of his public relation skills than any scientific ones. His research heads, like Ian Childs, expend much of their creativity in finding ways to achieve results with the barest minimum of cost.

The BBC played a part in the Eureka project, aimed to promote the European standard for HDTV in direct competition to the Japanese. The BBC provided programme material. The Engineering Research Department provided the means of acquiring it. The way these engineers went about establishing how this programme could be created showed what could be done with little time and almost no money.

Dr Moffat comes up against some of the same issues as Jim Coaton. Environmentally, the location of Research is vastly superior to most of the existing and prospective sites where other BBC staff could expect to work. The pace of life in the thirty-acre grounds seems relaxed and undemanding. However, visitors from the Corporation have to be induced. More often than not they come to Surrey to question the value-for-money equation. Value for money tends to be based upon immediate value for immediate money. No research organization stands up to this test.

So the engineers struggle, despite their professional reputation. They struggle for funds, for security, for a fair wage and for recognition. It is a long and hard struggle, but one that seems to keep them in good heart, and profoundly loyal to their own organization.

R & D and the Mainstream Business

The preceding two examples would seem typical of the issues which arise where R & D has been treated as a process of organizational apartheid, and has accepted this treatment as appropriate. The most successful R & D departments are those which are closely allied to the mainstream business, physically, professionally and psychologically. In 1982, Jay Galbraith published a paper entitled 'Designing the innovating organization'. His contention was that innovation requires an organization specifically designed for that purpose. He pointed out: 'An organization that is designed to do something for the millionth time is not that good at doing something for the first time.'[10] Later he states:

> Industry has a poor track record with this type (good ideas which do not quite fit) of innovation. Most major technological changes come from outside an industry. The mechanical typewriter manufacturers did not introduce the electric typewriter. The electric typewriter people did not invent the electronic typewriter; vacuum tube companies did not introduce the transistor, and so on.[11]

Galbraith went on to describe the problem of the interface between the innovating organization's need for differentiation and the operating organization's capacity for acceptance of new ideas for implementation.

This position was re-examined by Rosabeth Moss Kanter in *When Giants Learn to Dance*. She introduced the expressions 'newstreams' for the innovators, and 'mainstreams' for the orthodox businesses, and pointed out that the two have different logics. She wrote: 'It is in the nature of newstreams to be uncertain, bumpy, boat rocking, controversial, knowledge intense and independent – seeking their own course.'[12] The newstream requires committed leadership, patient money and planning flexibility. Mainstream requires detailed resource commitments, predictable return on investments, clear time-horizons and adherence to the game plan. So how do we keep them apart?

Galbraith uses the expression 'reservations' to describe the safe havens put aside for innovative organizations within larger mainstream ones and explains these as follows: 'Reservations permit differentiation to occur by housing people who work solely for the innovating organization and by having a reservation manager who works full time as a sponsor.'[13] Reservations can be internal or external, permanent or temporary. Where they run into problems is, of course, when they become organizations just like their customers, the mainstreams. This process of bureaucratization is not uncommon where R & D organizations of any size reach their maturity.

So many scientists and engineers in R & D feel insecure. In times of crisis or restraint, they feel even more insecure. There is little evidence that personal insecurity ever provoked greater creative productivity.

The Personal Fears of Research Scientists

A research focus takes scientists into some very narrow regions of knowledgeable expertise. They can fall into the trap of knowing everything about nothing. Such situations leave them feeling kings in their own domain, but paranoic about the possibility of giving up on that territory and moving to a new one. So the hardest activity for any research organization to undertake is to find legitimate ways of closing down programmes which are getting nowhere, without meeting enormous and often very articulate, very mischievous, resistance from the scientists concerned as they fight a rearguard action to protect what they see as their physical and psychological security.

A second fear that committed research scientists have is that the process of ageing will take away their capacity to have original thought. Worse, ageing might deprive them of their value as their subject discipline expands and evolves. The research they need to grasp expands beyond their capacity to abort it. Young scientists emerge to challenge their positions, which are in any event held only through a tenuous organizational tenancy. The young Turks' new thinking is unencumbered with the older scientists' weight of obsolescent conceptual baggage. Most scientists acknowledge that age takes away the edge of their speed of thought, once forty-five has been reached. Nobel Prizes for Science are seldom won by people whose prize-winning work was done after their forties.

In a transcript of a discussion on the BBC Third Programme on 25 April 1966 and published in *The Threat and the Glory*, Peter Medawar was asked by Dr J. W. N. Watkins: 'Are you at fifty still in your prime or past it?'

> . . . I am certainly less quick-witted than I used to be. I am certainly less analytically deft. If science is essentially an analytical procedure, if it depended upon let us say, the working of an inductive machine, then I would have to admit that I was going rapidly downhill. But another

factor has to be taken into account: an important element and this does not decay at the same rate as the other faculties of the mind. The critical faculty by which one puts one's imaginings to the test may deteriorate and perhaps it has done in my case, who knows? – but the imagination itself seems to persist.[14]

This compensating wisdom can come to some scientists but not all. No great study has yet been made of who will receive the touch of this muse, and who will not. Those who have been most creative most early in their career are the least likely to suffer the adverse consequences of age. The rule could well be: the better you are, the better you stay; the worse you start, the worse you get.

Peter Medawar, in 1977, had this to say on the subject: 'From the standpoint of academic administration, no sociological research could be more important than the attempt to ascertain what truth there was in the commonplace notion that creativity diminishes with advancing years.'[15] There is clearly an incentive to preserving physical health because, particularly in the older person, it is harder to maintain *mens sana* without *corporo sano*.

The third area that frightens the scientist is found where the more traditional single-channel career path operates. This is the fear of personal failure that comes when a person who feels perfectly competent and comfortable in one job is obliged to take another job (in order to get on) in which he has no idea how well he will perform. Few, if any, scientific research establishments offer the kind of comprehensive retraining that such a step should warrant. It is a very large step for most successful scientists to take, and their success or failure is often decided very early, with the judgement based more upon their interpersonal skills than on any other aspect of the research management process. They have reason to fear.

Conclusion

Mathematician Jacques Hadamard wrote a book packed with informed opinion about the creative process, *The Psychology of Invention in the Mathematical Field*. One of the most telling of his observations was his reference to the two conceptions of invention. After attending a meeting at the Centre de Synthèse in Paris in 1937 he quoted Claparède (a Genovese psychologist) as having said:

There are two kinds of invention: one consists, a goal being given, in finding the means to reach it, so that the mind goes from the goal to the means, from the question to the solution; the other consists, on the contrary, in discovering a fact, then imagining what it could be useful for, so that, this time, mind goes from the means to the goal; the answer appears to us before the question.

Now, paradoxical as it seems, the second kind of invention is the more general one, and becomes more and more so as science advances. Practical application is found by not looking for it, and one can say that the whole progress of civilisation rests on that principle.[16]

The first observation represents a core issue in the commercial management of the creative scientist. Pure research is the source of great advances in knowledge, and produces Nobel Prizewinners in numbers which encourage a sense of great social congratulation. Such science is seen as discovery even though everything that can be discovered is already there. The invention, the creativity is not in making it up, but in finding it out. Unfortunately, finding it out may have no immediate commercial consequence. Indeed, it could be said that the greater the genius applied to the problem, the farther from utilitarian advantage the discovery will be.

The essence of managing scientific creativity for commercial ends must be, first, the pre-selection of areas of interest which might a priori be considered to provide an appropriate commercial yield, and second, a closely regulated monitoring process designed to trap and exterminate potentially unproductive strays which use up resources and exhaust attention through the self-indulgent pursuit of red herrings. After that, the priority is the recruitment of those scientists most likely to produce under a benign regime of security of tenure and autonomy of method.

For scientists just as for the creatives in advertising, there needs to be an interpretive, sympathetic, but hard-nosed band of folk who act as mediators between the commercial priorities of the organization, the prevailing needs of the market and the indulgent, self-sustaining enthusiasms of the scientists and engineers themselves.

Perhaps because scientists and engineers are not always seen as so wild and anarchic in their self-expression as are the creatives, the need for a formal intermediary function is seldom seen. The mind-set of the organization man separates out the boffins from the rest, sees them as needing a quiet, campus-style country environment to deliver their best, and, as often as not, quickly and silently forgets about them until they next ask for more money.

Paul Valéry writes in *Nouvelle Revue Française*:

It takes two to invent anything. One makes up the combinations; the other one chooses, recognizes what he wishes and what is important to him in the mass of things which the former has imparted to him. What we call genius is much less the work of the first one than the readiness of the second one to grasp the value of what has been laid before him and to choose it.[17]

The point should not be missed, that the second of these two, the chooser, is exhibiting taste. Even in science, the choice is one of elegance, of beauty, of aesthetic feeling. Commercial value comes afterwards.

Notes

1 Jonathan Swift, *Gulliver's Travels* (Oxford University Press, Oxford, 1933), p. 12.
2 Shakespeare, *The Merchant of Venice*, Act 3, sc. 1.
3 Peter Medawar, *The Threat and the Glory: Reflections on Science and Scientists* (Oxford University Press, Oxford, 1990), p. 29.
4 Jacques Hadamard, *The Psychology of Invention in the Mathematical Field* (Princetown University Press, NJ, 1945), p. xii.
5 J. D. Fitzgerald, in F. H. Gross (ed.), *Decision-Making in Drug Research* (Raven Press, New York, 1983), p. 209.
6 Edward Regis, *Who Got Einstein's Office? Eccentricity and Genius at the Institute for Advanced Study* (Simon & Schuster, London 1987), p. 131.
7 Ibid., p. 136.
8 Medawar, *Threat and the Glory*, p. 65.
9 Ibid., p. 82.
10 Jay Galbraith, 'Designing the innovating organisation', in *Organisational Dynamics*, vol. 10 (Summer 1982), p. 543.
11 Ibid., p. 544.
12 Rosabeth Moss Kanter, *When Giants Learn to Dance* (Simon & Schuster, London, 1989), p. 203.
13 Galbraith, 'Designing the innovating organization', p. 552.
14 Medawar, *Threat and the Glory*, p. 9.
15 Ibid., p. 54.
16 Hadamard, *Psychology of Invention*, p. 124.
17 Ibid., p. 30.

6

Creative Organizations

The most important invention that will come out of the corporate
research lab in the future will be the corporation itself.

John Seely Brown, *Harvard Business Review*

Dr Rosabeth Moss Kanter has long been a critic of the rigid, self
supporting bureaucracy that limits Western organizations' capacities
to change and to harness innovation. In several books, numerous
articles and countless personal appearances, she has pointed out the
impositions and restrictions that large American organizations have
placed upon themselves by their inability to flex, to yield and profit
from change.

In *When Giants Learn to Dance*,[1] she introduces her theme by
highlighting the many actions that corporate America is taking to stay
alive in the new world. She points out the need for these
organizations to navigate a very narrow passage between thinking
ahead, taking in the big picture and, yet at the same time, being
obliged to make competitive short-term gains to ensure their
current attractiveness to investors. This requires that they take
business risks, but do not chance the business failing; become very
committed to, and focused upon, a shared, clear corporate purpose,
yet keep very flexible, able to switch direction at the drop of a
percentage point. They have to minimize their payroll, yet offer
security and good employment. They have to set up small autonomous
business units, yet keep the corporate core working well for all. They
have to innovate but stay as they are, only more so. They have to seem
big, but act small. They have to be all things to all people.

Trying to work their way through this maze of conundrums, the top managers naturally lean towards the short-term. Some take the short-term view in everything, giving up any concern for new sources of next year's profits. The corporate purpose has become focused on lowered costs, simplified structure and added value. Risks are things to avoid or share, rather than to take, even after calculation. The people who look the most relaxed are the ones who have been fired, who no longer have to live with the uncertainty of whether they will be the next to be let go. Organizations become more and more about personal power, less and less about merit or competence. It is a stark picture, but one which pervades all but the very best in the USA, and, to a lesser extent, Europe.

One of the driving forces behind this pressure has probably been removed, at least for a while; that is the junk bond. 'Leveraged buyouts' was a term of the 1980s which provided more insecurity, corporate crisis, and value-subtracting costs than any other item since the 1940s and asset-stripping. Organizations have since been obliged to consider only such matters as increase in earnings per share, sweating assets, looking for places to reduce expenditure, and essentially selling orthodoxy loud and hard. In these circumstances, innovation has no place. The innovative genius is not given the space or the time to evolve his thinking or to gather resources, or to take risks which cannot be defined except in terms which are beyond the top management's planning horizon. In the circumstances that have prevailed, only the strongest companies, or those who see their business as innovative, are prepared to afford the luxury of radicalism, of long-term research, or of risky design. It needs only a poor report from the ultra-conservative cadre of financial analysts, and the selling starts, the share price drops and the cost of purchase comes under the threshold of anticipation of waiting predators.

For the time being, this pressure has waned. Near-permanent fears of perpetual recession have watered down desires. A few dramatic failures have discouraged the desire to acquire. But the uncertainty remains, and the pressure on innovation has not diminished.

The focus is now on the ways in which organizations can deal with the problem of having to shore up the present with planks drawn from their futures. Some organizations need to be powerfully innovative to survive at all. Not always are these the obvious ones. Others, which would seem to need all the concentration in the world on being innovative, seem, to an outsider, to be unconcerned with making use even of what potential they have. Tapping innovation, making use of their genius, creating the conditions for such added value does require great effort and consistency of purpose. It requires maturity. It requires reflective thought. It requires time. It requires courage. These are not all common virtues in large organizations. The instinct in the Anglo-Saxon organizations is for transfixion. Their reaction to turbulence, to the dangerous, combative and unpredictable disorder of the outside world, is to go firm on the inside. It is to homogenize the organization's soul and at the same time emulsify its body so that it sets hard with a newly rigid consistency.

Establishments as varied as the BBC and the International Stock Exchange on the one hand, and the Prudential and BP on the other, continue their quest to capture a core culture and a core vision for the organization as a whole. They seek a concept that makes clear that here is a single organization, together with a collective purpose that tells the public why it should remain one. Once this is in place – usually put there by a new and newly high-profile chief executive – the overall strategic mission, the imperatives, the subordinate goals and the reward systems that are designed to reinforce the communication of this newly found order are packaged, sold and supported. This creates a semblance of stability. It provides a much needed feeling of comfort. It encourages people to relax and feel that for all the muddiness, ambivalence, and provisionalism of the outside world, at least *we* know where we are going.

The essential drift of this process is toward a new conformity. The essential consequence is that innovation is encompassed within the plan horizon. It is again constrained. It may well be killed altogether.

The missing ingredient to all this activity, which renders all its effort in vain is employee security. Each twist and turn throws out another band of ex-employees. Each time this happens, those who remain begin to take significantly less chances and shore up their own houses to keep their families leeside of the winds of change.

Organizations are beginning slowly to learn how to be creative themselves, how to produce a culture and a climate which sustains and nourishes creativity everywhere. But there is a long way to go.

There are many organizations in the commercial world which claim to be creative and innovative. None claim that they are not. But some are more so than others. 3M has made claim to its powers of innovation as a corporation longest and loudest.

The Case of 3M

Large organizations which proclaim an absolute commitment to innovation are rare in the Western world. The most consistently self-proclamatory over the past few years has been 3M.

3M was one of the original excellents in Peters and Waterman's 1982 volume, *In Search of Excellence*.[2] In 1980, it had sales of over $6 billion, with just over 10 per cent of sales as after-tax profit. It traded 40,444 products, with a hundred new ones coming out each year through forty different divisions. Less than ten years later, it passed $10,000 billion world wide sales, reached 50,000 products and operated in what it describes as 110 technologies. The company employs over 80,000 people in over fifty countries, including over 700 laboratories in eleven countries. 6.6 per cent of sales is spent on R & D, about half the rate of the big spenders, the pharmaceutical companies, but three times the rate of comparable, chemical technological companies. 3M appears in everyone's list of the most admired companies.

3M makes and sells tape and allied items, abrasives, chemicals, printing and recording products. The company support the proposition of Peter Drucker that 'whenever anything is being accomplished, it is being done, I have learned, by a monomaniac with a mission'.

In the nineties, 3M continue to voice the consistent view that innovation is their mission. At Bracknell, in the UK headquarters, this word is almost harder to avoid than the 3M logo itself. Executives at 3M frequently appear on the public stage. Whether they are personnel, line-management, engineers or research men, they say much the same thing, in much the same way, confident that they have got it right. They ask the same questions as many people in large organizations do: why is it that small companies have a much better track record in bringing new products to the market than larger companies?

John Cowland's speech to a conference in early 1989 was titled 'Creating innovators and entrepreneurs within a large organization'. He was the UK company's personnel director at the time, but has since moved back to line-management. His view of the issue is:

> . . . large organizations strive for efficiency, so resources become scarce. Innovation, on the other hand, is a rather messy, playful

process, with complexity of information being the overriding influence. Striking a happy medium between these two opposing influences is hard but must be achieved if ideas are to flourish.

The barriers, he suggested, include bureaucracy, the pressures for short-term profitability, line-by-line accounting orthodoxy, too much management, professionals who have lost their enthusiasm, rigidly constraining corporate objectives, procedures and processes; in summary, just too much control. So how does 3M avoid the consequences of its size?

It does have a long history of very public pronouncements that are hard to miss if you are an employee, and often sound a little pious. For instance, 3M chief executive of forty years ago, William McKnight is still quoted as saying:

> Mistakes will be made. But if the person is essentially right, I think the mistakes he or she makes are not so serious in the long run as the mistake management makes if it is dictatorial and undertakes to tell people exactly how they must do their job. Management that is destructively critical when mistakes are made kills initiative. And it's essential to have many people with initiative if we are to continue to grow.

Len Lehr, who was chairman of 3M in 1985, put it another way: 'Human beings are endowed with the urge to create . . . developing entrepreneurs simply means respecting that dimension of human nature.'

The organization is public about numbers in its promotion of innovation. The target for each product division is that in any given year 25 per cent of sales should come from products that did not exist five years earlier. One can imagine that there are ways of fudging these figures, since they are so important and so public, but the data is inspected. It is not easy to cheat and soon, if it has not happened already, the target percentage will go up to 35 per cent.

Over the years 3M has evolved a number of principles aimed to ensure that such goals are achieved. Autonomy is one such principle. Interaction is another, where all kinds of tactics are introduced to encourage people to bump into each other, to share knowledge, to influence across boundaries. Interaction is not allowed to take place naturally. If this were the case, it is believed, it would not happen.

Creative people can become very solitary. They need to be prompted into sharing. In Austin, Texas, 3M have designed 'interaction nodes' into their building where people from different units are induced to sit down with others with coffee and in comfort.

A third principle is reward and recognition of the innovator. This is done both in terms of offering career paths, which do not necessitate capable technical innovators becoming managers in order to increase their income and advance their position in the company, as well as public honours for successfully introducing new business. The R & D people get 15 per cent of their time to use on projects of their own choosing. In the UK this incentive has been extended to any senior manager, who can ask for sponsorship of up to £5000 to make an investigation into a project proposal. Finally, they encourage sponsors, people who look after people who are scratching around trying to find the time, resources and space to give birth to their pet scheme. This is a clear message of the organization, showing that it recognizes the hazards involved in being an innovator in a big company, even one that celebrates and demands innovation.

In 3M there are many stories of the man with the idea being crushed by bureaucracy, saved only by the often devious, and occasionally intransigent, activities of his friends and sponsors. A passing glance through Nayak and Ketteringham's book, *Breakthroughs!* shows how much effort and contrivance goes towards providing large organizations with the gifts of their future profits. The famous Post-it case started before 1970, with a polymer chemist called Spence Silver, and went through several hands, and much despair, before being pressure-sold by Art Fry to become one of the most famous products around.

Silver is quoted in *Breakthroughs!* as saying: 'In the usual cycle of things, the long-range research programmes were cut . . . all the discoveries [of the polymers for adhesives research group] were shelved.'[3] The authors go on:

> So he did what seems to happen frequently at 3M. He shrugged at the organization and he did it himself. He had to wage a battle to get the money just to patent his unique polymer. 3M eventually spent the minimum money possible. Post-it adhesive was patented *only* in the United States.[4]

One final quote from Silver:

In the fat times, these groups appear, and we do a lot of interesting research. And then the lean times come just at the point where you've developed your first goody, your gizmo. And then you've got to go on and try to sell it. Well everybody in the Divisions is so busy that they don't want to touch it.[5]

The story from 3M says that once Art Fry got into Post-it's promotion, the company backed him despite considerable technical difficulty and some bad market results. But this was after years of effort and frustration from its inventor.

To round up this short visit to 3M, it is worth listing their ten-point theory of the values that a large company should embrace in order to foster a climate of creativity:

- Allow people the freedom to do their jobs in their own way.
- Give them time to explore innovative projects of their own choosing.
- Let them learn from their mistakes.
- Honour the heroes of invention.
- Get things done by informal cooperation.
- Stay visible, accessible and open to new ideas while managing.
- Find more and more ways to reward innovators.
- Stay committed to the best ideas despite obstacles.
- Use strong cross-functional teams to bridge organizations' boundaries.
- Sponsor others in their efforts to innovate.

It is often the individual innovator who takes the biggest chance, not the company. 3M have spent fifty years encouraging themselves to be supportive of new ideas, and of the people who have them. Yet even here, people like Silver and others have to fight for space, and must show abnormal persistence to get their ideas accepted and built upon. If it is like this at 3M it is no surprise that so few companies in the world can get it right.

The Case of Celltech Ltd

At the time when 3M was a $6 billion company, with a 10 per cent yield in profit of turnover after tax, the state-owned National

Enterprise Board (NEB) announced the formation of a new biotechnology company to be called Celltech Ltd.[6] It was to have £12 million backing, and access to the Medical Research Council biotechnology research. The purpose of setting up the company was to encourage the commercial exploitation of leading science, something in which the UK had had a record of continuous failure for many years. There were some doubts about Celltech being set up, not only because it was very much a scratch organization, but also because it was seen to be undercapitalized and lacking in commercial focus. Its formulation was an attempt to create a science-based business in biotechnology, at the time a totally product-less research world.

The company was headed up for ten years by Gerard Fairtlough, who joined from the staff of NEB, and given its technical direction by Norman Cavey, aided by a cadre of his colleagues who joined him from G. D. Searle. The first of two technologies that started the company was for recombinant DNA. This involves recombining fragments of genetic structure to produce a new form of life. The second was hybridoma. This is cell-fusing, producing in quantities protein with unique properties. Cell-fusing is also known as monoclonal antibody technology. These two research streams have slowly merged, enabling products which are biologically completely new to be both created and mass produced.

In ten years, the company has never produced much of a profit, has grown to over £20 million turnover, employing around five hundred people, and devoting over a third of its income to R & D. In a small field, Celltech is a significant world player, and the major European one. It has registered more patents than some of the UK's major pharmaceutical companies over the same period. It has earned a reputation to innovate and do so at speed. This is an organization that was set up to be innovative, to produce new products and market them. What are the thinking processes that support such a company?

Fortunately Gerard Fairtlough, who has some very distinct views about organizations, has been more than willing to give them a public airing. Fairtlough uses the analogue of cell biology in communicating his view on how organizations should be structured. Compartmentation is the term used to denote the closing of a part of the organism from the outside world, but leaving specific connections available to develop relationships with other parts. The compartments can then go about their business intensively, and without the need continuously to seek help. At the same time they can communicate in a controlled way with others, the outsiders. Each cell has to follow a few universal rules which concern both competition for resources and cooperation in reaching goals. Each cell evolves continuously, but only the results of those mutations which are seen to benefit that cell *and* the collective needs of the whole organism (organization) will prevail.

Fairtlough put his views to good use at three levels, particularly in relation to the yield of communications. First, he concerned himself with the architecture, or the physical environment: the quality and structure of the built environment in which the scientists work. Second, he considered climate, which he saw as the morale, and the values held to support it. Third, he was concerned with systems, that is, the methods of direction and consultation. Each of these has an impact on the others, although clearly some are easier than others to change. His views corresponded with some of 3M's in relation to the architecture. This aspect has, over the past ten years, come to be seen as having a serious part to play in the innovation of organizations.

Openness at Celltech has had to suffer constraints as growth has proven to increase the cost of rapid and coherent sharing of information. The company operates a matrix in its R & D organization. Research staff are recruited to a group of like discipline, subsequently having their time and interests apportioned to appropriate projects. The choice between the discipline or project as a preference for the 'home' of the scientists is a constant source of debate in R & D circles.

Celltech has also followed the pioneers in offering dual careers to research staff. The post of Principal Scientist was introduced to provide the opportunity for personal growth for specialists, without occupational diversion. Salaries are negotiated on an individual basis, although there are informal fuzzy lines of differentiation. Appraisal is taken very seriously despite being very time-consuming. Many systems for sharing information are in operation, including informal but regular get-togethers internally, open contact with universities and other sources of ideas, stimulation and discussion.

Clearly the company has great commitment. There is a strong work ethic. People feel a part of the organization and seem to be clear about the role they play within their 'cell' as well as the contribution each cell can, and should, make to the corporate whole.

Size is again the potential killer. The amount and level of communication required to sustain a consistently far-reaching, leading-edge, collectively identified community such as this is very high and needs to have great fidelity. At the five-hundred level this must already be stretched. Sooner or later some fundamentally new systems will have to be put in place or something will change. If the cell analogy holds good, it could well be a cloning of the whole organization, elsewhere. Certainly, there seems little sign of any other form of growth or extension taking place. Celltech is due for some turbulent years.

The Lessons of Honda

Honda is often seen by the cognizant as being a truly creative organization. Commercially not without its ups and downs, it has consistently placed innovation as high on its list of values, and seems not to be just another Japanese company. The conventional Japanese organizational style, as it emerges from many investigations over the years, combines a benign relationship between the big company and its employees, with much interaction and hard work.

The company offers security and chances for personal and occupational growth. In exchange it asks for, and usually gets, loyalty, flexibility and a shared sense of purpose. At Honda, staff employees are trusted to get on with the things that concern them, and management employees help and share their work problems and solutions. Such security and intense day-to-day interaction could be expected to provide an atmosphere conducive to relaxed adaptive change.

In the *Honda Book of Management*, Setsuo Mito sets out the personal mottoes of the founders:

Be original
Do not rely on Government
Work for your own sake[7]

These were later supplemented by five golden rules:

1 Follow your dreams and keep a youthful outlook.
2 Respect theory, new ideas and time.
3 Love your work and make your workplace bright and positive.

4 Ensure a smooth flow of work.
5 Make research and dedicated effort a daily habit.[8]

The passion with which these fundamentals were upheld is demonstrated by Kiyoshi Kawashima's further checklist of appraisals. He insisted on the questions:

Are we giving the staff the chance to use their imagination?
Is there enough youthfulness and courage in the leadership to prevent the organization from becoming bureaucratic?
Are we being sufficiently receptive to the flow of new ideas?
Are decisions made at the right time?

Kawashima, made president of Honda at the age of forty-five, retired ten years later. It is rare in Japan, as in the rest of the world, to find a powerful executive willing to give up power on account of a principle.

Other characteristics Mito highlights include the joint boardroom, where the top thirty directors of the company each share their desks in the one room. Introduced in 1964, the intention was to encourage wider discussion of issues rather than have decisions confined to a single person or a chain of events and influences. It took time to get it right, but it seems now to work well.

In research and development, the talk is of markets and pragmatism. Mito writes of the R & D world:

The research personnel at Honda must have an irrepressible pioneering and innovative spirit. People who are wholly determined to reach some goal are bound to appear a little crazy to others.

To lead a group of 'mad' engineers, a supervisor must be as shrewd as 'an old fox'. He has to be quick to understand the moods and attitudes of the researchers, pampering them when they face disappointment, restraining them when they become impetuous, supporting them when they have personal problems.[9]

As Honda has grown, it has had to learn to export its culture of creative productivity. It seeks always to find ways in which individualism and teamwork are harmonized. It prefers to call employees associates. It works at de-emphasizing any and all status barriers, including asking that all wear the same white uniforms. It tries to keep security of employment. None of this seems arcane. It seems regimented rather than encouraging of individual creative output. Yet in a sense, only through insisting on conformity in all the 'important' things, like offices, job security, and symbols of status, can individualism emerge freely. Certainly there are lessons in Honda that can be learned by those who would match its success.

In *Fortune* magazine of 13 February 1989, Brian Dumaine wrote an article on succeeding through speed. He suggested lessons that competitive organizations needed to learn in order to keep their products ahead: start from scratch, rather than trying to put more effort into old practices; wipe out approvals, taking the new past and through the bureaucracy; try teams of mixed disciplines devoted to development of new product; work the schedule, to keep up the pressure on results; focus and vitalize distribution, which can be the killer in the tail of speedy market engagement; and last but not least, put speed in the culture. Honda comes up for especial mention in the last category. Dumaine wrote:

> Honda did [put speed in the culture] and it definitely helps. Though the company entered into Formula One racing only six years ago, Honda Engines have won this demanding annual circuit three times. By circulating young engineers though the Formula One team, Honda teaches its people the racing spirit, which means thinking about minutes, not hours.

Honda's forecast development-time for a new car was predicted to improve from five to three years. In the *Financial Times* of December 1990, Honda was reported as aiming to reduce model development-time to twenty-four months. America and European equivalent time scales were reported as five years, which is where Honda was in late 1988.

Siemens – Creative Conglomerate?

Siemens is another giant organization which is based on the solid foundation of engineering excellence. It has a world-wide manufacturing and sales organization in over 120 countries. The company receives half its business from outside Germany. Electronic products and systems account for over half its sales, of more than DM 70,000 million, and the work of 353 thousand employees. Its R & D expenditure runs to 11 per cent world-wide sales, on a par with most pharmaceutical companies' average. Of this expenditure in 1987–8, 7 per cent was on basic and applied research, 10 per cent went into basic manufacturing technologies, 28 per cent into software development, and 55 per cent into product and systems development. Seimens' R & D headcount totals 42,000 employees.

More significantly, Siemens publicly claims that 50 per cent of sales are generated by products introduced within the last five years. Siemens is an organization that was built up on the basis of engineering excellence. Some of its customers sell their equipment second-hand at prices greater than they paid for it five years before. Its way of innovating is to ensure that boundaries are constantly being approached and breached, boundaries of technology, of function, and of community.

Whenever new products are considered, Siemens will organize it so that people from each of marketing, applications, manufacturing and research, where applicable, are all involved. Its employees are constantly encouraged to converse, to exchange views, to promote, to display. At intervals, the whole technological base of the company is put to the test of peer review. On the last occasion, the Olympics stadium at Munich was hired to enable the various technology groups to talk to each other. It is systematic, orderly sharing. It demands order and commitment.

Siemens' problems can be expected to grow rapidly when the recently divisionalized organization begins to separate out into different identities. It is in too many joint ventures, in too many places, for there to be a shared community. It may maintain pockets of excellence for creative people, but they could well no longer have the consistent ear of their organization in future.

Managing Growth and Control in Creative Companies

Organizational size and complexity have to be seen as most important to the way in which creative genius is efficaciously managed. While 3M keep their many divisions by pushing hard and mightily for an overall philosophy that includes crossing boundaries, Celltech are already beginning to worry about growth and its impact on their culture with five hundred people on one site in Slough. Yet it seems possible for a company of the huge size and dispersion of Siemens to offer support to the creative engineer in ways which enables it to claim that 50 per cent of its product is less than five years old.

Clearly the public image of the company is important, as is its technical positioning. A chemist who was interested in innovation in the field of abrasives or adhesives could scarcely ignore the possibility that 3M might offer him greater opportunity than working in a university laboratory on his own account. The same could apply to the biochemist whose interests are ignited by monoclonal antibodies. Nor can the German computer buff who wants to develop parallel processing in a big way ignore the fact that Siemens owns Nixdorf. So the big company offers both opportunity and frustration to the young scientist.

So, with all this success, how do people go wrong? EMI was an organization that had its quota of innovative scientists and engineers. With Joe Lyons, it developed the first computer (LEO) put to commercial use in the United Kingdom. Its engineers developed the first colour TV cameras, brought into use some of the earliest manufacturing automation, were pioneers in radar, and in large-scale values, and had a good lead in viable electronic pattern-recognition back in 1960. In the 1970s they went for electronic body-scanning, and developed a very sophisticated system for so doing. It was fascinating, but it took up huge sums of money, upsetting the fine balance that Sir Joseph Lockwood had maintained between the cash-generative records business and the cash-retentive electronics side of the company.

When General Electric encouraged President Carter to introduce legislation against importing competitive technology, EMI was finished. The company tried to sell its medical technology arm to Thorn. Thorn said: 'Why not buy EMI?' Thorn bought EMI. Soon afterwards, they sold the Medical Division to the United States. EMI's essential support for the individual creation or the creative individual did not die. It merely went underground. It is still there, in 'Thorn-EMI', and it is successful. But it is largely subversive.

Advertising agencies run into the same kind of problem at regular intervals. When things go well the creatives are on top, they spend over-optimistically, as all creative people tend to do when things are moving, expanding, pushing at the frontiers of investment, but losing track of the cash flow, and of the contingency plans. The dialectic is always between creation and control. Between the tightness that prevents haemorrhage and accounts well for income and expenditure, and the looseness that enables people to make changes, follow things up, make mistakes and enjoy themselves, there is constant friction and permanent ebb and flow. This is the essential paradox for the creative organization: if they let their creativity loose and take their eyes off the till, they stand to lose their licence to operate as an independent whole by being taken over by those who did not. If they keep their creativity under close wraps, then they stand to lose in the gamble for the next leap forward. The choice is a cultural one, and change is not easy to manage.

The Case of the Morgan Car Company, Non-creative Non-pareil

Lessons can be learned from the example of companies where resistance to innovation is so endemic and great that even most creative people become anodyne and ineffective. What brings about such a result? It is not size. Some of the smallest companies insist on retaining the status quo despite all the signs that it is a policy with no future.

Non-creative organizations are not as rare as might be imagined. John Harvey-Jones, ex-chairman of ICI, made a series of TV programmes with the BBC in 1988. He visited six organizations in the UK, seeking to assess, help and guide the fortunes of those as varied as the Shropshire District Health Authority and Apricot Computers. In the course of making these programmes, he was constantly frustrated by the unwillingness of the individuals he interviewed to see themselves as failing (in all cases, Harvey-Jones was pessimistic about their future), or to look upon innovation as something they should naturally seek out for themselves.

Possibly the most non-innovative of all of the organizations he visited was the Morgan Motor Company. The company was founded in Malvern in 1910 by H. F. S. Morgan. His son Peter was still running it at the time of Harvey-Jones' intervention. Grandson Charles also works there.

Morgan appears to have had a few crises in its history. It lost out spectacularly to competition from the Austin Seven in the 1920s. It had no orders after breaking off production to produce munitions during the Second World War, and its domestic market remained poor, its performance being sustained only by US orders, which themselves dropped off severely in the 1960s.

Peter Morgan remembers his father telling him always to keep demand slightly ahead of supply. His one major innovation as chairman was to develop a new covered car with a fibreglass body for the home market. It flopped. Morgan remains a hand-built, highly traditionally designed car, with exports all over the world and a five- to ten-year waiting list. It turns over better than £5 million, with less than 10 per cent of that retained as profit.

In his book *The Trouble Shooters*, Harvey-Jones wrote:

> In a way Morgan has the problem of success. The car has a tremendous following, it generates great enthusiasm, and there is an enormous waiting list. The car sells all over the world, and half the output is exported. But I sense that the company isn't going anywhere, and, sadly, companies which don't go anywhere are usually heading for trouble.[10]

Harvey-Jones spent almost a year intermittently trying to provoke an innovative response in a company he describes as follows:

> Morgan has a keen and loyal workforce. It's the biggest collective love affair I've ever seen. Everybody loves the car, loves the factory, loves the business. There is a passion about the car which is wonderful to see and a great strength . . . I have never seen anywhere where there is such total Conservatism with a little 'c'.[11]

He concluded:

> I have been involved with Morgan for less than a year, but even I am having difficulty letting go. What are my final impressions? I am so conditioned by my low expectations that I am grateful for almost any change that is proposed in this most Conservative of factories . . . they cling to the idea that they have a mission in life to provide cars at a certain price to a certain type of person whom they happen to like. This kind of thinking is a sentence of death to any business.[12]

Such organizations are themselves a sentence of death to those people working in them who feel the need to make changes. The chief development officer, Maurice Owen, was quoted as saying that it took him eleven to twelve years to persuade the company to go over to rack and pinion steering. He thinks the way the car is made is wrong. He has to be a deeply tolerant innovator.

Non-innovating companies can become so because of their history, because the continuity of ownership and power kills off all attempts to introduce change, because their industry is a conservative one.

The Checo Company

One further example will suffice to show the differences that exist between innovative and non-innovative companies. It is a composite picture, in order to preserve confidence. It concerns a company in Holland which is in a profoundly conservative market, but which cannot continue in its traditional way. The world is moving on.

Checo produces and sells bulk chemicals. The company employs altogether 1500 people. A patent exists for the formulation of the product which is based on the discovery of the founder, Mr Cornelissen. The company's head office was moved to Rotterdam ten years ago. The production division has remained behind in Brabant where the factory complex has dominated the local community for decades. One of the preliminary steps to prepare for a substantial change was a deep analysis of the organizational culture. The patent is shortly due to expire and it looks as if the company's hitherto unassailable position as a supplier of chemical feeder-stocks will be rapidly undermined. The management will therefore have to turn the organization around and focus on the refined chemical market.

The next pages summarize some of the research findings from the study of the organizational culture of the Checo Company. The study was carried out in the first instance at the production division in Oost Brabant (the eastern part of the province of Brabant in the Netherlands). Later it was also conducted at head office.

The picture that prevailed, and which is propagated in all kinds of different ways, is the image of the drayhorses from Brabant which trudge on stolidly, pulling the plough behind them. Not hurried or fast but imperturbable. A horse of which people are a little afraid, but which would never do anyone any harm, even if they were to get out of line. In this prevailing picture, clashes simply do not occur. It is inconceivable that anyone on the staff would actually want to get out of line. On the odd occasion that something like this happens, it is denied. The horse ploughs on contentedly, so that any continuing sign of criticism automatically becomes ridiculous. At best you can ride along by sitting on the plough. That of course is not the idea, but the horse is so strong that nobody gets worked up about it.

Formerly, when the inventor and founder of the company was alive, everything was better. Mr Cornelissen was popularly known as Meneer Co (Mr Co). People referred to him with a mixture of love and respect. After all, was it not Meneer Co who had brought them such prosperity? He was a distinguished man, but he was also interested in his staff and in the ups and downs of their home lives. He himself came from Oost Brabant and was very fond of the area. He was generous to the church and to the village club. The village became a town with a real function in the region. Meneer Co saw to it that a hospital was built. He was joint founder of the sports association and of the brass band.

A lot of stories were told about what management was like when it was done in the Brabant way. The organizational culture at Checo is indisputably permeated by the culture of Oost Brabant. In Oost Brabant, unlike elsewhere, prominent figures are still respected. There is no desire to rail against one's immediate superior. A man like Meneer Co deserved your respect just as much as the priest and the burgomaster. They did not end up in the job they were doing just like that. They had studied for it, they had worked hard for it and they were called by God to their task.

As a result of the patent that Meneer Co managed to obtain on one of his most successful discoveries, prosperous times quickly ensued. Checo was an extremely good company to work for.

The worst mistake any employee can make at Checo is to bypass someone in the hierarchy. If a person has the courage to give voice to something about which he disagrees he will have to go to his immediate superior. Bypassing another in the hierarchy is immediately interpreted as a personal affront. The information flow usually proceeds step-by-step via the different hierarchical levels.

In an organization which is so hierarchically entrenched, the various departments know little about each other. Checo's production division has a great many miniature empires. People do not visit other departments. Criticizing another department is absolutely not done. Despite the respect for management and despite the hierarchical structure at Checo, many decisions are taken only after substantial consultation at departmental level. One manager put it this way: 'I never take a decision without having exchanged ideas in detail with my staff. Nor do I like to take a decision if this goes against the opinion of the majority of my people.'

People are generally very kind to each other at Checo. The unwritten rules are very strict. A member of personnel related that when she was appointed she was given to understand quite plainly that it was more important to visit and congratulate someone who was celebrating their birthday, and to take the time to drink a cup of coffee and eat a piece of cake with them, than it was to keep the personnel records up-to-date.

Checo behaves like a real monopolist. It is slow, with many time-consuming procedures. The sale of products has been guaranteed, so why should anyone worry. Punctuality and precision are more important than pace.

A number of people were asked how they were hired:

> I was taken on at the priest's recommendation. I realized this at the start because actually there was no work for me, as it soon turned out. Nevertheless, nobody said anything negative about it. My colleagues were extremely helpful in thinking up all kinds of jobs for me to do.

> The only way of getting a job with Checo was at the recommendation of the burgomaster or the priest. Or you had to know somebody personally from the Cornelissen family.

> I went to the same primary school as Meneer Co's son, we were in the same class. We always kept in touch, even though later I called him Meneer instead of Johan. So it was always on the cards that I would go to work with Checo.

Various members of staff admitted that responding to future developments and new markets was proceeding too slowly. They were afraid that Checo had already missed a lot of chances. They were primarily referring to head office in Rotterdam. Others on the other hand, agreed that they themselves played a role in holding back innovation because they did not want to take any big risks. One said, 'I cannot bear to think that on Monday we might have to take a decision about a problem on Friday; I become totally disoriented.' Another respondent commented: 'We use false arguments so as not to introduce innovations. That we are supposedly not ready for them or the time is not ripe, or something like that.'

This is an organization which almost glories in its resistance to change. People working at Checo realize that life cannot go on in this way for much longer. Intellectually, this is recognized in a way which is not the case with Morgan. But emotionally, the acceptance of the need to plan for innovation of all kinds and at all levels, as a matter of survival, has yet to be engaged. Perhaps when it is, it will already be too late.

The Lessons of Non-creative Organizations

The issues here, for both Checo and Morgan, are not about how happy people are. In both companies the employees are happy. In fact, it is likely that people working in non-creative organizations are, on average, always happier than those in the creative ones. Happiness is not often a characteristic that we should expect to find where innovation is the driving force. Neither is it an issue of success. Many innovative organizations seem no more successful, in the conventional sense, than those which are determinedly non-creative.

The main lesson to be learned from looking at creative and uncreative organizations is how powerfully effective the company culture can become in uplifting or depressing initiative. There is little doubt that the transfer of people at any level from the one style, say 3M, to the other, say Morgan, and vice versa, would cause immense distress to both. There are creative companies in all sectors of the commercial world, and there are non-creative companies. It is a factor of strategic intent, of carry-through, of habit and of coherence of mission. Creative companies exist where the company gives in to the smart individual, bent on change. In non-creative organizations it is the other way round. Creative companies are no more long-term in their philosophies, nor are they better in any technical sense. The virtue they have is that they have the power and the will to adapt. They do not depend upon the stability of the world around them to support their own continued success.

Conclusions

Moss Kanter's concern for the adaptive capability of US corporations focuses on large organizations. There is evidence, in companies like 3M and Siemens, for example, that large corporations can and do make very effective utilizers of their own inventive potential. This works well in mature industries, where the creative candidate can see his best opportunities within an established business, a member of a mature oligopoly, with a market place wherein end-usage is also mature and relatively slow to change. If the organization is aware of its need to stay technologically and scientifically ahead, size should be an advantage to it in these circumstances.

However, as is seen by Morgan, and by Checo – small companies whose emphasis is, or has been, on maintaining a market position and where the circumstances of its trade have emphasized the conservative – even the smallest, least corporate-like organization will inhibit and compress its inventive capability. It will lose that which it has, and it will have few chances to change. Such a chance is unlikely to come from anywhere but the top, or more likely, from outside.

The biggest problem for those who seek to sustain an organization which has creative endeavour as its core mission is that of keeping alive its vital spark. One of the features of genius that distinguishes it from the average is the burning desire for more, the insatiable ambition. When the flame of genius goes out, it is rarely re-ignited. Shorn of this passion, what is left is often an empty and misshapen husk. So when organizations expand on the basis of their creative will and inspiration, they run the risk of growing too fat and complacent, like IBM, or going out of control, like Apple Computers, or of having to compromise on the founder's vision, as have many organizations created and grown over the past generation.

Most people naturally reach a level of personal need-satisfaction where the edge of their ambition for more is blunted. In the global market place, this is quickly followed by a loss of initiative or market share. Somewhere there are people more hungry for success. However, it is so much easier to manage a company like Morgan, holding on to a place in a niche market shored up by nostalgia. Companies like Honda, 3M and Seimens have to constantly reinforce the message, invent new incentives, find refreshing inducements from the top down to keep their organizations from the almost inevitable consequences of ageing.

Notes

1 Rosabeth Moss Kanter, *When Giants Learn to Dance* (Simon & Schuster, London, 1989).

2 Thomas J. Peters and Robert H. Waterman, *In Search of Excellence: Lessons for America's Best-Run Companies* (Harper & Row, London, 1983).

3 P. R. Nayak, and John M. Ketteringham, *Breakthroughs!* (Rawson Associates, New York, 1986), p. 59.

4 Ibid., p. 60.

5 See note 4 above.

6 Mark Dodgson, *Celltech: The First Ten Years of a Biotechnology Company* (University of Sussex, Falmer, 1990).

7 Setsuo Mito, *The Honda Book of Management: A Leadership Philosophy for High Individual Success* (Kogan Page, London, 1990), p. 1.

8 Ibid., p. 7.

9 Ibid., p. 62.

10 John Harvey-Jones, *The Trouble Shooters* (BBC Publications, London, 1990), p. 106.

11 Ibid., p. 118.

12 Ibid., p. 126.

PART II

Reaching for an Understanding

7

The Nature of Creation

Creative is a term of praise much affected . . . it is presumably intended to mean original, or something like that, but is preferred because it is more vague and less usual. It has been aptly called 'a luscious, round, meaningless word', and said to be 'so much in honour that it is the clinching term of approval from the schoolroom to the advertiser's studio.'

H. W. Fowler, *A Dictionary of Modern English Usage*

People who have discussed, researched and contemplated the nature of creativity have worried and fussed over the definitions. Most experimental work has been done, and there has been an awful lot of it, with each theorist defining the creativity to be studied. Researchers in psychology have studied students of psychology in great depth, in the flesh, searching for those controllable and explorable elements that can be pinned to the laboratory bench. Others have defined creativity as that which people of eminence have demonstrated, for example, Nobel Prize winners. Yet others have given up the whole notion that creativity exists at all in people, believing that it only manifests itself in the products that they produce. The debate will ever continue about whether each of us could be creative, if only the potential were given the stimulus, or is creativity by definition limited to only a few, who have got there by an accidental combination of genes, heritage, upbringing and opportunity?

In this chapter, the terms 'innovators', 'geniuses', and 'creatives' are used in a way which the purist will find unhelpful. However, the purpose is to illustrate the more robust ideas and the more universally accepted notions that abound about the people who change lives through introducing novelty. Whether they should, or should not, all be called geniuses is less important than that we need them, and we need to get the best from them, all of them.

Probably the best working definition of creativity, and therefore of the product of creative people, was offered by G. M. Prince in 1970 in his book *The Practices of Creativity*.

> Creativity: an arbitrary harmony, an expected astonishment, a habitual revelation, a familiar surprise, a generous selfishness, an unexpected certainty, a formidable stubbornness, a vital triviality, a disciplined freedom, an intoxicating steadiness, a repeated initiation, a difficult delight, a predictable gamble, an ephemeral solidarity, a unifying difference, a demanding satisfier, a miraculous expectation, an accustomed amazement.[1]

All invention comes in three parts: the person, the intervention style (including process and purpose) and the product. The only way in which a genius can be defined is by the public acknowledgement of his product. This has to be given the time to show, and, unfortunately for many geniuses, this does not happen in their lifetime. A most famous case is J. S. Bach, who plodded on for a lifetime as a relatively obscure organist, appreciated as a star in his own community but never attaining the world supremacy he later enjoyed, in no sense perceived by his peers, nor even their grandsons, as creating any music of obviously greater merit than they.

So a creative product need only be new to be creative, but needs wide recognition if it is to be ascribed to the outcome of genius. Most creative products, however, are of necessity in the minor league. They are innovations which require a unique coming together of previously unconnected thoughts, processes, mechanisms, technologies, or philosophies so as to produce something which is both different and desirable. In examining the nature of invention, it is always necessary to keep in mind that the merit of any one product, style or person involved in its production depends indestructibly on the merits of both the other two.

The Qualities of Genius

1 Strange Temperament

If there is one enduring belief about people of genius, ranging all the way from Mozart to the most recent rocket scientist in the laboratory, and holding up over the centuries, it is that creators are mad. At the extreme of historical acknowledgement, Aristotle said that no mind of any eminence is free of madness. The genius of Newton and Einstein has provoked many efforts to uncover a parallel insanity to match their conspicuous accomplishments. Much has been made of Newton's protracted and unscientific association with alchemy, of his blatant egotism, of his social shortcomings. Anthony Storr, in *The Dynamics of Creation*, places Einstein among the schizoids. He writes: 'Although Einstein was a saintly character, he was not much involved with individual human beings. His passion was for causes, not people.' He quotes Einstein's first wife as saying 'He has never really needed human contact'.[2]

The workaday creative comes under the same diffuse umbrella of belief. When asked, 'How would I find the scientist you say is your one true genius?' a personnel director of an engineering division responded, 'You cannot miss him, he is the one who will be picking his nose.'

Neil Kessel, in *Genius, A History of an Idea*,[3] shows the continuity of this view. From the ancients:

There has never been any great 'ingenious' without some touch of dementia.

Through Dryden:

Great wits are sure to madness
near allied
And the partitions so their bounds divide.

and Griesinger:

Whenever I hear of an instance of genius in a family, I straight away ask whether or not an idiot is also to be found.

But Kessel leads the reader through the counter-indicators of Havelock Ellis:

> It is rare to find any true insanity in a man of genius when engaged in his best work.

. . . to the 294 German-speaking geniuses acknowledged since 1650, studied in great depth by Adele Juda and who led her to the conclusion:

> There is no definite relationship between highest mental capacity and mental health or illness, no evidence to support the assumptions that the genesis of high intellectual ability depends on psychological abnormalities.

Kessel leads persuasively to the understanding that was originally offered by George Pickering, who proposed that the relationship of madness and genius could be simply explained through desire. Where motivation is high and directed, and frustration the equal of it – the irresistible force meeting the immovable object – there can be only two psychological outcomes, both of which could well look like madness, but only one of which is. In his words: 'In brief, psychoneuroses represents passion thwarted, a great creative work, passion fulfilled.'[4]

The madness of which the commentators talk is the consequence of commitment, of determination and of focus. Francis Galton, one of the earliest people to study the biographies and behaviour of men of eminence, confirmed that the determining factors that lead geniuses to perform acts that lead to reputation, are capacity, zeal and a tendency to work hard. He writes:

> I do not mean capacity without zeal, nor zeal without capacity, nor even a combination of both of them without an adequate power of doing a great deal of very laborious work. But I mean a nature which, when left to itself, will, urged by an inherent stimulus, climb to a path that leads to eminence, and has the strength to reach the summit – one which, if hindered, will fret and strive until the hindrance is overcome, and it is again free to follow its labouring instinct.[5]

However, in a hefty, 700-page manual called *Abnormal Psychology* by Rosenhan and Seligman, creativity rates one mention only, but one which adds yet more fuel to the argument:

Being related to a schizophrenic may not be all bad. In fact it may have some distinct advantages. Reporting on a follow-up study of children born to schizophrenic mothers, and placed in adoptive or foster homes after birth, Heston and Denney note that the children who did not become schizophrenic were more 'spontaneous' , 'had more colourful life histories', 'held more creative jobs', and 'followed the more imaginative hobbies . . . ' than normals . . . [6]

The text continues:

A study of genetics and schizophrenics in Iceland by Karlsson observed that the 'genetic carriers' of schizophrenia often exhibit 'unusual ability' and display 'a superior capacity for association thinking' and proposed that society may even depend upon 'persons with schizophrenic constitution for its social and scientific progress'.[7]

Karlsson coined the name 'Supersphenic' for those people who link outstanding accomplishment with schizophrenic disorder.[8] So it seems that the notion – to be a creative person you need to be somewhat crazy and, by implication, to be a genius, you have to be completely mad, at least for some part of your life – is one so irresistible that it never really goes away.

The other favourite assumption is that of the manic depressive association. The same handbook on abnormal psychology highlights evidence of this state through the description of a highly successful manic artist describing this mood:

I feel no sense of restriction or censorship whatsoever. I'm afraid of nothing and no one. During this elated state, when no inhibition is present, I feel I can race a car with my foot on the floorboard, fly a plane . . . as an artist, I feel I can write poems and paint paintings that I could never dream of when just my normal self. I don't want others to restrict me during this period of complete and utter freedom.[9]

The manic-depressive, in his manic phase does not see limits to what can be achieved. But often there is no control. The discipline that shapes and orders the ideas that flow is missing. The depressive phase of the illness is often deeper than the level dropped to by the purely depressive, and the contrast can be quite devastating both to the manic-depressive and to those close to him. In the world of work, the hyperactive manic phase is probably the harder to handle, but in the victim, it is his despairing periods that provoke the most concern. The state can be very debilitating, leading to broken marriages, foreshortened careers, few friends, alcoholism and, more often than in any other psychotic group, suicide. However, under the right circumstances, and provided it is not so distressing as to be pre-emptive, much of the pace, the hyperactivity, the sheer energy put out by the manic-depressive in the manic condition can lead to the kinds of outcomes on which society places great value. Winston Churchill and Theodore Roosevelt have both been clinically described as manic-depressive people.

Taking all this together, it suggests powerfully that psychopathology is more likely to be found amongst highly creative people than within the general population. The question begged by this observation is whether creative genius is brought on by madness, or whether being mad is a precondition to becoming a creative genius.

Similarly, it would be useful to know if there is a relationship between the extent of madness and the ultimate creative product. Does a slightly mad creative person produce less creative output than a near totally mad one, one mad enough to be a genius but not so mad as to become incapable of communicating thought or action? Does being absolutely devoid of any symptoms of madness imply that creativity is beyond one's reach? There is some evidence for such a relationship. Many personality tests in frequent use have been used to measure differences. Among them, the Minnesota Multiphasic Personality Inventory, the Eysenck Personality Questionnaire (which measures stability/neurosis and introversion/extraversion) and Cattell's 16PF (personality factors) have all shown creative people (those perceived and nominated by experts as more creative in output than the others) to be statistically more deviant on almost every personality dimension than 'normal' people.

So the conclusion has to be reached that creative people in general, and geniuses in particular, do show psychopathology. The best explanation of their productivity is that this psychopathology provides a driving push to achieve, to reach their limits, and therefore to ignore the distracting niceties of everyday life that prevent normal people achieving abnormal ends. The emotional supercharge can drive the individual to madness and despair, or to great works of art and science, or to acts of sustained leadership. The difference is brought about either by strength of will, or social conditions in early life that prevent the pain of frustration from destroying before it creates.

Perhaps this is a good moment to recall the observation of Nathaniel Lee, the seventeenth-century playwright, as he was consigned to Bethlem: 'They called me mad, and I called them mad, and damn them they out voted me.' This is an epitaph which would be appropriate to the tombstone of many a genius, of whatever order of merit.

2 Powerful Drives

There is another commonly observed aspect of the creative individual: lack of modesty. Most creative people typically describe themselves, without shyness, as creative. The famous study done by MacKinnon in 1962, reported in some detail in chapter 3, sought evidence of difference in the self-image of samples of creative and non-creative architects. The creative group used adjectives about themselves such as inventive, enthusiastic, determined, industrious, whereas the control group pointed up such relatively mundane self-descriptions as responsible, reliable, and sincere. Those touched by genius are much more confident of the true value of the work they do than others.

One reason for the conflict that often arises between creative people and those they work for and with, is this conclusive arrogance. The frustration that the creators feel in not being recognized for what they have done is akin to the hemiplegic who has lost the effective use of vocal cords yet maintains full mental functioning. The strain of trying to communicate with people who seem both too ignorant to understand, yet also so patronizing as they shout and mouth and whinny in response to the efforts of the afflicted to make them recognize his truth and wisdom, magnifies the suffering beyond measure. The doubt is always there for creative people, but it is not about their ability to create, only about their sense of oneness with the object of their creation.

While being very proud of what they produce, they are also very critical of it, and are more likely than others to change direction when it is apparently nearly finished. In particular their self-image must be powerful enough to sustain them against antagonism from other, less obviously (to them) productive people, and to support the painful and protracted solitary periods of learning, of processing and integration that almost all productively creative people must go through.

Creative people must be workaholics, they must seek and find an unnaturally high proportion of their rewards, and their pleasures in life, in this working world. Just as alcoholics have bouts of drinking, and feel nervously deprived when separated from the object of their desire, no matter by what alternative attraction, so the person in the full flood of creative endeavour becomes addicted to the search. This must make them seem strange folk to more apparently balanced people.

C. M. Cox in 1926, after concluding her very detailed research into eminent men wrote in 'The early mental traits of three hundred geniuses':

> the following traits . . . are diagnosis of future achievement: an unusual degree of persistence, tendency not to be changeable, tenacity of purpose, and perseverance in the face of obstacles – combined with intellectual energy – mental work bestowed on special interests, profoundness of apprehension, and originality of ideas – and a vigorous ambition expressed by the possession of the highest degree of desire to excel.[10]

So the creative person is determined, focused, iconoclastic, ambitious, confident of his intrinsic worth and prepared to expend a very large proportion of life and resources on reaching his creative end.

The process and the product are dealt with in greater depth in later chapters. A warning for those who see the process as a matter of technique, and technique only, is to be found in Denise Shekerjian's work. In her book *Uncommon Genius*, Shekerjian followed up and interviewed forty winners of the MacArthur Award – the so-called 'genius awards'. This award was funded by the MacArthur estate, and serves to support 'the maverick geniuses' who drive America's social, material and artistic progress. Apart from demonstrating some special competence, and a perceived creative potential, their genius has to be recognized. The winners also have to be American. They are given money, and opportunity to explore what they will. One award-winner, Howard Gardner, advises:

> I think if you're going to write something about creativity for the public, one of the main points is to divest them of the nonsense you see advertised: 'Come for a weekend, learn to brainstorm, learn to free-associate, we'll make you a creative individual.' I mean, that just doesn't work. It's a serious business for serious people. Creative work requires, I think, being a certain kind of person, which includes being

able to work on things for years, a drive not likely to come to people who are paid 500 dollars for a weekend in a tent.'[11]

Creative ideas, products, theories or outcomes are always products of existing ones. Even the revolutionary positions reached by geniuses such as Copernicus came about as a result of challenging something which was already there. Creativity cannot be had from a vacuum. The creative product must be novel but also of use, or at least of value. The means of making use of it must therefore be in context. Furthermore, it must be recognizable as useful by the creator, and his customers, at least. The creator of genius must therefore have taste, and a taste, moreover, that comes close to matching that of his contemporaries for all but the most outrageous ventures.

In an earlier chapter Gardner is again quoted by Shekerjian:

> . . . and whether people are allowed to do something unusual and whether it becomes accepted or not is really a value decision made by the culture. Most cultures throughout human history have not liked creative individuals. They ignored them or they killed them. It was a very effective way of stopping creativity.'[12]

In other words, the product has to be seen as desirable, or as a workable answer, or as a fitting new start by numbers of others. It has to have an element of 'why didn't I think of that?' about it. If the product is simply novel, creative without context, adding no value to those around, then genius is an unlikely appellation to be applied to the creator of the product, no matter how *original* he might have been.

This element of taste, this just-in-time but never-failing connection with the world about, is the factor that separates the productive genius from the simply creative. It is why people such as Jean-Louis Gassée, one-time head of development at Apple Computers, look for research engineers who know about real-estate, who understand about markets, and have a feeling for people, as well as being capable of practical computing insights.

3   Strange Mentality

Anyone can re-combine old elements into new outcomes. It ought to follow that the more elements a person has to hand from which to re-combine, and the greater the permeability between the domains that house these elements, the more likely that person is to be creative. Brighter people with more accessible memories ought to be more often creative than others because they have a greater capacity to learn new things, and things which are significantly different from each other, as well as a capacity to assess them, and compare and contrast their components in the search for new connections. Theoretically, therefore, the brighter the person, the more likely that he should be a creator. Fortunately for the world at large, but unfortunately for calibrating theorists, such linearity of relationships is poorly represented in nature.

Intellectually brighter people may be faster at reaching a solution, but so are the famed idiot savants, within their limitations. There clearly is a minimum intellectual capability necessary if anyone is ever to reach a level of mastery over some disciplines and to be able to find the time, energy or opportunity to be creative within or between them. This is not so high as to be unattainable by more than 80 per cent of the well-taught population in science, maths and physics, or 65 per cent or so for language-based creativity.

However, intellectual capacity is not the greatest limiting factor for the 99 per cent of people who believe that they will not create anything of consequence in their lives: anything, that is, which is both significantly valuable to others and transparently novel. In fact, the case could be made for suggesting that the scales of intellectual and creative abilities are parallel and not interactive.

Just as people can be so bright as to find communicating with the average person to be disappointingly difficult and unproductive, so the potentially creative individual can easily lose touch with the ordinary and therefore produce great novelty, but nothing that people could possibly want.

The Manner of Invention

Before a creative act can begin, there has to be a person capable of bringing new associations, or stimuli or contrasts, and sufficient knowledge across a wide enough band of disciplines to be able to bring two or more things together that were not there before.

As long ago as 1926 the creative process was seen by Wallas[13] as four successive stages:

Preparation: the gathering of data, impressions, concepts that are related to the domain of the problem or opportunity.

Incubation: the passive, seemingly unconscious sorting and re-sorting of this material prior to:

Illumination: the sudden revealing of an answer, a flash of insight, the emergence of a new solution which reveals novelty.

Verification: the examination of the new thoughts, theory or concept against the existing framework of evaluation. Does it work, under what conditions? How is it an improvement? What refinements are necessary?

These stages have been looked at again many times since then without a great deal of improvement.

Stage 1: Preparation

Preparation is all-important. One of the reasons why brainstorming (discussed in chapter 10) is not as effective as it might be is because it is too rarely preceded by the kind of intense, prolonged and detailed study that preludes most creative endeavours.

One other aspect of preparation which is commonly seen to be a vital part of the whole creative process is re-defining the problem, and seeing the issue that might produce the greatest outcome. More than one of the creative scientists have looked at old problems in a new light. Sir James Black consistently looks at tables of results when reading research papers, rather than spending time examining the conclusions that others have drawn from their experiments. He looks for inconsistencies, for gaps that the researchers themselves might have missed because they were sure of their conclusions and concerned for experimental tidiness. He also exhorts his fellow scientists to recognize how much is already known but unused in scientific research. The world is full of people extending boundaries which have already been explored. Whole scientific conferences have been written off by middle-aged professional attendees, saying, with despair, not arrogance, that the experiments seemed to generate a sense of *déjà vu*.

The Lotus Advanced Engineering team, no doubt in common with others of like circumstance, gain a great benefit from motor-racing.

The day-to-day yield of working on the problems of cars that only a handful of people in the world can drive is that this provides the opportunity to confront the most testing of engineering issues. On the other hand, the majority of architectural schools will suggest that the most difficult task to set a student is to design an innovative private house for a typical family. The search for anomalies in existing output, theory or daily work, challenges that are beyond the orthodox framework of problem domains, and a willingness to transgress traditional boundaries are all part of the preparation stage.

The larger part of preparation must be the attainment of mastery over a domain or a sphere of knowledge, or a craft. Those who have not yet discovered the wheel will no doubt shout 'Eureka' when it dawns upon them. Much creative endeavour will continue to be rediscovery rather than novel discovery, as the breadth, depth and detail of recorded knowledge grows.

The second major part of preparation is the search for the problem, defining the approach, not taking first impressions or looking for the quick fix. Most major innovators have decided on a specific approach to an issue long before they have reached an outcome which others can recognize as a breakthrough. Preparation is both a long, arduous process and a willingness not to take no for an answer.

Stage 2: Incubation

Incubation has always been the most hotly debated of the component stages since it is often only implied, as in the anecdotal but spectacular evidence of Poincaré, whose revelation of fuschian functions was reached, he said, as he stepped on a bus, having thought about anything else but the issue for days.

The concept accepted by most theorists is that of primary- and secondary-process thinking. Secondary-process is seen to be under active control, primary- as being involuntary. Incubation is the art of letting go, of leaving the involuntary processes to search unattended through the mass of incompletely connected memory traces.

We owe to Freud the promotion of the concept of primary-process thinking. Most people experience it most often between being asleep and being awake. During this period, impressions, images, feelings and thought particles can rumble in one after another, sometimes producing outcomes which would be hard to reproduce in any other conditions. Freud saw primary-process thinking as a product of the id, the primitive, pleasure-seeking, self-serving part of the personality, most highly prominent in children, but gradually socialized into the background during the process of their upbringing. The ego, and super-ego, in Freud's terms, take over as the rational problem-solver and the moral interpreter respectively. So as children grow, their propensity to think freely under the profound and luminous influence of the id is inhibited and circumscribed. If the process of growing up is accompanied by the regulation of primary-process thinking, it might be no surprise to discover that so many creative adults seem so often to be like children.

Incubation could be seen as a peculiarity of the creative classes, indulged, encouraged, by prolonging or restricting sleep, looking into fires, having a notepad by the side of the bed so as not to lose the stray hypnopompic imagery, taking drugs, drinking too much tea, or being surrounded by the smell of rotten fruit. All of these have been used by great men to induce in themselves the productivity of incubation.

Hypnagogia is the state of consciousness between wakefulness and sleep. Hynapompia is the term used more rarely for the state between sleep and wakefulness – that is, prior to waking up fully. It is something that most people experience. It can include visual sensations of colours and cloud-forms, complex designs, people, animal figures, scenes, landscapes, words, writing or just nonsense. The real timing of these experiences is very short, seldom more than ten minutes. To most people, it seems much longer than this. The process is a tumble of sensations, merging, re-forming, and finally shifting into wakefulness, or sleep.

Andreas Mavromatis has written a book devoted exclusively to this subject. In it he quotes extensively from sources which show hypnagogic experiences to contribute much to creative outcomes. Brahms, Puccini, Wagner and Goethe have each described hypnagogic-like trances or states in which they created their best-known compositions. Mavromatis quotes E. Bernd on Edison as follows:

> Edison used to work very hard on his research – at beta, the faster wave frequencies. Then when he would reach a 'sticking point' he would take one of his famous 'cat naps'. He would doze off in his favourite chair, holding steel balls in the palms of his hands. As he would fall asleep – drift into alpha – his arms would relax and lower,

letting the balls fall into pans on the floor. The noise would wake Edison and very often he would awaken with an idea to continue his project.'[14]

Kublai Khan was supposed to have come to Coleridge while he was in a state of hypnagogia. Einstein's first true insight into relativity was said to have come to him as he got out of bed. The often quoted experience of Kekulé, who first envisioned the ring-like nature of the benzene molecule while dozing in front of an open fire was clearly a hypnagogic experience. Many of these experiences seem to be internally visual in form, whether they come to scientists, artists or writers. This may be one of the factors that have led people to the assumption that the recombining of relations, the bringing together of thoughts and ideas from different memories, many of which are verbal in nature, is achieved by creative people at these times because of their regression to subverbal words: grammar and syntax can be fearfully constraining to the orthodox.

Perhaps only by working within such a framework, or absence of framework, can such boundaries be crossed. People who need the rigour of convention find such processes frightening. Even those who favour the challenge of the new can find some threat in such input. William Least Heat Moon wrote in *Blue Highways*: 'Beware thoughts that come in the night. They aren't tuned properly; they come in askew, free of sense and restriction, deriving from the most remote of sources.'

The clues to the value of hypnagogia and other mind-releasing activities are best presented by Rhona Ochse in her book, *Before the Gates of Excellence*. First she quotes Jean Cocteau as a passive but eager receiver of these thoughts: 'The Poet is at the disposal of his night. His role is humble, he must clean his home and wait its due arrival',[15] having previously pointed out the most likely explanation for the phenomenon:

> . . . while actively engaged in solving a problem, one's attention is narrowly focused: one's range of awareness is likely to be relatively constricted. Even if one shifts the focus of one's attention, only a narrow range of cues will be utilized at any one moment . . . .
>
> When one is in a low state of arousal (during, say, a period of incubation), however, one's attention is likely to be wide and diffused, and a relatively wide variety of 'irrelevant' cues is likely to be simultaneously accessible to awareness . . . and bringing supposedly

irrelevant cues together in the current stream of thought may provide a vital link to a new perception of a problem. In other words, lowering of cortical arousal makes one open to simultaneous perception and association of hitherto unrelated items.[16]

So, only when *not* paying attention, is incubation, or our primary thinking processes, or creativity, likely to bring essential new insights to our problem-solving. This is precisely the opposite to the mentation recommended to, and rewarded by, our commercial and industrial managers and professionals. These people are conspicuously taught to think analytically, to route issues down logical paths. Where they have to follow heuristics, they learn to do so on a narrow plane of experience and on the basis of subjective probability born of the evasion of any risk.

Stage 3: Illumination

Illumination comes when the primary processes suddenly recognize that there is a reconfiguration that works. It is a very mystical-sounding process, and for those who have never had a creative thought, it seems profoundly unlikely. None the less, it seems to be instantly acknowledged as real by those who have.

Illumination is the answer, or at least an answer, which at least comes close to satisfying the constraints of the problem and the utility of the outcome. This is where creative minds come into their own. There is often an intuitive outcome, a gut reaction, a newly formed, but seriously held, belief. Philip Goldberg wrote a book called *The Intuitive Edge*. In it he points up the inhibitions which many people have about receiving those kinds of messages:

> Old hands suffer from what psychologists call 'problem set', habitually dealing with problems in ways that worked in the past. Thus the internalized operations that can free an experienced person to skip steps and make quick connections may also inhibit the kind of intuition needed to deal with novelty and ambiguity.[17]

Goldberg goes on, referring to the work of Ralph Keyes: 'many executives gather hard data not so much to help them make decisions but to obtain support for an intuitive idea and defend themselves in case it doesn't pan out.'[18]

Analytical thinkers plan, order, proceed through to an end in ways that enable them to retrace their steps. The intuitive play around with things they are not sure of, trying to sense and feel what the playing-field is like before choosing which game to play. They take chances. They take chances because taking chances has paid off in the past. To the analytical thinker, the intuitive can seem extraordinarily languid and unconcerned, even as the water appears to be closing over his head. Contrastingly, to the intuitive, the analytical seems dull and tense, focused and heavy, even when working at speed.

It was Max Planck, the physicist, who said that the pioneer scientist 'must have a vivid intuitive imagination, for new ideas are not generated by deduction but by artistically creative imagination'. Illumination can come after much preparation, after substantial, apparently fallow periods of incubation, and seem to have been no effort at all. Equally illumination can be ragged. It can be impossible to evaluate. It may seem impossible in practical terms, or irrelevant. But very rarely does the creative individual give up on it, once it is his. This is the danger point for many organizations.

Another danger point is that a good insight, produced through a real creative process of great quality and considerable potential, could look just as silly to the outsider as a dumb piece of cerebration from a self-serving crank. Not many creative thinkers will know the difference themselves, at first, but this does not stop them having a deep affection for their ideational offspring, and a highly protective posture in relation to any potential predator. How do organizations which are rational, orthodox, essentially steady-state and risk-averse bodies, ever apply their generalist evaluative skills to the product of a creative, unorthodox specialist, who insists that his idea is the greatest?

Unlike analytical thinking, it is not possible to make sound judgements about one person's intuition by applying that of another. Unlike analytical thinking, there is no going back to retrace mental steps. This is a source of deep frustration for those who reach this pinnacle without being able to learn from their passage down the path they have taken. Laurence Olivier once played Othello so well that everyone was stunned by his extraordinary brilliance. He left the stage at the end of the play, looking furious. 'But Sir Laurence,' they cried backstage, 'why are you so upset after you were so brilliant?' 'I know I was brilliant,' he said, 'but I don't know why.'

Stage 4: Evaluation

So we come to the final stage of the creative event: evaluation. In the scientific world, this stage could well outlast the rest put together. Chemists have to subject their theoretically perfect syntheses to elaborate measurements to ensure that nature has not, after all, deceived them.

Charles Darwin admitted that he could not remember a single 'first-formed hypothesis which had not after a time to be given up or greatly modified'. Anyone who has ever taken part in a series of experiments which have subsequently been explained or written about for those who were not present will recognize how time reduces the mistakes and the clumsiness, and the story omits mention of the shallowness of so many deliberations on false trails.

Creative copywriters in advertising can seldom forgo the torture of focus groups, public panels and recognition scores even before they find out whether their contribution to product promotion has produced a worthwhile increment in sales. Evaluation is the critical time, where the creator not only has to test the product of his creation against the interests of the real world, but has to put up with incursions on his private world by many others as well. It should be a time of joy, but is often a time of fear.

In the evaluation process, the need is to temper sympathy with objectivity. A favourite idea is hardly likely to be criticized by its originator with any bite or thrust. On the other hand, the bite and thrust of another could well destroy the possibilities of further exposure to the light of day. If the creator is smart and speedy, perhaps no one will ever know how good his idea might have been.

This is one reason why advertising agencies keep their creative departments away from sharp eyes, and interpose, between most of these denizens and their client staff, a group of intermediaries whose job it is to interpret client needs and market dimensions, and mother the creatives into producing the golden goose. They are there to support, provide preparation, husband during incubation, induce illumination and attenuate evaluation. It is a crucial and almost universal role in the advertising world which appears to exist rarely anywhere else in organizational life.

The Place of Chance in the Creative Process

Many thinkers on creativity have attached great significance to the factor of pure chance. The probability of landing on the right answer depends, as much as anything else, on the frequency of jumping. James Austin, one-time Professor of Neurology at the University of Colorado, is one of the few who have examined this aspect of creativity thoroughly, in his book *Chase, Chance and Creativity*.[19]

Serendip was the name given to Sri Lanka before it was Ceylon. It in turn gives its name to serendipity, which often occurs in researchers' explanations of original discovery. This means a happy outcome of a chance occurrence. Records everywhere show the extent to which serendipity figures in the lives of most acknowledged creative geniuses, of whatever silk. The conjunction of the old name of Sri Lanka with happy chance has less to do with the island than with a story that Horace Walpole discovered in 1578, again by chance. He had been told of a 'silly fairy tale about "The Three Princes of Serendip", who, in their travels, were always making discoveries, by accidents and sagacity of things which they were not in quest of'.

Walpole was a person who felt himself lucky, being able to reach conclusions, seemingly at the last minute, which were based upon observations that did not come from experiences at the centre of his attention. So serendipity was the word invented by a man who experienced it, to mean a gift for discovering things by accident or sagacity, while hunting for something else.

Curiously, the Three Princes story itself has more than a little Sherlock Holmes about it, since these princes solved every strange riddle posed to them, often through the process of analysis and deduction. However, Sherlock Holmes seldom admitted to accidental discovery in his analysis.

James Austin went on to describe what he called the three categories of chance (other than pure accident), which he named Kettering, Pasteur and Disraeli. The first of these is what most of us would call *pure* chance. He named it after Charles Kettering, an automotive engineer, because Kettering once said, 'Keep on going and the chances are you will stumble on something'. Pure chance assumes no intervention. Whatever will be will be. Keep moving even without any sense of where to, and you will change the odds in your favour, at least a little.

One of the most often quoted statements about research was made by Louis Pasteur, who wrote *'Dans les champs de l'observation, le hazard ne favorise que les ésprits préparés'*. This is always translated as 'Chance favours the prepared mind', a translation which loses significantly from the original. Pasteur was referring to busyness, activity, continuous search, even in unlikely places – the kind of alert busyness that stopped Fleming throwing away the dish on which was growing penicillin, even though all of the sensible scientific controls necessary to lead to any practical conclusion were gone. (He was away on holiday, and the dish was subject to all kinds of contamination and changes in temperature.) Free energy, persistence, and educated awareness mean that Pasteur's chances were better than those of Kettering.

The third level of chance, Austin named after Benjamin Disraeli, who said, 'We make our fortunes and we call them fate'. In this category the chances fall to the very few. These are the big ones, where opportunity comes to the person uniquely equipped to profit from it. This is the James Black and the Paul Ehrlich category. Ehrlich and Black, like many applied scientists everywhere, tested hundreds of compounds because they 'knew' what the effect they were seeking had to be. Both went back to early compounds which had failed, and re-tested them. Both found an early compound which failed only because the experiment was improperly conducted. In both cases, no one else in the scientific community rushed to compete in the search, because they were not prepared to deal with the unorthodox thinking that was required. So it is a chance, in the sense that it is a discovery. But it is not chance, in that the search is a very narrow one, and a very individual one.

Serendipity is often perceived as pure chance, the product simply of good fortune, or at most good fortune married to Kettering's proposition. From the original stories, however, it would more nearly describe the experiences of those fortunate (but not lucky) few who follow the Disraeli principles.

Conclusion

In considering the nature of invention, a choice has to be made between fine and robust interpretations. A genius becomes recognized as such by those who have an understanding of his domain (and these can be a very few, as few as those who can read *Principia Mathematica*, and are able to explain the contents to a lesser mortal), and, beyond that, by those who accept that he is a special person because of what he has added to collective culture and understanding.

Recognising a genius of the stature of Mozart or Einstein or Newton is one thing; classifying levels of genius or defining at what point a person is not to be classified as one, is another. Are all geniuses eminent people? Are all eminent people geniuses? It is certain that we cannot classify them by their intellectual standards, since by any measure this is too varied. Very bright people rarely end up being recognized as geniuses. Not all those recognized as such are really very bright. The answer has to be pragmatic.

Creative people are essential if we are to survive. We need them. They need us. Whether they become recognized as geniuses depends on a number of factors.

- Are they sufficiently 'psychopathic' to devote an abnormal amount of their time, effort and attention to learning about one domain (field of endeavour) in order to master it, without being so psychopathic as to be unable to relate to the rest of the world?
- Are they provided with the necessary intellectual opportunities and internal drive to make them want to achieve as much as they are afforded the wherewithal to achieve?
- Do they then find themselves in situations which provide them with both the opportunities and the problems from which to make something for, and of, themselves?
- Are they lucky enough to find a place that no one else has noticed, or have the key to the lock that no one else can open. Have they serendipity?

Without these conditions, most creative people probably follow what Donald Campbell[20] called his 'blind variation and selective retention' model. Campbell's view was that all new knowledge requires first the means of producing variations, variations moreover which are blind, unconnected with others – mutants. These mutants are akin to illuminations, insights gained from accidental comings-together.

These illuminations, wrote Campbell, are subject to the same natural selection process as attributed by Darwin to the survival of the fittest. Finally, he proposed the concept of retention. New ideas with survival value are preserved, then become part of the orthodoxy. Once there, they become the subject of mutation again.

Thomas Kuhn also held that ideas become preserved in orthodoxy. He extended Campbell's position by calling each evolutionary plateau a paradigm. Unlike Campbell, however, he felt that 'Cometh the how, cometh the man' was not purely an accident of fate, a solution waiting for its time, but that individuals could have a real influence on events, albeit not without supreme effort. Kuhn was concerned only with scientific creativity. He referred to the conflict between the fixed paradigm, the prevailing orthodoxy, and the threatening innovator as reflecting the essential tension in all creative people. He believed that the scientist must simultaneously display the characteristics of the traditionalist and the iconoclast if he was to prove successful.

In today's competitive world, most organizations cannot afford the possibility of chance happenings, or even chance aided by motion. They need serendipity with extra sagacity. They do not have the resources to look under every independent stone hoping to find a jewel. They have to make much more effective use of their potentially creative people and find better ways of reaping their fruit without killing the tree.

Notes

1 G. M. Prince, *The Practice of Creativity* (Harper & Row, New York, 1970), p. xiii.
2 Anthony Storr, *The Dynamics of Creation* (Atheneum, New York, 1985), p. 65.
3 Neil Kessel, in Penelope Murray, (ed.), *Genius: A History of an Idea* (Blackwell, Oxford, 1989), pp. 196–212.
4 George Pickering, *Creative Malady*, (Oxford University Press, New York, 1974), p. 309.
5 Francis Galton, *Hereditary Genius* (Appleton, New York, 1869), p. 33.
6 D. L. Rosenham and M. E. Seligman, *Abnormal Psychology* W. W. Norton, New York, 1984), p. 489.
7 See note 6 above.
8 J. L. Karlsson, 'An Icelandic family study of schizophrenia', in A. R. Kaplan (ed.), *Genetic Factors in Schizophrenia* (Charles C. Thomas, Springfield, Ill., 1972), pp. 246–55.
9 Rosenham and Seligman, *Abnormal Psychology*, p. 346.
10 C. M. Cox, 'The early mental traits of three hundred geniuses', in L. M. Terman, (ed.), *Genetic Studies of Genius* (Stanford University Press, Stanford, Ca., 1926), p. 180.

11 Denise G. Shekerjian, *Uncommon Genius: How Ideas are Born* (Viking Penguin, New York, 1990), p. 141.

12 Ibid., p. 52.

13 G. Wallas, *The Act of Thought* (Watts, London, 1926).

14 Andreas Mavromatis, *Hypnagogia* (Routledge & Kegan Paul, London, 1987), p. 186.

15 Rhona Ochse, *Before the Gates of Excellence: Determinants of Creative Genius* (Cambridge University Press, Cambridge, 1990), p. 232.

16 Ibid., p. 201.

17 Philip Goldberg, *The Intuitive Edge: Understanding and Developing Intuition* (Turnstone Press, UK, 1985), p. 90.

18 Ibid., p. 91.

19 James H. Austin, *Chase, Chance and Creativity* (Columbia University Press, New York, 1978).

20 Donald Campbell, 'Blind variation and selection retention in creative thought', *Psychological Review* 67:6 (1960), pp. 380–400.

8

Dimensions of Creativity

Genius does what it must, and Talent does what it can.

Owen Meredith, Earl of Lytton

Every modern manager has to understand how to reap the benefit of the human resource, whatever and wherever it might be. In a world dominated by change, this manager needs all the help he can get to ensure that his unit will anticipate, adapt to, and defend itself against the adverse consequences of the turbulence around it. He does this through constantly coming up with renewed ways of winning. In other words, he has to maximize the creativity of his charges. If he does not, others will win. They will win because they keep doing the same things better, or because they think of better ways of doing things differently. They will come up with products which offer that bit extra, with machines which are that bit more efficient, or with organizations which are marginally more efficacious. Each innovation that competitors put in a place ahead of us is another challenge to our competitive capacity. It is a challenging world, and the need for creativity in dealing with it has never been more pressing.

No one could disagree with the need or the urgency. Furthermore, there is little doubt that much work, effort, intelligence and ingenuity has been applied over the years to grasping and understanding the subjects of creativity, innovation and their management. Almost all of this work has been undertaken in the United States and in Europe. Yet it is clearly the Japanese who are the innovators of the 1990s.

Many books and articles have been written about innovatory organizations and creative people. Yet most organizations do not use their creative potential well, and most admit to not doing so. There is clearly a gap between the need to compete within a global tide of innovation, and our grasp of the essential insights required to make our vast innovatory potential work for us. Part of that gap comes from a misplaced optimism that something will turn up; that 'muddling through' has always worked in the past, and will continue to do so in the future; that is to say, there is a lack of the perception of need. A second component in the gap is the lack of realization of how much insight, intelligence and capability exists, in one way or another, which could be of help to those who feel the sharp draught of cold reality.

This is not entirely the failure of those most in need of understanding. Over the years, debates between the experts have ranged over how much creativity exists within the average man; what creativity is, and how it is different from innovation; how it comes about, how to improve on it effectively; how to attempt to reach it, and how to recognize it when you see it. Research into creativity and innovation has become a fearfully hazardous endeavour for the professional student. It is a minefield for the professional manager seeking, in the small time available to him, ways in which to get better at being creative, and of inducing creativity in his organization.

This chapter aims to package creativity, to provide a framework for understanding where it can be found, and how, in its different forms, range and complexity, it can be tamed. It is intended considerably to broaden the concept, which has become too focused, with the result that creativity and innovation are seen as the properties of the chosen few, and to have no place for the average organization man.

The Dimensions of Creativity

To try to encompass all the variety of interests and endeavour in the domain of creativity and innovation is not an easy task, and if we are to make the best use of the information, we need an algorithm. Three dimensions are proposed:

1 The creative attribution: creative people.
2 The style of intervention:
    (a) the creative process
    (b) the creative purpose
3 The outcome: creative products

Each dimension has its scale of variation. Exploring these variations is important to finding a correct diagnosis, for the efficacious treatment of one is often the tragic poison of another.

The Creative Attribution: Creative People

The creative attribution has been the subject of many and varied researches. The word attribution is used because it is often impossible to separate the person from the process or the product, except by attributing him with the powers of creative thinking. The creative person is a person who is attributed with the capability to create. The proposed scale reads:

Everyman : Adaptor : Innovator : Prodigy : Genius.

It is a scale of perspective from the eyes of the beholder. It includes the two concepts introduced by Michael Kirton[1] (Adaptor/Innovator) and has, as its extremes, Everyman, who is assumed by most to make relatively little mark on the changes adopted by society, and the Genius, who is often defined by the observation that he has made a major impact.

There is no implication of any co-variant scale of intelligence. However, there is one of the potential to influence, and one of perceived importance. By definition the Genius is a rarity, and Everyman is commonplace. The Innovator here defined is the person who challenges what is and seeks to put in plan or in hand something different. On one side of the Innovator is the Adaptor, who seeks to find ways of improving on things by nudging and following through, working with the grain rather than (as the Innovator would) against it.

Kirton introduced his concepts of Adaptor/Innovator (A/I) in 1976 and his work has been the subject of much review since then. He looked upon the two as meaning the *style* of decision-making, problem-solving and creativity, although specifically not the *capacity* to create as such. He described Adaptors as producing just enough ideas through pushing at the boundaries of the existing positions. 'Doing better what is done' is the best description of their endeavours.

As Kirton identified them, Innovators have 'a taste for proliferation of ideas', are more likely in the pursuit of change 'to reconstruct the problem, separating it from its enveloping accepted thought, paradigms and customary viewpoints, and emerge with much less expected, and probably less acceptable solutions'.

Convinced Innovators and Adaptors have some differences in their personalities. Innovators are seen to be insensitive, riding roughshod over the views of others. They are impatient. The Adaptors are more pedestrian, but more agreeable, less profligate with their world, but essentially conventional.

Research on the A/I scale shows the interaction between the creative attribution and the nature and environment of the organization. Civil servants, accountants, banks and local government employees tend to be more adaptive. Those in organizations which are stable and live in quiet waters also tend to have a more Adaptor-like profile. Studies show how groups of people gradually (over years) become more self-similar, rejecting or influencing those whose conformity to the A/I profile does not match their own.

The Prodigy is a rarity. This is the person who has developed, or perhaps inherited, the talent which could bring genius within his grasp, but who, for one reason or another, has not achieved this potential. Maybe he will be accorded that appellation one day, perhaps after his death, but not now. The *Shorter Oxford Dictionary* defines prodigy in terms of wonder: 'An amazing or marvellous thing, anything which causes wonder, astonishment, or surprise'.

The Prodigy is often seen as one whose exceptional talent is sadly unconsummated. It is possible for such people to have too many options, to have so much versatility that they feel unable to choose to follow anything through. Alternatively, they could become so deeply committed to the mastery of one 'domain' that they find themselves unable to wrest a genuine new idea from out of the intellectual congestion.

Chance plays an inevitable part in the attribution of creativity to individuals. There are abilities and behaviours that must be present if a person is to make it on to this scale at all, but how far up the scale of creative attribution they ultimately come is a result of many other factors. Intrinsic to this dimension is that the position on it of any one person cannot be determined without examining the product of his output. There are many people of exceptional aptitude in MENSA, for example, who seem to have spent their lives behaving as conventionally as the most orthodox person could hope for. Equally, there are people who are given the title 'Genius' whose personal attributes could be seen as well short of prodigious.

Geniuses can be described as major and minor, depending upon the scale of their impact and the uniqueness of their position within their domain. Such attribution could be the result of an accident of timing, or of opportunity, or just pure accident. For example, society has irrevocably linked only the name of Alexander Fleming with the discovery of penicillin. In fact, the Nobel Prize for Medicine, which he received in 1945, was shared with Ernest Chain and Howard Florey. Fleming discovered the existence of penicillin as a substance of some significance in 1928. The sequence of circumstances which led to this have been described as equivalent to a winning run of blind bets on seven outsiders in succession. Yet although he explored many of the properties of penicillin, including its important anti-bacterial effect, Fleming did not use penicillin for therapy, and made no effort to push for its application in clinical practice. Alexander Kohn, in *Fortune or Failure*, observes: 'Among his 27 papers and lectures published during the decade after the discovery, he only once mentioned penicillin as a potential therapeutic agent.'[2]

Florey and Chain began their research on penicillin in 1938. They concentrated the substance and injected it into terminally infected mice and cured them. Kohn goes on: 'The results were published in August 1940 in *The Lancet* and caused a sensation. Fleming immediately went to Oxford. Chain, hearing of the visit, is supposed to have said: 'Good God, I thought he was dead'.[3]

Fleming took up the torch. In the US other researchers found a new strain and manufacturers then produced sufficient quantities to make a significant impact on the war effort. Most of the creative aspects of the ultimate design of penicillin as we know it was the work of many others. But, with the passage of time, Fleming's name forever overshadows those who made the therapeutic breakthroughs. Kohn concluded, about Fleming:

> Perhaps he was not a genius, but he had the power to see what was really there and the more mysterious flair for distinguishing between the important and the trivial. But would penicillin have been there to save the lives of thousands of World War Two soldiers and countless civilians thereafter if it hadn't been for Florey and Chain?[4]

History is replete with similar examples of people seen as geniuses who owe so much of their success to so many others. Similarly, history is empty of people who have had the compulsion and capacity of the truly exceptional, but in some way did not make it into the public arena that would give the critical mass to their fame.

The Style of Intervention: the Creative Process

Set in an organizational context, innovation can be brought about by a very wide variety of interventions. None of them should be treated as of lesser significance than the others. Some writers believe that at least two of these very distinctive styles need to be present if the hard natural crust of organizational resistance is to be successfully cracked. The dimension has been given five positions, as follows:

Inventor : Entrepreneur : Intrapreneur : Champion : Sponsor

Reading from left to right, there is an increase in organizational norms and involvement, and at the same time a diminution in direct creativity of thought. The Inventor focuses on making something different, the Sponsor on creating conditions under which something different becomes something relevant.

The Inventor as a concept usually includes the 'aha' component. The notion of a somewhat harebrained, garret-living solitary outsider, playing with novelty, and becoming obsessed by its exploitation, and paranoid about its theft, is a deep and irresistible one.

The Entrepreneur extends this towards the outside world, seeking to make commercial advantage of the innovation he feels he commands. Not all Entrepreneurs would be innovators. However, they do have in common this need to turn what they have to their commercial advantage. Some Inventors are Entrepreneurs, but not all; it depends how much the pleasure of the idea or of its exploitation dominates intentions. On this scale, the Entrepreneur is being used to describe the innovative exploiter, the idea pioneer, the creative person who seeks personally to control the practical consequences of his ideas. Such people do not usually survive in commerce for very long.

More often than they succeed in commercial ventures on their own account, they will sell out to larger organizational interests. The many failures pass into obscurity daily. S. R. Ovshinsky in the USA and Sir Clive Sinclair in the UK are examples of inventors becoming

Entrepreneurs in the pursuit of their dreams, but ultimately falling foul of their own ambitions, usually more than once.

Intrapreneur was a word invented by Gifford Pinchot III to describe the Innovator who operates inside a corporation: an *intra*corporate entre*preneur*. An employee who feels a powerful need to improve on, change, create or innovate while remaining inside an organization was offered several life-guides by Pinchot in his book *Intrapreneuring*. He listed the differentiating characteristics of the Entrepreneur, the Intrapreneur and the Traditional Manager. Under the heading 'Courage and Destiny' are the following:

Traditional Manager
Sees others in charge of his or her destiny. Can be forceful and ambitious, but may be fearful of other's ability to do him or her in.

Entrepreneur
Self-confident, optimistic, courageous.

Intrapreneur
Self-confident and courageous. Many Intrapreneurs are cynical about the system, but optimistic about their ability to outwit it.[5]

Pinchot saw the traditional manager as one who strives to avoid mistakes, or to delay recognizing them for what they are for as long as he can get away with it. The Entrepreneur, at least while he is still hungry for success, takes mistakes and failures as opportunities to learn better how to make progress. The Intrapreneur, Pinchot says, is 'sensitive to the need to appear orderly in corporation. Attempts to hide risky projects from view so he can learn from mistakes without the political cost of public failure'.[6]

The Intrapreneur is almost always the originator of the new approach, who becomes, and has to become, passionately attached to it. He often retires from the organization a lonely disappointed man. Anyone who feels that this is his lot should study Pinchot's text. On page 31, there is a questionnaire to help him to assess how much of an Intrapreneur he already is. On page 22, he can read the Ten Commandments that will help him to learn the rules of personal and professional survival. The first of Pinchot's Ten Commandments for the Intrapreneur is 'Come to work each day willing to be fired,' the seventh, 'Never bet on a race unless you are running in it', and the eighth, 'Remember that it is easier to ask for forgiveness than for permission'. For all this, he commends the role of Intrepreneur as 'the dreamer who does'.

The Champion is recognized by the organization as one of its own. This innovator is assigned by the organization, and encouraged to take the role of internal irritant. Companies that recognize Champions understand that their organization, like most, if not all, is a giant obstacle to change.

Organizations need to introduce mutants and invasives to enable them to adapt to their changing worlds. However, most organizations' immune systems are resistant to such a seeming parasite. The Champion is the equivalent of the enzyme systems that prevent a new mother aborting her foetus, or the medication given to transplant patients to prevent them from rejecting the foreign tissue. Champions have to have a pugnacious and determined style. More than Intrapreneurs, they have to be street-wise. Much more than Intrapreneurs, they have to be objective about those in their care. They should not feel so emotionally attached to the innovations they are charged to pursue that they become totally blind to the issues and problems that attend their introduction.

The Champion is not often a creative person who produces the original ideas that make for the substance of innovation, but he has to be a person who creates the pathways which will make it happen for others who are. He is a lover of new ideas, not just a passive supporter of their delivery. He is more the surrogate mother than the midwife. He admires inventive people, even envies them. Vicariously, he shares their insight, passion and excitement through becoming part of the chase, and the kill.

The Sponsor is the midwife. He knows that the organization needs to profit from providing a stream of challenges to the status quo and the comfortably familiar. But he is very much part of the fabric of the organization. He would not seek to come up with ideas of his own, but he will listen to those of others. He will provide the cover they need to ensure that they have the time and space to cultivate their progeny. He will prepare the ground for their acceptance, using the organization systems with care and sensitivity to ensure that they do not turn against him. Sponsorship has a level of risk, and takes up time and effort which may well detract from the prime needs of the Sponsor's position. The Sponsor must feel safe enough in his position to take such a chance.

Some Sponsors are would-be Intrapreneurs who lost their

courage, or whom luck did not favour and who are keen to balance the books. Most are people who know that no organization will survive for long if those in power seek to use that power only to ensure that they keep it. The Sponsor is the least creative in the sense that most people see the nature of the creative act. He probably has the most important part to play, however, in the creative successes of the majority of organizations.

An Inventor can succeed where there is a Champion. An Entrepreneur can succeed if he has a Sponsor. An Intrapreneur is often his own Inventor and his own Champion, but this is a very tiring combination of roles. There is endless evidence of organizations which turned away the very substance of their own renewal. If the nature of these intervention styles was better understood, and the interactions between them were built and lubricated, then many of these errors would not have occurred.

The Style of Intervention: the Creative Purpose

One of the more unhelpful outcomes of modern organizational practice is the tacit assumption that research and development (R & D), go together. The skills required of each are as different as marketing is from selling. They are nearer to each other than they are to manufacturing, but are nothing like as close as their universal coupling would suggest. In viewing creative aim as a separate dimension, consideration has to be taken of the purpose and motivation of the individual innovator as well as of the objective of the organizational unit to which he belongs. The positions on this dimension reads as follows:

Pure Research (R) : Applied Research (d) : Development (D) : Commercial Development (CD) : Organizational Enhancement (O)

Pure Research can be scientific, artistic, commercial or political. Its principal characteristics are that its pursuit is more often than not driven by a personal need, and that its completion date is both hard to calculate and to influence with any confidence.

If research is the aim, then the research aimer is somewhere between selfishly indulgent and keenly evangelical. Many individuals and organizations have sought to make people in Pure Research become open to the influence of their broader remit. They have offered bribes. They have harnessed them together with marketing men. They have sought to make them understand the hard commercial world. Mostly they fail. If research (that is, Pure Research) is to be successful in any terms, it will be because it is driven by motives which owe nothing to ultimate utility and everything to insistent and patient curiosity. It is not a large field of endeavour. In many parts of the world, it is sinking fast.

Pure Research has always been an indulgence, either of the rich, or at least the well-to-do, like Darwin and Huxley. Latterly, however, devoted researchers have taken advantage of opportunities created by expanding global markets. For example, from the competition for new drugs between pharmaceutical companies, large and small, have arisen many openings through which scientists pass to follow through their own interests. Basic researchers have become ever more worldly as they seek funds to provide for their research platforms. They have sought to set up their own protective institutions.

Zaltman King[7] proposed some dimensions which fit neatly into place in this summation. Innovation can be 'programmed' and 'non-programmed'. In most research establishments, the programmed quickly overcomes and drives out the non-programmed. All people like to have their time structured. Most hate the possibility of going to work tomorrow with no idea what to do. Programmed innovation is naturally less likely to be creative, since it is tight, focused and forecast.

Non-programmed innovation can be promoted because there are slack resources, and someone is drawn to put them to use. A sudden priority will bring into play an action which has not been pre-set. Finally, there could be non-programmed innovation because someone sees something coming, and brings forward an innovative initiation to cover the anticipated need. As this scale is ascended, the more the innovation has to be programmed.

Zaltman also suggested a conservative/radical dimension for innovation, which is about degree risk and novelty. Conservative innovations are those which take a new but small, safe step into the dark. Their recognition is accompanied more by the 'ah' than the 'aha', and certainly not the 'Eureka'. But they are the stuff of organization growth and competitive performance.

Sir James Black, in his Premio Nobel in 1988, noted that when he joined ICI's Pharmaceutical Division in 1958, he had 'gone there to pursue a very clear project that had been developing in my mind for several years. I wanted to find a beta-receptor antagonist.' Later he adds, 'In 1964 I went to Smith Kline and French Laboratories to pursue another project that I had been thinking about for some time.' This is the embodiment of the research mind: focused, determined, knowing, insistent. It is emotionally programmed, but intellectually free. It is not a mind that is easily turned, nor should it be.

With such exploratory innovation, the decision to support or manage or accommodate should not be made on cost benefit–analysis, but on the basis : how much can I afford to lose, and how long can I afford to go on losing it? The judgement then needs to be made as to whether the person who is costing all this time and money is the best there is for the research arena into which he delves. Beyond these questions and the promise of their answers, there is nothing that an organization or its representatives can or should do. Neither of them can be expected to produce a perfect, analytically sound answer.

With Applied Research there is a hypothesis, a target, a budget. Again there may well be no opportunity for cost/benefit analysis, but at least it is not a pure punt. This is the aim which takes the answer to the research question from 'What is it?' to 'Can we make something of it?'

Applied Research is not expensive if it has intermediate targets. It can become quickly and irretrievably expensive, both of finance and of time, where there are no recognizable intermediate positions. Where this emotional focus becomes tunnel vision, problems arise. Black communicated this to *Omni* when asked in an interview why he had to revisit early experiments when developing Cimetidine. He said:

> You have an expectation, a prejudice that drives what you do. For histamine at SK & F, I was using the same kind of operation that worked for me with adrenaline. But I took the analogy too literally and rigidly. I hadn't yet learned that when you make a sound method and your expectations are not fulfilled, you have to retreat and say 'What's wrong with my expectations?'. I was still pushing, pushing, because I was so sure my image was right. It took a long time before it gradually got through my thick head that we were attacking the wrong end of the histamine molecule.[8]

Some research scientists can convince their sponsoring organizations that they have only to keep the funds coming and one day a pot of gold will await them. They become Principal Scientists. They produce papers. They become stiff with an unshakeable belief in their own value, and rigid in their determination that it will one day be recognized. Many organizations find it very difficult to prove otherwise, and very hard to terminate the programmes that such people maintain. They have neither the knowledge that they are being deceived, nor the willingness to make void the sunk fund resulting from years of endeavour.

Development (D) as a creative aim is the point where time and money take over from fun and games as the primary forces of direction. The skills of project management, of administrative control and of financial accountability all move into the frame. Development is only intermittently creative. Problems arise that need to be overcome, but they are more often logistical than structural. This is the point in science, art and commercial endeavour when rigour takes over from serendipity.

In the pharmaceutical world this is where animal, pre-clinical and clinical trials enter the picture. The search for the successor molecule begins. The push for successive layers of protective registration takes over. The big money starts to be spent on what is conventionally called drug 'research'. Creativity here is about legal drafting, marketing, lobbying and tight strategic defence. It is about anticipating the unforeseen obstacle. It is about making things happen.

Commercial Development (CD) brings in a wholly different approach to the world of innovation. This is the innovation world of Peter Drucker: the 90 per cent effort regime. This is where deep familiarity in any domain of knowledge has a short half-life. This is also where the money to pay for innovation gets to be made or not made. It is probably where creativity is most underestimated. Perhaps the following example will illustrate the point:

> A corporate financier has the country's leading toothpaste producer as a client. His client's toothpaste business was extremely successful, maintaining its market share despite the level of competition through the brand loyalty of its customers.
>
> One morning, as he was squeezing his toothpaste along the bristles of his brush, an idea struck him. He suddenly saw a way of increasing his client's toothpaste sales by 10 per cent with no significant outlay.
>
> He conducted some swift and conclusive market research which confirmed his brainwave, and made an appointment to present his idea to the board. He arrived for the meeting clasping a slim briefcase. 'In

here', he said 'is a sure fire way for you to increase your toothpaste sales by 10 per cent with virtually no expenditure required.' This got their attention. 'Tell us', they said. 'Not yet,' he said, and produced some papers from his case. 'I will tell you, but only if you sign this document, whereby you agree to pay me a percentage of your increased sales if you adopt my idea.'

After a brief debate the directors agreed to his terms. 'Now tell us.' From his briefcase he produced a drawing of a toothpaste tube with the company's branding. 'How the hell is that going to increase our sales? It's identical to what we've already use!' 'Not quite,' said the financier. 'Let me explain. Your customers are brand loyal, right?' 'Yes.' 'People tend to spread their toothpaste down the length of the brush, right?' 'Certainly,' they agreed. 'Do you still not see the significance of these two facts?' They did not.

In Commercial Development, many ideas such as this are brought to the surface daily. They seem small at the time, but are often immensely valuable over the longer term. The engineer who invented the intermittent windscreen wiper is a case in point. A small modification to an existing piece of machinery had vast commercial consequences. The size of the subsequent pay-off from those manufacturers who had exploited this idea without compensating the inventor shows the enormity of its commercial value.

The financier's explanation, for those who did not immediately recognize it, was:

The difference between my toothpaste tube, and the ones you use is barely discernible, I agree. However the circumference of the nozzle is 10 per cent greater. The toothpaste comes out 10 per cent faster. It'll be used up 10 per cent sooner. And people will come back and buy it 10 per cent more frequently.

The idea was implemented, and sure enough sales rose. The financier increased his earnings by considerably more than 10 per cent , but not as much as he would have done if he had done a deal that had included a percentage of all the other possible applications.

The judgements made at this level of creative aim can cost very little, but make a huge impact. Market research has a part to play, but it did not help Ford Motor Company in the market acceptance of the model Edsel. Their introduction of the Sierra in the early eighties, when the fortunes of motor manufacturers were at their nadir, can be looked back on as a huge and dramatic demonstration of Ford's faith in the future. Their chief designer, Uwe Bahnsen, believed that this was so. The company needed to present a huge symbol of rebirth to the market at a time when the world of Ford and many others seemed near a dark edge. Sierra fulfilled that purpose.

Ford of Europe had a history of success built upon engineering orthodoxy and marketing flair. The idea that it should go for a mid-range replacement of the fabulously successful, but astonishingly average Cortina, with a car as innovative in its outward and inward design as the Sierra, was an extraordinary example of creative Commercial Development.

Whether it was an aberration or an adventure is hard to tell with certainty. One of the marketing executives who was responsible for making the Sierra a success was very concerned about the fierce complaints of its 'inverted jelly mould' shape, and its low sales. Even deep discounts and predatory marketing were not producing results. He spent secret days trying to find ways of improving its looks with stick-on stripes and figurings. The argument continues today between the authorizers and between designers - was Sierra a car ahead of its time, or evidence of a car-maker out of its mind? A symbol of defiance, or a gross error of judgement? These are the unknowns of most creative decisions in Commercial Development. Like Classic Coke, their value is never entirely proven. The one-time Ford executive's tinkering was done in secret because he knew that the Sierra's novelty had become established as the organization's orthodoxy. He referred to the car's 'imperfect market receptivity' when what he really meant was that it was unsaleable.

At the top end of the scale of the creative aim – Organizational Enhancement (O) – is the constriction of the creative environment. There is what has been described as the 'learning organization', where the Argyris principles of double-loop learning apply. The organization not only learns to adapt this time, but how to adapt better next. There is the high-profile, publicly innovative organization, like Apple in the Steve Jobs era, where the whole organizational ethos is encouraged, even forced into maintaining a posture of iconoclastic creative offence.

The means by which creativity and innovation can be influenced at this level are many and various, but hard to measure. This is cultural. Innovation can be part of the cultural environment of a whole community, as in Silicon Valley and Route 128 out of Boston in the

United States, and in several parts of southern France, or around Cambridge in England, or where the technical universities of Germany began to act as the motivating centres of engineering innovation a hundred years ago. Alternatively, it can stem from one man, or woman, determined to make their organization pursue throughout its breadth and depth a style of continuous refreshment.

The creative aim can be diffuse or focused. It can be long term or short term. It can be deeply intense and self-consciously thorough. It could be presented as natural, unaffected and lightly held. There are as many ways of creating creativity at an organizational level as anywhere else. The effect, however, can be heroic.

John Langrish,[8] in 1972, attempted to identify factors which enabled some firms in Manchester to succeed in innovation. The factor which they discovered occurred more frequently than any other was 'the top-person phenomenon': an outstanding individual in a position of authority who contributed more to the variation in innovation performance than anything else. This applied in cases from all industries investigated, chemical, electrical, mechanical and craft alike. It was also the most frequently occurring factor in the few examples examined of cases of large changes in technology. Some of these people drove their organizations into innovation, some provided cover and succour for others to innovate freely. There is little doubt, however, that the quickest and most effective route to increasing creativity and innovation in an organization is through the personal impact of the man at the top of it.

The Outcome: Creative Products

There will always remain a confusion between the creative person and the creative product. Among the evolutionary theories of innovation are those which suggest that the innovator is purely a passive link in an inevitable chain of events; that Einstein was only ahead of his time, not outside of it. If he had not made his contribution to physics when he did, it would simply have postponed the time when it arrived. It is in the nature of things that people will try something new, and that some of these will be more new, or more original, than others.

Just as Darwin registered the evolutionary power of natural selection and the consequent survival of the fittest, so those original features which are seen to be better will naturally be taken up, and those conventions which are seen to be no longer valid will be dropped. These theorists suggest that there is no need to invent the concept of creativity, either in people or in product. It is no more necessary to the world of creativity than is the concept of God to the evolutionists. They say: Just accept innovations as a natural consequence of the natural order.

Such a position is tenable but unhelpful. If creativity is to be managed competitively, finer distinctions need to be made. Classifying the product of creativity is not often a feature of creativity research and, when attempted, often shows a degree of confusion in its results.

Research into the nature and qualities of Beethoven, Einstein and Darwin are placed side-by-side with laboratory research into Mr and Mrs Average. In the latter, the psychology student is aiming to measure statistically the circumstances affecting the fluency of idea generation. For example, they ask their subjects to come up with new uses for a tea bag. It should be no surprise that the results of research at the two ends of this spectrum do not often tally. Because they do not match up to the products of the giant, the temptation is always present to dismiss the poor output of the ordinary man as trivial, and therefore uncreative. This is one of the biggest mistakes that people of the Western world can make. There are three aspects to judging the quality and quantity of creativity without denying its nature. These interact to produce the central judgement as to the value of the product as a creative outcome. They are *originality*, *impact* and *timescale*.

Originality

Creative outcomes can range from the local product or process modification to a paradigm shift where whole ways of looking at the universe are revolutionized or overturned. Reactions could vary from 'Why didn't I think of that?' to 'This is heresy'. Each end of this scale adds novelty and value, to the extent that what is *now* is a step beyond what was *then*. If creativity is the subject, not just massive creativity, then the word applies throughout the scale. It was Abraham Maslow who first lent academic weight to this argument by suggesting that a cake made from an original recipe, created and presented with professional style by an ingenious housewife, should be accepted as having more creative worth than any picture quickly drawn by an artist of acknowledged genius without any concern for its originality or merit.

Impact

This expression is intended to define the extent to which the innovation affects the lives of the people on the planet. Thus, the impact of the products of such people as Baird, Marconi, and Edison are clearly up at the monumental end. The small band of scientists who introduced the mathematical science of Chaos might well collectively turn out to have an impact on thinking at least as significant. The original views of Karl Marx and of Maynard Keynes in their different ways created political, economic and social impacts which far outweighed their intrinisic creative worth either as thoughts or as new products.

Elsewhere, there are people who work very hard on ideas (the better mousetrap?) which, by comparison, could be enormously more original than anything that the above luminaries managed. But at the end of the day, the results of their work and thinking affect little more than the survival of a few trees in the Amazonian rainforest, or a few more Deutschmarks per ton to a manufacturer of specialist steel in Upper Saxony.

Time-scale

The final consideration in measuring the creative product is how long it lasts before it becomes superseded or obsolete. For many innovations everywhere, their time is shortening in places exponentially. The half-life of some products is measured in weeks. This compression applies to people as well as products. A Ph.D. scientist has spent up to eight post-school years proving master of one domain of human understanding. Current views suggest that the half-life of this education is not more than five years. Half of what this student will have learned in eight years will be redundant before another five years has passed. This is the soft underbelly of the creative process.

This can encourage the formation of attitudes which weaken the resolve: 'What does it matter if we are not innovative, because the rewards of innovation are so short, and the effort to achieve them so great?' The alternative approach could be: 'If that is how the competition is pacing my business, I have got to find better ways of beating them to it. I have to learn to be in the market before my competitor with innovations at least as novel and profitable as are his.' This is the hard route and too often it is not a route which European and American interests, especially in manufacturing, choose to take.

Conclusion

There has been much debate about the nature of creativity and innovation in the commercial context. Confusion has prevailed over reason, because different approaches have produced conflicting outcomes, and the field is a large and complex one. There is often a distinction made between creativity and innovation which is neither consistent nor clear, and it is seldom fruitful. To bring into being or 'to form out of nothing', as Johnson defined the word 'create', is not so far from 'to make new, to change or to bring in something new', which is to innovate, yet many writers consistently keep the two apart. One reason for this has been the division of research on the subject between the specialists, with economists and sociologists claiming innovation as their legitimate area of enquiry (the spread of innovation, the evolution of technology), and psychologists and psychiatrists focusing on the nature and causes of creativity in people. This division does not in any way help the end-user of the research thinking to profit effectively from its application.

In offering four dimensions to cover the creative person, the creative aim and style, and the creative product, the following assumptions have been made.

- All people have the capability of being both creative and innovative, and almost all can be helped to improve on the value of these talents. It is a self-limiting, self-conscious, and socially supported inhibition that keeps individuals from the profit of their own originating talent, and the inflexible, oversized and insensitive organizational environment that prevents people from making the creative best of themselves.
- Innovation and creative change can be seen as an integral part of any and all positive approaches. From the Inventor to the

Sponsor, from Pure Research to Creative Organizational Enhancement, each contribution needs to be taken as offering its particular specialism. All make a contribution which has value. None can be treated in the same way as any other. We have very few Geniuses but very many ordinary people. The capacity of both to help keep organizations competitive in a changing world is suppressed in many different ways. In turbulent times, organizations must contrive to move the focus of their management of their human resource from the less creativogenic towards the more. If each person becomes one step more creative than he is now, then what could not be achieved?

Organizations need to make their average non-innovators become more Adaptor-like, their Adaptors more like Innovators. Their Prodigies need to become their Geniuses, and their Geniuses secured and managed like the crown jewels. They need to move their researchers more towards applications. Pure Research is not the most appropriate use of most commercial organizational time or resources.

Project Hindsight asked why the US Navy in 1969 should spend money on theoretical research by pure scientists operating in universities. Their claim was that such research provided the advances in knowledge that led to breakthrough defence applications. The enquiry showed clearly that at least in warfare, technology advanced out of prior technology. Success came where there were aims and a mission for the innovation, and not where a curious scientist had thrown up a novelty.

Organizations need to make their Inventors Entrepreneurs and their Intrapreneurs Champions. The products of this shift will look after themselves. A massive increase in organizational innovation could cause the user, the customer, the client, to become the selective agency, and thus leave the market to choose which innovation it wants to keep. This gives the earliest, and most convincing, confirmation that value has been added.

Langrish has suggested that technological innovation can best be seen as the interaction of three systems:

(a) An existing technical system together with an imagined improvement.
(b) An advantage system, in which some form of advantage of the technical improvement over the old can be clearly established.

(c) A resource system that determines whether the controlling organization has the capability to exploit the better concept and thus profit from its advantage.[9]

Langrish points out that where any one of these systems is missing, the possibility of the innovation taking up its place is severely diminished. So the cure for cancer, almost certainly over-funded over the years, has still to find the first of the conditions listed above. There is little doubt that the advantage of a cure for cancer over no cure for cancer is the ultimate in clear advantages, and, if only an effective technology could be found, the resources system would not be found wanting.

Notes

1 Michael J. Kirton, 'Adaptors and Innovators', in K. Gronhaug, and G. Kaufmann, *Innovation: A Cross-Disciplinary Perspective* (Norwegian University Press, Oslo, 1988).

2 Alexander Kohn, *Fortune or Failure: Missed Opportunities and Chance Discoveries in Science* (Blackwell, Oxford, 1989), p. 86.

3 Ibid., p. 87.

4 Ibid., p. 94.

5 Gifford Pinchot III, *Intrapreneuring* (Harper & Row, New York, 1985), p. 54.

6 Ibid., p. 55.

7 Zaltman King, in M. A. West and J. L. Farr (eds), *Innovation and Creativity at Work* (John Wiley, Chichester, Sussex, 1990), p. 48.

8 *Omni*, November 1990, p. 126.

9 J. Langrish, in *Creativity and Innovation Yearbook* (Manchester Business School, 1988), p. 19.

9

The Genius of Nations

A nation never fails, but by suicide.

R. W. Emerson

Jewish people are substantially more frequently represented in the hall of Nobel prize-winning fame than others. Conversely, Roman Catholics are significantly under-represented in proportion to their populations in any of the prize-winning nations. Of the four or five million patents issued since the US Patent Office opened in 1790, women have received only about 1.5 per cent. Even in the latter half of the twentieth century, this proportion has barely reached two per cent. Despite Japan having the foremost technologically-based growth over the past forty years, very few of the world's top scientific and engineering prizes have been won by Japanese. These observations all pose questions of culture. There are no certain conclusions about cause and effect. These are statistical variables. However, there are lessons to be learned, and there are aids to such learning which most organizations can put in place. For example, differences in national culture suggest that a basic research venture would be better run in an Anglo-Saxon environment than in a Latin one.

Percy Barnevik led a merger in 1987 of Swiss, Swedish and German interests in forming a huge electrical and power-generation business called Asea Brown Boveri (ABB). Barnevik quickly chose English as the lingua franca for the company. Senior executives at ABB commented to *International Management* reporters in June 1988 that English 'contributes to more frank and open discussions – it's much easier, and often takes a lot less time, to say something difficult or even unpleasant in another language than your mother tongue.'

Also that the substitution of English for German 'has removed some psychological barriers.' German is a very structured language and when speaking it, it is difficult to be informal, which is an absolute necessity for a group trying to foster a multinational culture.'[1] This one decision almost certainly significantly changed the creative style and thrust of its overall operations.

If a chief executive wanted to implant a culture into his company which would improve the creativity of his organization in a deep and enduring way, there are clear and practical guidelines to help him to do so.

Creative culture is not only about the culture of creative organizations. Culture is about the acceptance of common practices by people of otherwise uncommon characteristics. If an organization insists on a strong and determined dependence upon the orders predicated by the past, then the most creative and determined mentor of that organization will either succumb to this pressure to conform, or he will leave. The more homogenous the culture, the more that the majority conform, and the more resistant to change that culture will be. The less there is a perceived threat, the more will people hold on to the old values; they worked before, so why should we change them now?

Cultures change only very slowly. Their impact on the way people behave in countries, companies and organizations has only in the past ten years or so become fully recognized. There are a number of luminaries who have combined a background of industrial experience, academic authority, an understanding of social anthropology, and the exposure to cultures around the world which enables them to speak and write on this subject in ways that are both learned and helpful. One of the best of these is Geert Hofstede. It was he who made a study of the survey of work-values of IBM employees in fifty countries in the 1970s. His first book, *Culture's Consequences*,[2] explored national cultures in great detail.

In his latest book, *Culture and Organizations* subtitled *Software of the Mind*,[3] he has explored this data further, and added to it the investigations he and his team made into corporate culture in the Netherlands and Denmark in the 1980s. Part of this chapter is a summary of Hofstede's thinking, part that of others. The cultural dimensions he introduced will be used in the following pages to explore the culture of creativity around the world, and in Chapter 12 to explore corporate culture.

National Cultures

People normally grow up within a family unit, then, if the society has the educational resources, they develop further in an effectively closed society such as a school. Finally they are exposed to a working world very much conditioned in its assumptions by those exposed to the same social influences as their parents. This accumulation of conditioning is a highly complex process. Early on in their development, most people absorb a sense of the values of the community in which they live. They learn what is clean and what is dirty, what is success and what is failure, which pleasures are attended by the risk of pain or punishment or guilt, and which can be taken freely. They learn a language which predisposes their way of thinking, and subtly and distinctively shapes the world they live in.

They acquire a concept of themselves from their willing, or otherwise, membership of groups of similarly conditioned people. They come to believe in a Britishness, or an Americanness. They perceive differences between their group, say working class, or Catholic, or English or professional, and the other groups which are seen to be competitive. They learn to recognize the symbols and the rituals which illustrate that difference, and which help provide the comfort of belonging. They attribute reasons why people in membership of other groups are so different. They create stereotypes which attach a certain permanence to the conclusions they have been led to believe in: stereotypes about people, about things, about judgements of all kinds. These stereotypes are shorthand, and seldom if ever do people unpack them to be exposed for re-examination. These are the sources of prevailing cultures. Groups of people will differentiate one from another as long as people recognize that there are some people who are like them, and others who, in some significant way, are not. These stereotypes might be positive or negative – but they are most often negative. The French and the British each have a view about the Germans which has some part in common but is otherwise unique. The French and British will not each have the same view of the Germans, since each is seeing the other from a different starting perception.

As the observer comes closer to the field of play, so different levels of differences emerge. In Germany, the Bavarians have a perception of the Prussians which reflects both their different historical and cultural backgrounds and, maybe, their geographical and climatic differences. In their turn, the citizens of Swabia will see considerable differences between their culture and what most would call the rest of Bavaria. And so, no doubt, the long-standing residents of Stuttgart will see themselves as very different to the city's young newcomers.

Four Dimensions of National Culture

In analysing the data from the world-wide IBM survey, Hofstede identified that most of this could be most effectively interpreted at a national level and along four dimensions. Clearly there are other ways in which it could be analysed, such as by religion, sex, or occupation, but none of these produced as consistent a pattern. Nationality is a highly recognizable characteristic, and one which most people do not deliberately or fearfully conceal. These dimensions he named as:

Power-Distance (PD) : Uncertainty Avoidance (UA) :
Individualism/Collectivism (IND) : Masculinity/Femininity (MAS)

None of these terms and concepts were invented by Hofstede. All of them had been used before. What he did was to bring them together, and to use them to characterize the major variabilities he found within the IBM data.

Power-Distance (PD)

The three survey questions which formed the basis for the calculation of a country's position on the scale of power-distance were:

- Answers by non-managerial employees to the question, 'How frequently in your experience does the following problem occur: employees being afraid to express disagreement with their managers?'
- Subordinates' *perception* of their boss's actual decision-making style (a score was based upon the percentage choosing the description of either an autocratic or a paternalistic style out of four possible styles, plus a 'none of these' option).

• Subordinates' *preference* for their boss's decision-making style (percentage preferring an autocratic or a paternalistic style, or a style based on a majority vote, but *not* a consultative style).

The differences the IBM employees reported in responding to these questions showed wide variation between nationalities.

PD is defined by Hofstede as the extent to which the less powerful members of institutions and organizations within a country expect, and accept, that power is distributed unequally.

In some countries, subordinates feel able to disagree with their boss. In his turn, he finds their disagreement no source of embarrassment or discouragement. It is part of life's rich fabric. In other countries, there is a culture of formality and distance, where subordinates do not feel able to criticize or, in extreme cases, even to address their boss. He assumes that his rank gives him privileges, not least of which is that his subordinates subordinate.

Countries which scored very highly on this dimension (i.e they were more like the second condition above) included many of those in the Third World, still agricultural in their essential economy, or only recently emerged from it. The highest scores were shown by Malaysia, Guatemala, Panama, Philippines and Mexico, with the Arab countries and India close followers. Apart from Yugoslavia and Singapore the country with the highest position on the PD scale in the developed world was France, closely followed by Belgium and Portugal. Of the ten bottom places topped by Britain and Germany, four were the Scandinavian countries. Israel and Austria were lowest.

Hofstede looked at occupational differences in the PD dimension where he could. He found that the less educated, low-status employees in various Western countries hold more authoritarian values than their bosses. Both professional workers and their managers were well down on the dimension. They were less willing to accept large differences in power. Power-Distance as a cultural factor shows itself at all levels, from early family life, through schools, to the workplace. PD does affect the way in which French research managers are different to the German and Scandinavian research managers. Creativity in France is an organized, intellectual activity. Researchers of status are respected for their views, and are given the benefit of the doubt by their subordinates and not often challenged where they might be mistaken. In Scandinavian countries, creativity comes from a debate between equals, an open interchange, free of the constraint of position. The hierarchy in France is more emotional in texture. Feelings often run high. Egos are definitely involved.

PD varies with climate. By and large the hotter the climate, the more likely that PD will be high. Additionally, the Romance languages are more predictive of a high PD culture than the Germanic. PD is also correlated with the national prevalence of poverty.

In terms of our knowledge of 'conventional' creativity, and of the circumstances which favour it, we have to assume that it would always be more likely to flourish in Israel, Denmark, Switzerland, than in Mexico, Arabia, India or West Africa. In Spain, Portugal, Belgium and France, if creativity is sought, it must be managed. It will rarely happen there in a vacuum, as it might in Britain. In the high PD countries, it could be expected to happen of its own accord only where there are isolated small groups of persistent people, doing their own thing well outside the normal rigidity of those countries' naturally prevailing bureaucracies.

Individualism/Collectivism (IND)

Like PD, this dimension is bipolar. At one pole is the highly individual culture, wherein each person is expected to look after his own interests and, at most, those of his immediate family. Highly collective cultures are the opposite. People are integrated into supportive and cohesive groups, to which they are expected to commit great and permanent loyalty in exchange for the continued collective defence of their interests. The individualist focuses his concerns at work on having control over his life, on his approach to his work, and to a sense of personal accomplishment. Collectivism is correlated more with a greater emphasis on using and developing skills and working in a supportive and pleasant environment.

In Individualism, the scale was led by the USA, Australia, Great Britain, and Canada. These were quickly followed by the majority of the developed European countries, propped up by Spain, but with Greece well across into the Collectivists. The more Collectivist countries were largely South American, African, and Far Eastern. Japan and India, close together, come in the middle. The Individualist culture favours the lone inventor: the Western concept of the absent-minded professor and the academic don. It would encourage competition amongst individuals seeking the same goals. It would support the giant-leap-forward type of innovation, as against the incremental style.

There is a correlation between large PD and Collectivist cultures, supporting the belief in the symbiosis of group coherence and powerful leaders. Leaders need to have committed followers. The followers need their heroes, and the power of the myths that they bring. Heroes raise the level of a group's own self-worth. If an individual in a group can identify easily with that group, so can the group in its turn easily identify with any leader of merit and charisma.

France and Belgium are slightly out of line, having a comparatively large PD, yet being at the same time almost as Individualist as most other North European countries or their colonial cultural derivatives. The explanation for this is given in the third chapter of Hofstede's book, where he quotes the French sociologist Michel Crozier as describing this aspect of his country's culture as follows:

> Face-to-face dependence relationships are perceived as difficult to bear in the French cultural setting. Yet the prevailing view of authority is still that of absolutism. The two attitudes are contradictory. However, they can be reconciled within the bureaucratic system, since impersonal rules and centralization make it possible to reconcile an absolutist conception of authority and the elimination of most direct dependence relationships.[4]

This is further explained by the understanding that the status and advantage conferred on the Frenchman by whatever rank achieved is seen by him as having a concomitant and traditional obligation. As Hofstede puts it, 'It is not so much what one owes to others as what one owes to oneself. It is stratified individualism.'

Clearly there is very likely to be a substantial impact on the nature and quality of creative events in countries of differing positions along this scale. Thomas Kuhn[5] theorized that scientific history could be divided into periods of steady development within a simple set of adjusted concepts, which he called a paradigm, and intervening periods of revolutionary change where a paradigm is shattered and subsequently replaced by a new one. He convincingly showed that the notion of advancement of scientific knowledge being progressive and rational is completely false. He showed scientific progress to depend on the culture, the values and the subjective beliefs of its community. Paradigms are built by scientists and others who create scientific orthodoxy and fixed models of the world and then defend them, sometimes to the death, against any attack, rational or otherwise.

A major step (or a 'paradigm shift') in scientific understanding in a Collectivist environment would be likely to be much more difficult to achieve than in an Individualist one. Just thinking about a new scientific thrust could feel like heresy.

The elite group are almost always sure that they hold the truth in their hands. Collectivism is strongly anti-deviant, defensive, sharing, about being together. All of these characteristics in some sense work against most forms of creative thought. On the other hand, where teams of researchers need to share their insights and cooperate emotionally as well as intellectually, the Collectivist culture would become an advantage. As mankind's knowledge-base increases, the evolution of a further professional specialization is inevitable. The rate at which the average person learns or uses learning is not increasing. If new knowledge is to be put to use, it requires that the emerging specialists share their insight more and more with professionals of a different stripe. As this picture unfolds then the creative solution of the problems of tomorrow may well proceed more quickly in those countries where Collective ways are the cultural norm.

Collectivism makes for efficiency and adds value where the unique capabilities of several or many individuals need to be brought to bear on an issue. While one end of the scale provides better bedding for breakthrough thinking, the other could well enhance and develop the advantage of the technological or the artistic revolution so gained, and perhaps reap the greater reward for being a good second.

Americans believe in the frontier spirit, in the freedom of the individual to do what he chooses. The Chinese, on the other hand, are taught that Individualism is bad, because it shows no discipline and focuses on purely selfish ends instead of on the greater good.

In days past, with much original creative thought being well within the grasp of wealthy prominent individuals like Darwin, with time on their hands, and opportunity taken with well-prepared minds, there has been a correlation between Individualism and economic success. Tomorrow, however, the newly industrializing countries, like South Korea and Singapore, where Collectivism is fed on a diet of readily available and up-to-date knowledge and technology, may soon begin to out-perform any of the rich Individualist nations of today. Westerners might take comfort from the fact that there is some evidence that the richer countries become, the more they move towards Individualism. It is slow and there is a lag, but it is a clear pattern.

Uncertainty Avoidance (UA)

This is a concept with a long pedigree in social science. It is a dominant part of any assessment of a person's beliefs and behaviour. People are always surrounded by uncertainty, to a more or less equal degree. They differ in how tolerant they are of this uncertainty, and how much they feel stressed by it if it is left unattended.

One of the questions in the IBM questionnaire was: 'How often do you feel nervous or tense at work?' The response to this question varied very predictably from country to country. For example, occupation for occupation, Germans were always more nervous than the British. A second question was: 'To what extent do you agree with the statement "Company rules should not be broken even when the employee thinks it is in the company's best interest."?' The third contribution to this scale was: 'How long do you think you will continue to work for IBM?' Each question endeavours to assess the level of anxiety and of tolerance for living in the unknown. The more anxiety that is created by this sense of a lack of control, the greater the defences that are put in place to overcome this feeling.

The scores for Uncertainty Avoidance showed Latin countries at the high end, led by Greece and Portugal. Japan and South Korea were also high. German-speaking countries were in the middle rank. Asian, Anglo-Saxon and Nordic countries occupied the lower ranks. The lowest was Singapore. However, there are some doubts about the validity of the Singapore scores.

Uncertainty Avoidance is an emotional need, motivating a search for structure, relaxing fully only when ambiguity is seen to be eliminated. It is not about eliminating risk, but about keeping down the level of ignorance that exists about risk. Students in higher UA countries want and expect their teachers to be experts, and their trains to run on time. In the words of Hofstede: 'Intellectual disagreement in academic matters is felt as a personal disloyalty.'

In respect of creativity Hofstede writes:

> Weak UA countries are more likely to stimulate basic innovations as they maintain a greater tolerance towards deviant ideas. On the other

hand they seem to be at a disadvantage in developing the basic innovations towards full-scale implementation, as such implementation usually demands a considerable sense of detail and punctuality.[6]

On this evidence, the strategy that science-based organizations should adopt is to confine the location of their research effort, their breakthrough, blue-sky creative endeavours either to such countries as Britain, India and North America, where a competitive environment prevails, or to Scandinavia where a more caring, mutually supportive climate is preferred. Once the development of a hard new idea, or the formulation of a product is reached they would be well advised to quickly transfer the focus of its development to Japan, or one of the Latin European countries (including Belgium for as long as it includes Walloons), or failing these, to the German-speaking countries.

Alternatively, if the new idea requiring further research calls for a very collaborative team, where the professionals exhibit natural instincts to work together, all other things being equal it would be as advantageous to set up the project in Hong Kong or the Philippines. These more Collectivist societies would add further value to advantages that come from their weak UA.

Masculinity/Femininity (MAS)

In this scale, the contrast is between the behaviour most commonly ascribed to the male of the species on the one hand, such as motivation for achievement, challenge, assertion, competition and public recognition for personal success, and on the other, the traditional 'feminine' concern for good relationships, tenderness, cooperation, good environment, and security. This was the only dimension on which men and women consistently scored differently. These differences are very small in more Feminine nations, but they grow wider in those nations which are nearer the Masculine end of the scale.

In the most Masculine nation, Japan, the average woman seemed substantially more Masculine than the average man in Sweden, Norway, Denmark or Holland, who together prop up the table as the most Feminine. Austria, Italy, Great Britain and Germany were high (Masculine) on this scale. France and Spain were lower, along with East Africa, Uruguay and Guatemala.

Salesmen and professional engineers and scientists were higher on MAS than unskilled or office workers. The high MAS person is more likely to be a workaholic, drawing most of his life's satisfaction from his employment. He would look for steep career paths, be strongly rewarded by status, and enjoy winning above all else. Those who know the Japanese would recognize these characteristics as very typical of their nation.

This dimension could influence the motivation to create. For example, persistence and determination to succeed in a work environment gives to those communities high on MAS an edge over the more cosy, collaborative peoples of the lower MAS nations. Competition for status would emphasize, and put pressure on, the need for education and learning in everyone.

The form of incentives offered to the creative individual in the different communities will have a differing impact. Thus, organizations in high MAS countries could do well to reward their creative achievers with distinguishing marks: strong, visible evidence of their pre-eminence, such as prizes, lecture tours, award ceremonies and tough new assignments. In low MAS countries, this could be a debilitating approach. Modesty is in order in Holland, not bragging. Caring for the weak and the unsuccessful is the approved behaviour. In such communities, rewards for creative productivity are more likely to be effective if the creative achiever is returned to his research group, to share what limelight there is with his peer group, to be rewarded with time and resources to start up a new line of research and to encourage his colleagues to build on their success. The balance of MAS and Collectivism has an important outcome. Japan is quite high on Collectivism and very high on MAS. There, recognition of success is vital, but never for the outstanding individual. He has to keep his place. None the less, at the same time, competition is fierce and unrelenting, and rewards must be carefully managed.

There seems to be a universal relationship between age and relative MAS scores. The young are more competitive and more personally assertive. After the age of fifty, both men and women tend to hold predominantly Feminine values. Between being young and becoming old, men clearly lose their Masculinity faster than women lose theirs. This effect should be taken into account in managing the productivity and motivation of creative people over the lifetime of their rewards and incentives. The practice is the reverse of good sense in Western communities, where older successful individuals tend to be offered the more Masculine rewards and the younger the more Feminine, or none at all.

Fifth Dimension: Confucian Dynamism

Michael Bond is a long-term Far East culture researcher working in the Chinese University of Hong Kong. He responded to the Western bias of the IBM research by asking a number of Chinese social scientists to prepare a list of at least ten basic values for the Chinese people. From these he put together the Chinese Value Survey. This was translated as carefully as possible, and administered in twenty-three countries. Twenty of these countries had also been covered by Hofstede's IBM survey. Comparing the two results showed correlations with PD (concern for seniors and juniors), Collectivism (concern for self and group) and Masculinity (gender). These are the most fundamental of human-value constructs. However, there was a dimension which did not match the IBM results. Bond called it Confucian Dynamism.

Hofstede lists the essential elements of Confucian values and beliefs as follows:

- The stability of society is based on unequal relationships between people.
- The family is the prototype of all social organizations.
- Virtuous behaviour towards others consists of not treating others as one would not like to be treated oneself.
- Virtue with regard to one's tasks in life consists of trying to acquire skills and education, working hard, not spending more than is necessary, being patient and persevering.

It is hard to avoid the conclusion that this same list could be attributed to the teachings of Judaism, if not its theology. Bond separated out the values with a long-term orientation from those with a short-term. Persistence, observance of order, and thrift were long term. Personal stability, respect for tradition, protection of 'face', and the reciprocation of greetings and gifts were seen as shorter-term led. They were concerned with the past and present, whereas the former group were all about the future.

Dividing Confucian Dynamism into long term and short term led to a curious distribution of scores in the twenty-three countries. Unsurprisingly, China was well in the lead. Hong Kong, Taiwan, Japan and South Korea followed. The top European country of the sample was Holland. The table was propped up by Pakistan, showing values which were predominantly short term. Bangladesh was in the middle rank.

As a place to find creative people, able and willing to exercise their talent, there is a strong suggestion that the longer-term cultural environment is the better bet. As shows up again and again, persistence is an important element of creative productivity. The very nature of innovation determines that it has its yield tomorrow, not today.

One final aspect of this research which is important to consider is the reason why, in the Chinese study, Confucian Dynamism displaced Uncertainty Avoidance as the fourth dimension. This is because of the different relative concerns for truth and virtue which exist in East and West. In the Western world, predominantly monotheist over the past two millennia, the search for the one Truth has been the driving issue in discovery and innovation. In the East, the concentration has been on what is done and for whom, rather than on what is believed, no matter when.

Hofstede explores this thinking, offering the following conclusion:

> During the Industrial Revolution . . . the Western concern for Truth was first an asset. It led to the discovery of the laws of nature, which could then be exploited for the sake of human progress. It is (un)surprising that Chinese scholars, despite their high level of civilization, never discovered Newton's Laws: they were simply not looking for laws. The Chinese script betrays the lack of interest in generalizing: it needs 5000 different characters . . . Western languages need only about 30. Western thinking is analytical, whereas Eastern thinking is synthetic.
>
> By the middle of the twentieth century, the Western concern for Truth gradually ceased to be an asset and turned into a liability. Science may benefit from analytical thinking, but management and government are based on the art of synthesis.[7]

The current thinking in management in the Western world continues to go against this teaching. The search for Truth in management continues, instead of the search for virtue. Already Japan is passing the USA in numbers of patent applications. When will China pass Japan?

The Cultural Conditions for Creativity

Silvano Arieti examines many aspects of creativity in his book *Creativity, the Magic Synthesis*. Among his most valuable researches was into that of the relationship between the sustained creativity of a community and the nature of that community. The question that has taxed many philosophers is whether great men make the culture (as Galton believed) or whether society makes great men (as Herbert Spencer decided).

Arieti quoted William James in 1880 as writing:

> For a community to get vibrating . . . many geniuses coming together in rapid succession are required. This is why great epochs are so rare – why the sudden bloom of a Greece, an early Rome, a Renaissance, is such a mystery. Blow must follow blow so fast that no cooling can occur in the intervals. Then the mass of the nation grows incandescent, and may continue to glow by pure inertia long after the originators of its internal movement have passed away.[8]

So James's belief was that the accidental coming-together, the chance arrival at a point in time of a critical mass, of men of genius created a newly sharpened and directed culture. But then James was a psychologist. Others, such as Leslie White, are given an airing by Arieti. White offered the opposing view, which Arieti shares. This is that it is the readiness of the culture which enables the individual to offer the creative act. White said: 'When the culture process has reached a point when an invention or discovery becomes possible, that invention or discovery becomes inevitable.'[9] Supporting this hypothesis, he quoted the more or less simultaneous promulgation of the law of conservation of energy by Mayer, Joule, Helmholz, Golding and Thomson, of sunspots by Galileo, Fabricius, Scheiner and Harriot, and respiration by Priestley, Scheele, Lavoisier, Spallanzani and Davy.

So what are the societal conditions that favour creative genius? What are the culturally creativogenic (Arieti's word) conditions? Arieti lists nine probable candidates:

1 The availability of cultural (and certain physical) means: it is not possible to be Beethoven without having a piano.

2 Openness to cultural stimuli: in the Dark Ages, cultural media were confined to the clergy. Geniuses were therefore rare, and where they existed, devoted to theology.

3 Stress on becoming, not just on being: a culture that emphasizes only immediate satisfaction, and neglects growth and aspiration, loses its creative thrust and potential.

4 Free access to cultural media for all citizens, without discrimination: the greater the restriction of opportunity, the less creative potential can be utilized. Women, ethnic minorities, religious groups have all suffered from some form of restriction.

5 Freedom, or moderate discrimination after severe or absolute exclusion, is an incentive to creativity: a factor which shows up in history time and again is that there is a surge in creative output in a people who have been given release after a long time under tight control.

6 Exposure to different and even contrasting cultural stimuli: the interaction of the old and the new is a great source of restimulation, avoiding the potential downturn due to the comfort of unchallenged mind-sets and customary thinking.

7 Tolerance for, and interest in, diverging views: this is about native curiosity, the response of intrigue rather than fear, when faced with unfamiliarity. Such tolerance needs to exist at all levels, not just in the elite.

8 Interaction of significant persons: the creative society will throw up people whose views will reinforce and reflect those of the others. When this takes place, the consequences are that creativity is significantly and potentially magnified.

9 Promotion of incentives and rewards: as Plato said, 'What is honoured in a country will be cultivated there.'

This list of circumstances is not presented as demonstrable truths, but only as guidelines based on historical observations. Arieti suggested that only the first factor is an absolute necessity (by definition), but all of them together are not sufficient to produce creativity. Nor, if all were absent (except the first), would there be no creative outcome. Serendipity will always play some part. This is the field of probability and observation.

Jewish Creativity

Arieti made an examination of creativity across the history of the Jewish people. They have not excelled in creativity when under persecution, nor where no significant cultural means are available. But they have done so at other times. The culture supports literacy and education. The religion is much more abstract, ethical, yet earthbound than most. It keeps its people more open to new ideas than those religions which manifest a more devotional, personal and rule-bound focus. The culture supports scholarship, and encourages interchange. Jews are widespread, yet interlinked, and manage to absorb, yet not be overrun by, a wide variety of cultural influences. In respect of each of Arieti's cultural factors, Jewish people have been subject to these more often than most. Insofar as they can be measured, the results are clear.

Over a seventy-year period to 1970, in proportion to the population, Jewish physicists were around seven times more frequent winners of a Nobel Prize than the next most frequent group. In the same period they also won more prizes for medicine. Since 1940, the proportion of Jewish prize-winners per head of Jewish people has accelerated at a phenomenal rate, passing 1.5 per million. The equivalents for French, German, Italian, and non-Jews alike have fallen over the same period to less than 0.1. The data are presented in detail by Arieti.[10]

Japanese Creativity

Akio Morita has been among the most valuable of the many people, Japanese and otherwise, who have sought to explain the phenomenal economic global performance of Japanese technology over the past forty years. Perhaps he came nearest to an explanation in his book *Made in Japan*.

> We Japanese are obsessed with survival. Everyday, literally, the earth beneath our feet trembles. We live our daily lives on these volcanic islands with the constant threat not only of a major earthquake, but also of typhoons, tidal waves, savage snowstorms, spring deluges. Our islands provide us with almost no raw materials except water, and less than a quarter of our land is liveable or arable.

Therefore, what we have is precious to us. And that is why we learned to respect nature, to conserve, to miniaturize, and to look forward to technology as a means of helping us survive . . . We Japanese feel that all things are provided as a sacred trust and are actually only loaned to us to make the best use of. To waste something is considered a kind of sin. We became skilled at Crisis Management . . . We are also great savers, and not just savers of money . . . [11]

Of course, this is but a small part of the origin of Japan's economic miracle. To a degree it does not need to be explained. The Japanese technology was never very far behind that of the Western world, except where it cut itself off during the Shogun era. Peter Medawar caught the essence of the layman's view, however, in an observation made in 1977 and noted in *The Threat and the Glory*:

My favourite (pop sociology) is the kind of brash declaration which can be heard at the bar of almost any suburban tennis club populated by young executives: 'Of course the trouble with the Japanese is that they have no really inventive powers, they can only imitate others.'

I have heard this with my own ears at a time when it should already have been clear to the meanest intelligence that Japanese scientists and technologists are enormously inventive and imaginative as well as inexhaustibly ingenious; and that their very common tendency to allow other nations to bear the costs of research and development, while they apply their inventive skill to improvement and further development, is a trait which does great credit to their common sense and business acumen.'[12]

Sheridan Tatsuno contrasted American and Japanese ways of supporting, exploiting and managing creativity in Japan. Under the heading, 'The Yin and Yang of Creativity' in his book *Created in Japan*, he contrasts the Western approach as breakthrough, spontaneous, unifunctional and Cartesian, and the Japanese approach as adaptive, cultivated, multi-functional and fuzzy. The Japanese are the incrementalists, re-combiners, applications people. Morita's sin-of-waste factor shows in their approach in contrast to that of the United States. Scrap is the biggest export from New York to Japan. Wastepaper is a vital part of this commodity. Some of this recycled scrap provides the packaging for the high-technology equipment shipped by Japan to the USA.

Tatsuno describes a contrast between creative fission and creative fusion:

> If cultivation is the mother of Japanese creativity, teamwork is its father. The goal of Japanese creativity is not just to create new products and ideas, but also to build teamwork and a sense of harmony . . . Individuals are encouraged to contribute ideas for the benefit of the team, not to be overly spontaneous or different . . . Western creativity is like nuclear fission, in which individual brilliance has an opportunity to shine, while Japanese creativity is like nuclear fusion – ideas from many people are gathered, assimilated, and squeezed into a new product . . . [13]

Later, he adds:

> Western creativity is rapid-fire, awe-inspiring, and often engenders the zeal of religious faith. Westerners delight in spectacular displays of genius by individuals . . . Anything short of spectacular quantum leaps is considered 'ho-hum' science.[14]

There have been very few totally new products initiated in Japan by Japanese. This is changing. They are changing. But they are looking after their strength. Tatsuno again:

> After the 1985 yen shock sent Japanese exports plummeting, Matsushita gathered a group of female engineers, product designers, market researchers and interviewers to explore the possibility of new home electronics markets. After conducting extensive interviews with working women and housewives, the group discovered market demand for an appliance that could make bread overnight.[15]

Saatchi & Saatchi in the UK organized a similar activity some years ago for Black & Decker. They hired lay people by the day, pre-screened for their creative potential. These were put together in small groups and given assignments. For example, one group was asked to dream up new products using small horsepower motors in the home. The cordless hand-held vacuum cleaner was one outcome. The experience of the teams recruited was a compelling one, both in terms of its productivity and in the impact it had on the groups themselves. Despite its success, however, the UK experiment was not repeated. Only recently have Western organizations thought to bring together manufacturing, design and market specialists in evolving and considering new products. Traditionally, new products were dragged through different departments in sequence. Good ideas were followed up by applications departments. Once the product idea was developed, maybe it would be offered to the design people. Then, when most decisions had been made, it could be discussed with the specialists from the manufacturing division.

There is not the time in the later twentieth century for this slow and hit-and-miss sequence. Furthermore, the modern pressure on innovative productivity and incrementalism pushes the creative advantage into the path of Japanese strengths, and away from the transformational patterns of innovation found in the West. On the other hand, in the Japanese environment the unwillingness to challenge authority, the need to be part of the herd, the disadvantage, even the shame, of being different, all conspire to make original research, fundamental creativity, or basic discovery difficult for young scientists or designers. It is much harder for the young to break through to enjoy the facilities that lead to success. Perhaps this may be a cultural weak link. But it is one the Japanese are very aware of and are seeking to strengthen. One way in which many of the larger manufacturers are using their new economic strength is by setting up basic research institutes in the West, recruiting the best Western engineers and scientists, and providing the proper opportunities for their creativity. The adaptive, fuzzy, group-think of the East has no problem taking advantage of the direct, individualistic, great-leap-forward approach of the Western cultures.

Conclusion

National cultures have been the subject of intensive investigation over many years. Only relatively recently has their impact on scientific and commercial creativity been considered.

The outcome of these studies shows a striking consistency between the qualities of national culture and the strengths and weaknesses of their innovators. The Anglo-Saxons are the competitive individualists. The people who create and who are applauded are the Edisons, the Franklins, the Flemings. Very few people from the Anglo-Saxon countries will think of creative talents in terms of more than two at a time. This competitive individualism is appropriate to basic research, to isolated inventors, to battles of will between individual and organizations. Anglo-Saxon innovators also tend to be self-indulgent, to live for today rather than tomorrow. Equally, an innovation can be the result of years of intense devotion to discovery, but, once the discovery has been made, the discoverer will find no satisfaction in improving on it.

Different countries adapt their creative output to fit their national psyche. The Germans and French respect expertise, and tend not to challenge the deeply knowledgeable expert. This can have two outcomes. It can inhibit challenge to existing authority and thus suppress new thinking; but it can also elevate the attraction of learning, and therefore increase the stock of well-educated people. This in turn can increase their creative potential.

All of these points lead to the Collectivist, the adaptive, the incremental culture as being where creativity will have most effect economically, at least for a few more years. The lessons of analysis of different national and pan-national cultures to those who seek economic advantage through the exploitation of creative genius become clearer by the week.

As knowledge expands, so the need for intensive education and specialization within the community increases, at least in the sciences and the technologies. Furthermore, the probability of breakthroughs diminishes, just as new building in heavily populated countries tends towards in-filling rather than new estates. Totally new towns are possible, but these take huge resources, and are not for the local builder.

So the Collectivist countries, like Japan and China, who do not seek after Truth, but only for virtue, and who concern themselves more with tomorrow than with today, will inevitably corner the world of creative science and technology. Only in fashion, in artistic revolution, in the communication and political arts will the West continue, for a while at least, to have the ascendency. Time is very short, if there is the will to seek a better balance in the global economic health of the twenty-first century.

Notes

1 *International Management*, vol. 43 No. 6 (June 1988).
2 Geert Hofstede, *Culture's Consequences: International Differences in Work-Related Values* (Sage Publications, Beverley Hills, Ca., 1980).

3 Geert Hofstede, *Cultures and Organizations: Software of the Mind* (McGraw-Hill, UK, 1991).

4 Ibid., p. 55.

5 Thomas S Kuhn, *The Structure of Scientific Revolutions* (University of Chicago Press, Chicago, 1962 and 1970).

6 Hofstede, *Cultures and Organizations*, p. 122.

7 Ibid., p. 172.

8 Silvano Arieti, *Creativity, The Magic Synthesis* (Basic Books, New York, 1976), p. 299.

9 Ibid., p. 301.

10 Ibid., pp. 328–34.

11 Akio Morita and the Sony Corporation, *Made in Japan* (Collins, Glasgow, 1987), pp. 227–8.

12 Peter Medawar, *The Threat and the Glory: Reflections on Science and Scientists* (Oxford University Press, Oxford, 1990), p. 52.

13 Sheridan M. Tatsuno, *Created in Japan: From Imitators to World-Class Innovators* (Ballinger Publishing Co., USA, 1990), p. 22.

14 Ibid., p. 49.

15 Ibid., p. 68.

PART III

Searching for the Answers

10

Enhancing Personal Creativity

Magic is a great hidden wisdom – reason is a great open folly.

Paracelsus, 1493–1541

Creativity started life as a religious concept, and has since extended to the artistic, the scientific, and now to the commercial. In the modern competitive world of high-speed change, it could well become a property of all, an essential ingredient of the democratic world, a *sine qua non* of the free-market consumerism of the late twentieth century. Writers and practitioners in the world of creative understanding are fundamentally divided in their views of creative potential. On the one hand, people like Ochse believe that creativity is a rare product of intellectual, emotional and circumstantial influences that is denied the man in the street. How can someone or something be nominated creative if it is within the reach of anyone who chooses to opt for it. On the other hand, people such as Abraham Maslow and Carl Rogers have supported the view that creativity is within the reach of all, and that creativity is in everyone. The task is to release it, because it is inhibited, rather than accepting its absence because it is so seldom easily found.

One way of dealing with this division of views is that proposed by Zalaznick. He believed that creativity is qualitatively different from innovation. Its most distinguishing difference, he wrote, is that it is rare, whereas innovation is more plentiful. Innovations are bounded novelty. He called them bricolage, or tinkering. Innovation is the work of the bricoleur, or handyman. Creativity, in contrast, is over or beyond boundaries not held to the social structure. Zalaznick proposed:

> Creativity and innovation involve different modes of thinking. The movement in thought processes is vertical in creativity, from highly structured and disciplined to loose, associative and symbolic. The vertical movement is from secondary process thinking, which is sequential as well as logical, to primary process thinking, which is characteristic of the unconscious. The innovator applies horizontal modes of thinking. While horizontal thinking uses analogies and past experiences, it depends on a limited number of styles of thinking, the most predominant being linear reasoning and successive trials. Innovation therefore involves lower levels of emotion and less anxiety.[1]

This is a fine distinction. In fact, it is much finer than this explanation might suggest. Certainly it does not entirely help to pinpoint where the boundaries between innovation and creativity are to be located.

Organizations and commercial leaders buy remedies, and are always proffered them optimistically by determined practitioners. It should come as no surprise that a considerable industry exists offering increased creativity to all those who are prepared to apply, with no entrance qualification required. Most of these facilities centre around individual practitioners who have managed to package mind-enhancing programmes developed from a few pieces of theoretical precept. Some of these have been rigorously researched for efficacy. Others are uninspected but successful because of the magic of the presenter's name, image and reputation, and his capacity to galvanize in ordinary people the belief that they have, for that moment at least, an extraordinary potential.

How Many Ways?

Most creativity-enhancing programmes are based around the assumption that people are intellectually and emotionally constipated by the routines and habits of everyday thinking. The remedy for constipation is laxative.

The expression 'unblocking' is a common metaphor for 'releasing creative tension'. Roger Von Oech, one of the gurus of do-it-yourself creativity, wrote a book called *A Whack on the Side of the Head*.[2] There is an assumption that creativity is good, and that in the process of growing-up, it has become trapped, out of reach. Normal problem-solving has some strict limitations. It almost forces us to the conclusion that education and experience is a diminishing process rather than an expanding one. This position is echoed by Rudy Rucker, in his book *Mind Tools* where he introduces the chapter on the laws of thought with a story, and a conclusion:

> In one of the Marx Brother movies Chico and Zeppo get themselves into some terrible predicament. They're locked in a room and pacing desperately. 'We've got to *think*!' cries Zeppo in his toffee-toned voice. Chico makes a dismissive hand gesture. 'Nah. We already tried dat.' Much the same can be said about logic. On the face of it, the application of formal logic might be expected to resolve all kinds of disagreements. As it turns out, though, the known laws of logic are too few in number to be of any great help.[3]

Scientists of all disciplines are still a long way from understanding the structure, character and capability of the human brain, but it is becoming increasingly clear that conscious application of rigorous analytical devices to the problems facing everyman, using the normal routines of language, is probably the least sophisticated of the many more arcane cerebral facilities built into the pack.

The Gestalt scientists were the first to order and generalize the need for perceptual order and completeness. They were the scientists who showed the propensity which people have for filling in gaps and perceiving wholes. Roger Sperry will always be credited with being the first neurologist to confirm that each of us has complete memory patterns retaining, often in dramatic form, an imprint of the experience of our lifetimes. All the schools of psychoanalytic thought have made great play of the significance of memory patterns in the unconscious and the part they play in our waking and dreaming behaviour. It is not the subconscious brain that cannot handle this volume and variety, but the conscious one. The conscious brain has to manage the more crude decisions and follow the needs of the lowest common denominator of physical functioning – the ability of the mouth to form and produce words, say, or of the arm to mechanically cut the fat from the meat.

The conscious mind has to be a slow, dull, predictable thing, because it is an executor in real time. Meanwhile, around and beneath it are all the other amazing things people do as they think, worry, react and conclude, go about their business, creating, confirming, and combining.

To increase their creativity, it is said, ordinary people have to find some new ways of learning the techniques of producing from their unconscious. But unpractised as they are, they must also increase the robustness of their conscious mind so as to cope with the product of this unconscious potential. To do the first, without the second, is liable to be at best illusory and at worst hallucinatory. Experiments with 'mind-releasing' drugs have shown that the creativity they were felt to release proved shallow. Only while actually under their influence do people dosed on these drugs feel that their creative power is released. Afterwards, the products which they thought were creative breakthroughs prove only to be weird. Just as people need the critic, so the conscious mind needs to be practised in its evaluation of the various emissions of the unconscious. The subconscious output has to be put to the test of taste, if it is to be seen as good, and creatively good, rather than random, ill-constructed or lunatic.

Keith Johnstone teaches dramatic art. He wrote a book called *Impro*, which probably contains as much helpful advice on improving creativity as any, and includes the following passage:

> Schiller wrote of a 'watcher at the gates of the mind', who examines ideas too closely. He said that in the case of the creative mind 'the intellect has withdrawn its watcher from the gates, and the ideas rush in pell-mell, and only then does it review and inspect the multitude'. He said that uncreative people 'are ashamed of the momentary passing madness which is found in all real creators'.[4]

The two most famous creativity enhancements are probably brainstorming and lateral thinking. The first of these was invented by Alex Osborn and published in *Applied Imagination* in 1957.[5] Edward De Bono is credited with the origin of the term lateral thinking, and has written many books over the past twenty years illustrating its nature and application in one way or another.

In his work, Osborn stated that group brainstorming produced 44 per cent more ideas than individuals working alone. His rules for effective brainstorming in groups were:

- All ideas, but especially way-out ideas, are welcome.
- Critique is discouraged until the creative phase is deemed to be complete.

- Quantity and pace of idea generation is sought after.
- Adding to, combining and multiplying the ideas of others is encouraged.

Usually a brainstorming session takes around thirty minutes, after which the idea-sifting and evaluation process is added.

Brainstorming is supposed to include five to ten people, one of whom is very new to the problem being discussed, and have a recorder who writes down the ideas as they arise. Some observers say that brainstorming always produces answers, but they are rough answers to rough problems. Many researchers have examined the productivity of brainstorming in groups and have consistently found no advantage over the same number of people working on their own over the same period of time. There is much evidence to suggest that people in groups tend towards conformity. Their thinking comes together rather than spreading to make more novelty.

This seems to be the predominant factor in brainstorming. It might be fun, and it might be popular. But productive of new ideas it is not. Its popularity comes probably from its age as a technique and its ease of application. If it is important to get many original ideas from many people it would be more advantageous to engage in 'brainwriting' and have each of them note down their ideas individually, then pass them to each other for any additional insight.

Brainwriting encourages people to build on the ideas of others, which brainstorming often does not. It allows people to think more deeply, which is particularly relevant where the problem at issue is a complex one, and it encourages better contributions from those less able to cope with high-speed interactions, or situations demanding social skills. Brainstorming needs leadership from a practised facilitator and is most successfully applied where broad-brushed conceptual breakthroughs are sought which could benefit from the rapid verbal interaction of some highly varied specialisms.

Edward De Bono is a Maltese medical academic, a gifted teacher, well qualified as a psychologist and a physiologist. He published *The Use of Lateral Thinking*[6] in 1967 and never looked back, annually producing another book on some derivative of his principal theories. De Bono defined thinking as: 'the purposeful exploration of our experience maps'. He explained that logical analysis was a very limited way of thinking. If we are to find creative solutions, there has to be a deliberate attempt to find alternatives. We must not accept that there is one answer. We must challenge things which seem acceptable. We have to look for different functions to serve the same purpose, and different purposes for the same function. De Bono could not find a word for 'looking for alternatives, where there is no obvious need to find them', so he invented the term 'lateral thinking'.

Curiously, despite great European attendances at his lecture tours, and the constant presence of at least a handful of his books in most bookstores, De Bono earns only a passing reference in the all-star gallery of creativity gurus. Perhaps being a European limits his fame, but it could also be that students of creativity expect greater creativity in their heroes than they perceive De Bono to have offered. While he may have made much of his initial idea, De Bono was predated by three years by the publication of Arthur Koestler's classic, *The Act of Creation*. Koestler wrote: 'Habit is heir to originality, without the hierarchies of organized habits, life would be chaos. Creativity means breaking up habits and joining the fragments into a new synthesis.'[7]

Koestler used the word matrix as denoting any ability, habit or skill of ordered behaviour governed by a 'code' of fixed rules. All coherent thinking, he said, was equivalent to playing a game according to a set of rules. He introduced the word, 'bisociation' to describe the point where the independent, autonomous and habitually determined character of two otherwise distinct and separate matrices are brought together in the creative act. 'Associative' thought, on the other hand, he said, was thought that operated within pre-existing matrices, within the rules.

For Koestler's 'associative', read De Bono's 'vertical'. For Koestler's 'bisociation', read De Bono's 'lateral'. Lateral thinking has a sweet and evocative ring to it. Bisociation sounds like a word which needs to be carefully explained. Bisociation, for all that, is a more versatile and valuable concept. Koestler used it to explain everything from a mildly humorous jest to a major scientific breakthrough.

A year after the publication of Koestler's book, J. G. Bennett wrote *Creative Thinking*, based on a course he ran in London in 1964. He believed that creativity was a natural attribute of all men. He concentrated on the element he called 'spontaneity'. 'Real' thinking is spontaneous, he said, it does not come from anything that is already present in us. Spontaneous thinking must not be interfered with by what is already there, which, in his terms, meant there must not be interference from a word of any kind. If a thought is new, it has to be outside of words. Bennett concludes:

But this non-verbal thinking is very hard to recognize, chiefly because we have this very strong habit of verbal thinking but, more fundamentally, because of the inability of most people to bring their inner sensitive screen to the state of empty receptiveness, unencumbered by words.[8]

So here are the three bases of most of the experiments and training designed to induce creativity in everyman:

1 Improving ideation: generating the flow of new ideas. This is done through letting the censor drop enough to allow playfulness and unreason to enter the field without losing total control. The process is encouraged by group interaction like brainstorming and enhanced by systematic extension such as brainwriting.
2 Crossing habitual boundaries of thinking. This encourages the abandonment of direct association, asks that people push hard against the rigidity of their normal way of managing their world. There are various instruments to help this. De Bono's suggestion of randomly interposing the word 'Po' in speaking so as to break up habitual flow of language is one. There are also various techniques of 'reframing': exercises aimed to change the structure or direction of thinking and provide the initial leverage into a new order or approach.
3 Ultimately, there is the search for the technique of reaching inner resources through releasing intuition, insight and imagination, through imaging, so as to escape the chains of cerebrally governed verbal expression altogether.

These three form the basis of all creativity training in one way or another. They are worth exploring a little more.

Improving Ideation

Brainstorming as a technique assumes that the individual needs relatively little encouragement to let his creative juices flow. This is of course true of some people. Brainstorming was devised by an advertising executive for advertising people. One can assume that they are probably more creatively juicy than others.

George Prince introduced synectics as a means of creating the greater pressure required to push most of us into the frame of mind necessary to become productively creative. Synectics is a proprietary creative problem-solving process which takes days to complete, and requires considerable investment to succeed. It is problem-centred, using the group to find many ways of reaching a solution to one issue at a time. Central to the process of synectics is de-focusing. The group is asked first to consider the problem, then encapsulate it in a word or a concept but in a context which is from a totally unrelated domain. Ideas resulting from examples elicited from this distant world are then explored, looking for relatively few 'Absurd Ideas', and trying to see how, working on these, and slowly applying them to the original problem, solutions can be evolved for the original problem. Much of the strength of synectics is its drill. Central to each session is a client figure: the person who owns the problem. Rules govern how he should behave towards the others and them towards him. It is a highly structured, even a painful means of reaching for a novel answer.

Matti Bergström, a Finnish professor of neurophysiology, questioned the fact that our brains could produce any new, unexpected thought patterns at all. Why should data input and data output not be exactly related, as the 'brain as computer' would have us believe? He suggested that the brain-stem, which is the older part of the brain and, in evolutionary terms, the more primitive, generates continuous disorder, it is the 'chance generator'. The cortex, which lies above the brain-stem, is the orderer, the means by which we manage our thoughts. Bergström saw the interaction between brain-stem chaos and cortical order as a 'battleground' between the two poles of the brain. Our complex patterns of information (sets, associative memory patterns, etc.) are constantly bombarded by these impulses. Occasionally one gets shattered, and we have new ideas.

Bergström explains different levels of creativity in people by their various levels of competence in handling this random barrage. At one extreme are the psychotics whose cortical function is so impaired that chaos painfully and shatteringly takes over. At the other extreme is the person who is so heavily acculturated, or who has been taught cerebral control to such an extent, that his thinking processes are impermeable to pressure from a new idea. Creativity in such people is stimulated when they let a little go and let a little chaos in. Bergström said that every new idea must fight for its existence: therefore the ones you want to keep have to be given some assistance. Other writers and explorers of creativity consistently repeat the message: creativity cannot be cultivated, it has to be trapped. Its source is a wild energy present in everyone. If we want to put it to use, we have to lay up snares, not lay down pasture.

So how does brainmapping help? It helps people who want to increase their ideas without losing control over their generation. It is simply a way of unpacking the fearfully constraining but totally necessary high-level concepts we use day-to-day, in order to re-examine them and, where it makes most sense, repacking them in a more creative way.

In brainmapping, a single key word is taken, for example, 'computer'. The key word is written down, and the first word or concept associated with it written on a line drawn out from the word, say, software. Software itself has some associations: Lotus 1, 2, 3, or Graphics could be one direction, or the word 'unbreakable' might start another chain of thought. At the end of twenty minutes' exploration, the mindmap will begin to look like a tree-root, viewed from above. The remarkable part of this process is that, with relatively little training, people with the very minimum amount of free-floating creativity can tap some creative energy quite quickly. They are cutting under and into the associative unconscious, but without in any sense losing control. Furthermore, they are made acutely aware of the highly varied substrata of what they previously saw as simple and straightforward beliefs and concepts.

Rudy Rucker put the essence of brainmapping beautifully in his book *Mindtools* with the expression: 'Life is a fractal in Hilbert space'.[9] A fractal is a fundamental feature of Chaos Theory. Fractals exist because the appearance and data offered by any one object depend on how far away it is when it is seen. Each step taken towards it offers more detail or creates a different perspective or insight. Some fractals are self-similar, as in a series of Russian dolls one inside the other, each with exactly the same appearance. Others vary dramatically: a map of a shoreline as perceived from a spaceship is very different from one drawn from a helicopter.

As an example of the complexity underlying simple actions Rucker takes the statement, 'I picked up a cigarette and took a puff'. Simple enough, but the smoker existed. He was alive. He had many states of understanding surrounding this simple act. He was multidimensional, like Hilbert space, a mathematical concept wherein space can accept infinite dimensions. Rucker examined the connections around this act figuratively, as though operating a menu-driven programme which can be pulled down at will. The first menu produces a narrative, 'I am smoking a cigarette, etc.'. A new menu might be brought up by taking one of these words, say cigarette. Under cigarette might be a menu listing: brands, experiences, places where it is allowed, knowledge of tobacco, feelings about cancer. Move the menu around feelings about cancer, and the listing might include: people I have known who died of cancer of the lung. This can be extended:

> Jim was a friend. He was born the day after I was. He went for a holiday with his wife, and had to return early because he felt suddenly very ill. The doctor found he had lung cancer. He was treated, and was cured. But later they found he had cancer in a brain tumour also. All this time he kept smoking. And his wife and three children all smoked.

This narrative can go on for some time, or a picture arising from it might provide a need to pull another menu, say, 'children smoking – why do they do it?', or, 'why did I do it . . . ?' – endless shifts of focus and direction, infinite branches of infinitely ranging size. Human life is a fractal in Hilbert space. Brainmapping has the great virtue of helping the relatively tight-brained people of this world to loosen up – to explore their own packages of beliefs, knowledge association and experiences, and search comfortably, and in their own time, for those new connections which can help them resolve creatively the problems which resist their normal approaches.

While mindmapping helps explore existing, but implicit, mental structures and boundaries in a controlled way, it does not open up new ones. For this, the creativity teachers offer a range of structuring techniques. Structuring is the formulation of an issue or a problem in a way that provides an opportunity to see where new entry points can be discovered. Where brainmapping helps expose and explore existing understanding from the inside, structuring seeks to characterize the external dimensions, so as to ensure that all potential opportunities are given their chance to be examined. The most common structuring method is through the development of matrices.

Its use is an everyday event in product development. All existing product capabilities are listed in the left-hand column on a sheet of paper, and a range of market opportunities written across the top. Examining the extent to which the product is used, or has a possible use, in each of these market segments can stimulate ways of looking at new applications. It is a simple enough method, but such unthreatening means of generating ideas have their place in conditions where people have come to believe rigidly that all avenues have been explored.

Morphological analysis is a slightly different way of structuring, where lists are produced under each of several headings, such as processes, properties, varieties, and forms. Under each heading all possible existing outcomes could be listed. For example, in pharmaceuticals, under *form* could be: pills, lozenges, liquids, capsules, injectables, suppositories, etc.; under a heading such as *disease target* might be: heart, liver, stomach, intestine, skin, brain, kidneys, etc. The object of listing items in this way is again to stimulate ideas as to where a new market for the product might be found, or a new product for an existing market might evolve. It is important that all listed items are chased through all of their potential combinations and possibilities.

Scenario building is another of these processes, where possible futures are constructed, and the kinds of opportunities that each might present are examined. Too often people make simple, and thereafter unexamined assumptions about the future, and are caught unprepared by the events which actually arise. By creating a range of possibilities without assigning probabilities to them, the range of responses is widened and creative flexibility of anticipation enhanced. It is important in scenario building to start with a 'what if' and reach a consensus as to both the outcome, and the appropriate response. Just thinking about 'the future of . . . ' tends to be unhelpful, and also increases the chance that there will be only one outcome to the thinking. The purpose of this process is to widen forecast horizons, not narrow them.

The use of tree diagrams as a general management technique assists creativity in some measure, since it enables consequences to be explored without funnelling down on to one outcome or issue. Thus, if the objective is to increase earnings per share by 15 per cent over the next three years, at the highest level of analysis there can be two ways of doing this: increasing revenue and decreasing costs. If we take each of these to the next stage of analysis, increasing revenue could be achieved through price increases or price reduction. Decreasing costs could be broken down to include eliminating products, transferring manufacture to another site or country, or subcontracting, and so on. Only through breaking these out and examining the contribution of each to the overall objective can managers be certain that there is not an element of opportunity missing. The process magnifies the detail, but by keeping levels symmetrical and interlocked, new routes can be illustrated and explored.

Crossing Habitual Boundaries

As Koestler and others have graphically pointed out, habits of thinking help us to manage our daily lives without being overcome by the shifting diversity of it all. Non-creativity is necessary where stability reigns around us. For the most part, this stability is there. The sun rises. It gets dark. We need to eat. Our children are recognizably the same day-to-day. Our signatures need to match the ones held by the bank.

However, the more adapted we are to today's circumstances, the more difficult it will be for us to succeed in tomorrow's. We need to keep the boundaries permeable between our sets of assumptions, our packages of knowledge and our chunks of information. We need to be open to cross fertilization, able to yield to the need to adapt.

It is this field of provision to the would-be creative which is most significantly well supported by books, by training courses, by consultants and by advisers. Mostly the books offer lists, many of which, like those in James Adams' *Conceptual Blockbusting*, Roger Von Oech's *A Whack on the Side of the Head* and Savory and Ehlan-Miller's *Mindways* are aimed to offer ways of shaking people out of their routines. Alex Osborn offered a range of suggestions as to how to bend a concept through brainstorming: magnify or minify, rearrange or decombine, turn on its head or make it go backwards, were suggestions he made.

Roger Von Oech's book, subtitled *How to Unlock your Mind with Lateral Thinking*, listed ten mental blocks which he considered were the prime inhibitors to creative thinking:[10]

Blocks	*Unblockers*
1 The one right answer.	Look for the second right answer.
2 That's not logical.	Think poetic, try metaphors to break from the prison of logic.
3 Follow the rules.	Every act of creation is first of all an act of destruction (Picasso).

4 Be practical.	Ask what if . . .
5 Avoid ambiguity.	Everything can be made ambiguous – try it.
6 To err is wrong.	The man who never made a mistake never took a decision worth taking.
7 Play is frivolous.	The next time you have a tough problem, play with it.
8 That's not my area.	Be ever curious, someone else has probably already solved your problem, but his way.
9 Don't be foolish.	Humour is a subset of creativity.
10 I'm not creative.	If you say so, you will be so.

The whole emphasis of this and other formulae is to find ways of multiplying the frameworks that are put to use, and to deny the closing-down activities associated with the uncreative response. Here are some examples of problems designed to get people out of their frame, or set, or functional fixation as it has been variously called:

A man who lived in a small town near Bradford in Yorkshire married twenty different women of the same town. All were still living, and he has never divorced one of them. Yet, he has broken no law. Can you explain?

Another man and his son were in a serious road accident. Both were badly injured, especially to their heads. On the way to the hospital, the man died. His son was rushed into surgery. However, the neurosurgeon refused to undertake any operation, saying, I cannot do it, that is my son. Can you explain?

At a golf match on a very dry but windy day, a ball played by Nick Faldo landed on the green just as a paper bag went by. The ball rolled right into the paper bag, out of sight, but barely three feet from the hole. How can Faldo get to his ball with no risk of a penalty?

For those who can happily move from one frame of reference to another, the answers are obvious, but readers who come to these questions with their routines and habitual sets fully intact would find them troublesome. In the first case, they have to think of another sense of the verb *to marry*. In the second, they have to overcome sexist notions. In the third, they have to imagine other ways of removing a bag apart from the purely mechanical.

All of the procedures which are readily available as training devices, aimed at enhancing creative thinking, are based on this kind of problem-solving, through challenging prevailing assumptions. So, while mind-expanding (or more appropriately, mind-exercising) techniques can help push people out of rutty thinking and broaden their scope of attack on a problem, they seldom threaten or cause any pain. To be effective they demand effort, and time, and a real sense of need to change, but they will in any event prove helpful.

Releasing Imagination

The real business of becoming more creative has to start with an acceptance that it will only become a competitive advantage when the risk is taken; that the creative momentum, once released, cannot be closed down at will. True creativity for everyman must be accompanied by risk, and by pain.

As Frank Barron has pointed out, it is a brave person who takes the path that commits him to a life of demanding creativity. But for most people a time will arise, and more frequently than in the past, where genuine creative insight would be a very considerable bonus to either work or leisure, or both. So how do people get to release their creativity, in depth? There are numbers of ways proposed, each of which is the more difficult for those less immediately favoured with the orientation and talent to exercise it.

Malcolm Wescott worked extensively on intuition in the 1960s. Intuition was defined as successful decision-making arising out of a medium of insufficient data to reach an analytical conclusion. Inference, jumping to conclusions, backing a hunch, taking a flier are all suggestive that intuition is taking place. Wescott categorizes people into four groups:[11]

Intuitive thinkers	who with little information managed to be very successful problem-solvers.
Wild guessers	who with little information were typically unsuccessful.
Cautious successes	where excellent in.ormation helped those people to reach quality answers.
Cautious failures	where people were unsuccessful at reaching good answers despite having received excellent information.

Testing these people using a series of conventional personality and other psychomatic tests, Wescott found that the intuitive thinkers, compared to the others, were more likely to be independent, spontaneous, unconventional and proud of it, and willing to take criticism. They were willing to change direction, never not simply as a result of being told to do so, but only if they were themselves convinced of the need.

One definition of intuition was offered by Philip Goldberg: 'Intuition can be understood as the mind turning in on itself and apprehending the result of processes that have taken place outside awareness.'[12]

If an individual feels uncomfortable with considering these feelings, if he feels that he *must* make a decision quickly, to get it out of the way, or that he will need all the data before he can reach an answer in which he would have confidence, then this is always going to be an impediment to intuitive thought for as long as it predominates. Taking ourselves and our thoughts too seriously, not recognizing absurdity, not being willing to be playful, all preclude intuitive thought.

Intuitives are prepared to suspend judgement until the last minute. They can do this because they are confident, as a result of previous experience, that the right answer has always arrived before time was up. Confusion reigns in their minds with comfort, because they know it will resolve itself, usually just in time.

Later, Goldberg quotes the work of J. W. Getzels of the University of Chicago in his discussion of successful artists: 'the artist's actions reveal that they are working in a goal-directed way but without full conscious awareness of what the goal is . . . they cannot tell what the drawing will be, but their behaviour shows that at some level the goal is quite clear.' He concludes: 'In the early days of any enterprise, it sometimes pays to temporarily set aside the demand for order, the compulsion to do things by the book, and the need for a quick resolution.'[13]

Some researchers have concluded that there are four levels of creative imaging, of which only at the fourth level can true intuition be brought into play voluntarily. The first level is where life is lived, on the surface, habitually forming the patterns we expect to see and following reflexly with our learned or automatic responses. At the second level, abstraction and self-consciousness become possible. At the third, there is integration, a re-evaluation of what is, a potential coming-together of disparate parts into a new whole. Only at the fourth does a search for a new pattern actually take precedence over the old. Most people do not get beyond the third level. Brainstorming often does not assist people to think beyond that level. To get to the fourth there has to be a conscious uncoupling of conscious control. It takes time, and it takes courage for those who do not have the confidence borne of success. But it is always likely to be worth the effort.

Keith Johnstone wrote a whole chapter on spontaneity in his book *Impro*. In it he recalled an experiment where some businessmen were shown up as very dull on word-association tests. They were then asked to imagine themselves as happy-go-lucky types. They were retested, and immediately showed up as far more imaginative. So, it is possible to turn unimaginative people into imaginative people just like that. Teaching in schools has always aimed to limit imagination, to teach children the right answer. Their fantasy, their imagination, their spontaneity, needs to be subdued if they are to enter the adult world. Johnstone offered some rare views:

> My feeling is that sanity is actually a pretence, a way we learn to behave. We keep this pretence up because we don't want to be rejected by other people – and to be classified insane is to be shut out of the group in a very complete way. Most people I meet are secretly convinced that they're a little crazier than the average person ... They understand that their own sanity is a performance, but when confronted by other people they confuse the person with the role.'[14]

Later he makes a telling point on originality:

> The improviser has to realize that the more obvious he is, the more original he appears. I constantly point out how much the audience like someone who is direct, and how they always laugh at a really 'obvious' idea. Ordinary people asked to improvise will search for some 'original' idea because they want to be *thought* clever ... Ask people to give you an original idea, and see the chaos it throws them into. If they said the first thing that came into their head, there'd be no problem.[15]

The advice is sound, and consistent with other supporting evidence. Creativity, insight and intuition are all lost to those who try too hard to reach for them. However, if people are to open themselves to their own creative capability, they need to feel safe, they need to feel that their unprotected output is not to be threatened or attacked. The risks are all too clear. Rollo May, in *The Courage to Create*, emphasizes the harsher aspects of the process:

> Creative people, as I see them, are distinguished by the fact that they can 'live with anxiety', even though a high price may be paid in terms of insecurity, sensitivity, and defencelessness for the gift of 'divine madness', to borrow the term used by Classical Greats. They do not run away from non-being, but by encountering and wrestling with it, force it to produce being. They knock on silence for an answering music; they pursue meaninglessness until they can force it to mean.[16]

May offered the concept of 'encounter' which he saw as a central element to creative thinking. There must be passion, intensity, even real pain, if qualitatively significant creativity is to be sustained. This is the hardest part: to be emotionally intense at the same time as intellectually prepared *and* mentally and psychologically open is a task still beyond all but the most determined.

There are further ways around the inhibition of habits, of words, and of routine conceptual framework. Hypnosis has been tried, transcendental meditation has proved helpful, at least in reaching for the openness of the senses if not to the passion or the learning. Attempts have been made to use music and art, encouraging people to try to express themselves in ways which are non-linear, which are outside their normal communication media. But above all, there has to be time, quality time, peace, the opportunity to let the whole brain do its work, not just the part we call consciousness. To find that time, there is a need to place a much higher value on solitude.

Organizing for Creativity

Many attempts have been made to create the organizational conditions under which people's natural creativity can be elicited. These range from the oddly titled 'skunk works' where a fully complemented organization unit is set up, dedicated to a single task and given its head, to Raytheon's new products centre, where the untested ideas of entrepreneurial employees are given concentrated attention. Honda has a system where first-time failures, mistakes or brilliant but unusable ideas are kept in sight for possible re-examination. Honda also makes specialists generalists, pushing them into considering the broader issues of the firm and so encouraging their ideas to widen their shape. Means by which ideas are swapped through networking are becoming more prevalent. Dow Chemical are reported to offer venture capital and to seek outside technology to discourage the 'not invented here' rejection of new ideas. Exxon do the same.

Thomas Allen, back in the 1960s, showed clearly the impact of spatial positioning on inter-technical communication. He proved that if people were separated by 60–70 feet, technical flow of communication was suppressed by two-thirds. If moved a further 70 feet away, 90 per cent of the possible technical communication between them had been effectively eliminated. There were no obvious differences whether the gap was 3000 feet or 3000 miles. Companies noting these very real inhibitions on creative integration have asked architects to ensure that the physical positions of staff that can benefit from working together accidentally are given the best chance of facilitating that accident.

The skunk works are a high-profile attempt to beat bureaucracy through having a simple option unit. The team is close-ended, pressed for delivery, and focused. It is separated geographically and economically from the parent organization. All talents needed at the outset are a hundred-per-cent allocated. Each is like one of Gerard Fairtlough's cells.

Computers have been brought to bear on the problems of managing data, and of reconstructing data in a form which makes the issue more open to creative thinking, cutting out the chores on the one hand, and increasing creative potential on the other. Some of this can be a mixed blessing. Many patents fail because inventors have not the time or the patience to search through existing rights. This can be made easier through computers and data bases (there is a world patent index). Over 3000 on-line data bases exist which are accessible with a personal computer, a modem and a telephone line. Most of them are bibliographies, which can be searched through simple logical commands.

Computers also offer graphic design facilities which can aid both artistic and scientific creativity through three dimensional presentation, although experts consider there to be some loss of creative edge as a result of the ease with which such patterns can be produced. The Apple Macintosh PC has revolutionized graphic design, but perhaps at the same time it has created a dependence which rubs smooth all but the most startling novelties. The more these aids are provided, the higher the minimum level of creative entry becomes. So while the price of entry becomes even higher, the distinction, that special best that comes from real creative endeavour, still shows clearly in a crowd. It is very clear that although so much more of the effort can be automated and enhanced, the human brain is the still only true arbiter.

The one thing that communication and computers can do is save time. The creative outcome will arrive through that saved time being used well by the people it is intended to help.

Conclusion

Creativity and innovation are perceived to be the central concern of a few, and for them it can become a passion. As organizations increasingly recognize the need for better, swifter, more innovative responses by their employees to the changing world, so this group will widen, and the pressure to search for creativity in working people will demand more and more. At the same time, in many parts of the world, the supply of well-educated people is not rising; the state investment in such creativity-supporting activities as research and tertiary education is often declining. The cost of re-entry into research-based industries to those who lose their lead grows enormously year by year, and the volume of information increases exponentially. This pincer movement can only result, in the long term, in the gradual removal from the first division of post-industrial nations of the losers in the global battle.

It must be imperative for people and organizations wishing to engage in this battle to find ways of maximizing the potential for creative thought and innovative output from themselves and others close to them. At the core, this requires genuine effort and commitment. Denise Shekerjian put this bluntly in her book *Uncommon Genius*:

> What everyone wants is magic . . . what they want is The Trick to creativity so that they will be assured of a richer, more satisfying life . . . The trick, if there is a simple useful thing to say about it, is to identify your own particular talent and then settle down to work on it for a very good long time.[17]

Creativity becomes a habit, a willingness to develop a capability, and then to trust to its judgement through tapping it intuitively. All of the many games offered by teachers of creative thought cannot work on nothing. All truly creative people have developed a talent, a knowledge base, a depth of interest and understanding without concreting it over and assuming that their knowledge is now complete and their problems perpetually solved. Dealing with this contradiction, of being knowledgeable and admitting ignorance at the same time, and living comfortably if not painlessly with such uncertainty, this is what enables creative thought to flourish.

Organizations and managers of creative people can find ways of suppressing the naturally inhibiting quality of structure, of norm-forming, of orthodoxy that all hierarchies tend to impose on people. There are many ways of going about this, but few will work if the people who are offered them have neither the talent nor the will to make profitable use of the opportunities to innovate.

Tests of creativity are rare and relatively infrequently applied. They exist, and can help to find the right people where urgent innovation is the order of the day. However, creativity as measured by tests can only seriously operate as an eliminator. There is little doubt that some people have such a resistance to creative endeavour that no amount of supporting system or technique will bring them to the point of releasing the creative purpose that everyone has somewhere within him.

Notes

1 A. Zalaznick, in R. L. Kuhn, *Handbook for Creative and Innovative Managers* (McGraw-Hill, USA, 1988), p. 39.
2 Roger Von Oech, *A Wack on the Side of the Head: How to Unlock Your Mind with Lateral Thinking* (Angus & Robertson, London, 1983).
3 Rudy Rucker, *Mind Tools: The Five Levels of Mathematical Reality* (Houghton-Mifflin, Boston, 1987), p. 198.
4 Keith Johnstone, *Impro: Improvisation and the Theatre* Eyre Methuen, London, 1981; reprinted Methuen Drama, 1989), p. 79.
5 Alex F. Osborn, *Applied Imagination* (Scribner, New York, 1953).
6 Edward De Bono, *The Use of Lateral Thinking* (Penguin, Harmondsworth, 1990).
7 Arthur Koestler, *The Act of Creation* (Hutchinson, London, 1964), p. 639.
8 J. G. Bennett, *Creative Thinking* (Yorkshire Coombe Springs Press, Ripon, 1964), p. 15.

9 Rucker. *Mind Tools*, p. 178.
10 Von Oech, *A Whack on the Side of the Head*, p. 9.
11 Malcolm Wescott, *Towards a Contemporary Psychology of Intuition* (Holt, Rinehart & Winston, New York, 1968).
12 Philip Goldberg, *The Intuitive Edge: Understanding and Developing Intuition* (Turnstone Press, UK, 1985), p. 137.
13 Ibid., p. 159.
14 Johnstone, *Impro*, p. 83.
15 Ibid., p. 88.
16 Rollo May, *The Courage to Create* (W. W. Norton/Bantam, New York, 1975), p. 108.
17 Denise G. Shekerjian, *Uncommon Genius: How Ideas are Born* (Viking Penguin, New York, 1990), p. 1.

Managing Creativity

Ignorance has always been a good friend to me.

Peter Jones, BBC Radio 4

Managing creative people is never easy. Managing genius is effectively impossible. Managing people who have the talent and potential to be more creative than they are is vital. Being creative can be painful, but managing creativity can be a no less discomforting activity. It can be personally threatening. Creative people seldom manage to sweeten their criticisms and complaints, but can at the same time show a massive sensitivity to even token criticism of themselves.

This chapter explores how those given the responsibility to manage creativity learn to recognize genius, to bring out the best in it, and to construct an organizational climate which will encourage their people to take the chances to show what they can creatively accomplish.

First, what are the likely features of the life and nature of a genius? No one should make the mistake of thinking that being a genius is a comfortable, happy or totally rewarding experience. On the evidence there is, being a genius requires most of the following:

An early life that:

- promoted a pleasure in non-conformity and a very early willingness to challenge assumptions, whoever should offer them;
- provided a cultural environment sufficiently rich and varied to offer the opportunities to explore and interact with stimulation and challenge;

- provided a father who has a professional occupation;
- offered an independent, determined, ambitious, autonomous mother (a great asset to the would-be genius);
- offered an economic milieu which is not perceived as so well-off to encourage indolence, but not so poor as to focus needs too closely on financial security;
- was Jewish in cultural style if not religious and probably male;
- was part of a small family, or early in the order if part of a large family;
- was in a family that placed great value on achievement, but offered relatively little emotional comfort in the sense of warm cuddliness; this produces a person who combines robust personal detachment with a strong need to make an impression on the world.

The putative genius shows these early signs:

- If the area of genius is to be in a field of knowledge or expertise, rather than as a leader, attained an education to bachelor degree level (and not much further; it was Einstein who wrote: 'I shall not become a Ph.D. . . . the whole matter has become a bore to me'). If in the field of leadership, or pure invention, it is best not to have graduated at all.
- Demonstrated very strong evidence of an early fascination for a particular subject or skill, which was relentlessly followed through to later life.
- Showed, where tested for intelligence, a score above average, but with a clear bias in intellectual style, not a balanced one.
- Indicated emotional volatility, probably with some signs of temperamental disorder, especially manic-depression, and a preference for solitude.

These characteristics need to be present to a considerable extent if the drive, the preparation, the 'divine dissatisfaction', and the talent is to be sufficient to make the high level creative breakthrough in later life.

As an adult, the would-be genius could be expected to show:

- Taste – this is a very necessary and consistent feature. The ability to quickly recognize the elegance, the beauty, the emotional satisfaction of the creative product exists whether the genius is in the sciences, mathematics, art, music or design.

- Within the extremes of the choleric temperament, only a rare exhibition of relaxed cheerfulness. Happiness is not often the lot of the genius: more typically, brief ecstasy occasionally interrupts the protracted struggle for perfection and continued dissatisfaction with results.

- Emotional and intellectual independence, which leads to behaviour that is almost always non-conforming and unconventional. This independence is formed very early, fostered by parents, or provoked by overly-demanding early socialization. It seldom shows much sign of diminishing.

- A driving focus on work, immodesty about its value, and clarity as to his superiority over that of peer groups.

- Great dedication to work, showing most of the indicators of workaholism; a capacity to work for long hours over protracted periods, resenting interruptions.

- '. . . sheer egotism. Desire to seem clever, to be talked about, to be remembered after death, to get your own back on grown-ups who snubbed you in childhood, etc., etc. It is numbing to pretend that this is not a motive, and a strong one. Writers share this characteristic with scientists, artists, politicians, lawyers, soldiers, successful businessmen – in short, the whole top crust of humanity.'

George Orwell[1]

In summary, the potential genius needs to have a cultural heritage, and to be inspired early by the values of achievement. He has to have an unusual talent, and to be somewhat above average in intelligence as it is conventionally measured. He has to have been subjected to some stress, either emotional detachment, or inferiority feelings, or rejection, which encourages the development of persistent, independent, intellectual activity, and the desire to excel. He has to have developed the habit of working alone and relying on his own judgement. He has to have worked hard to acquire a high level of competence in a specific domain. He has to want his peers to rate him very highly. The diagram below summarizes what is, in a sense, the trap into which these people fall. There is no end to the cycle of perfectionism and the desire for mastery, except sudden fame or the consequences of wealth and age.

Figure 11.1 The Circle of Genius

To be recognized as a genius is clearly not an automatic outcome of the conditions shown in figure 11.1. A substantial proportion of them are necessary, but may still not be sufficient to create genius. The drive to succeed, to compensate for feelings of powerlessness or detachment, may produce the motivation but it will not provide the opportunity.

The genius has to recognize and react swiftly to signals, to take the chances that arise, and to pursue them to the end. Public success often adds distraction, envy and misunderstanding to the social isolation and sense of emotional rejection so often inherent in the preconditions of genius. Clearly there are compensations, but the perpetual search for perfection, the deep sense of solitariness, and the driving need to be master in one domain carry with them many more of the elements of stress than of relaxation.

Perhaps the most favourable circumstances for the development of talent are where the genius has found a profoundly capable person as a mentor and learned from him. The mentor was prepared to teach the genius that he had the potential and that the mentor was the most likely person to develop it in him. More important, the mentor helped him to convert his latent talent into a public achievement that turned the aspiring prodigy into the accepted genius.

How do you turn Great Talent into Creative Genius?

For those who find that they do not have the talent, parentage or upbringing that produces the potential for genius, there are ways open to them which will at least allow them to expand the creativity of those in their charge.

These are some of the pre-conditions:

- Increasing creative potential is never easy, and is often painful. As with most things, if it costs nothing it is worth nothing.
- All learning is a complex process of moving understanding, through rehearsal, from ignorance to ignorance. The first ignorance is not knowing, the last is knowing so well as to not to be conscious of knowing. Creativity demands that this process is occasionally but fluently reversed. Creative people are not afraid of taking this risk, so managers of the potentially creative need offer only a little extra encouragement.
- There has to be time, and solitude. While some people can be forced, by deadlines or by economic pressure, to come up with prescribed but creative output, they are few in number, and probably always wholly dissatisfied with their own creative product. Creativity requires extensive solitude. Creative output can and must be shared, but it is usually singular in its origin. It is not often born of a group, only stimulated and rewarded by a group. The manager of the creative person should expect little vicarious pleasure from the creative process, and look only to enjoy its product.
- The manager must allow that there must be a willingness to look away, to defocus, to step aside from doing, if people are to exploit their creativity. Most worthwhile creative products arise from sub-conscious processes. Fiercely holding on to consciousness, rejecting anything which is not rational or capable of verbal expression, and believing that the conscious mind is the one and only vehicle for solving problems, will each prevent any creative thoughts from emerging, ever.
- As with all things, there are trade-offs. The greater the personal satisfaction from creative output, the lesser will be the comfort of the social rewards of relaxed friendships. Most people are made uncomfortable by creativity. They need the predictability of relationships, of behaviour and of orthodoxy. This is how they get by. Creativity is upsetting to them. The midwife has to observe the inevitable pain of childbirth, showing sympathy but communicating strength. So has the manager of the creative process at work.

The actions that are possible to enhance creative potential are many. However, it is worth assessing how difficult the process of enhancement might be, before embarking on the journey.

First of all, check, or have others check, the extent to which particular personal behaviour is habitual. Ask how important is it to the aspirant creator that:

- he goes to work the same way, eats at the same time, reads the same newspaper each day, and in the same order;
- he looks for quick decisions, prefers simple problems, reaches judgements quickly, and sticks with them, and dislikes complexity and ambiguity;
- he works only in the present, seldom working through implications, or second-guessing those of others as they might affect his future.

The first step in fostering creative advancement is to recognize that endorsement of any of the above makes the task significantly more difficult.

Second, consider these factors in terms of self-image:

- Creative people believe themselves to be creative and have often done so from very early in their lives and careers. Yet there are people who believe themselves to be creative who are much less so than they imagine. However, it is unlikely, if not impossible, that a person who does not believe himself to be creative will ever father a creative thought by accident.
- People who like and enjoy the way they are, who do not challenge their personal values, and who do not feel that they could be improved upon as people, are unlikely to change. By the same token, if this is how they are, their creative potential is very difficult to improve.
- Those who compete with themselves and with their own accomplishments are more likely to prove to be creative than those who compete with others, who believe that winning is more rewarding than self-improvement.

Of course it is possible for those who are happy with themselves, who see themselves as uncreative, and who prefer to win rather than get better, to improve on their creative potential. But each of these features makes it that much harder for them.

Many people have been on training courses which have aimed to improve their creativity, and come away profoundly depressed at their lack of potential. They need not be, since they are probably well-rounded, stable and perfectly competent in their day-to-day lives. There should be no judgement of creativity in any individual as good or bad, any more than a person of genius should attract disapprobation from the orthodox just for being different. The secret is for everyone to learn the profit of diversity.

There are no certainties in improving personal creativity other than that if it seems easy, it is because it is not happening. People who allow their creativity to work for them know not from where it comes, nor can they legislate either for its arrival or for its purity. Here are three examples:

Omni: Have you ever discovered drugs in your dreams?

Sir James Black: I don't think so, but I have absolutely no idea where my ideas come from. For all I know they come from comets. They creep up on me. The most creative thing your brain does is dream. It synthesizes totally new pictures of experiences you never had, manufactures them down to the smallest detail, and you are not in control of it all.

Interview in *Omni*, November 1990)

In creative thinking, a lot of things come from the dark side. If you try to control your darker impulses, you risk losing their positive value to creative thought.

Jean-Louis Gassée, ex head of R & D, Apple, 1990.

. . . those hypotheses which have stood up to critical assaults and have, so to speak, been received into the repertory, came to my mind fairly suddenly and in a form not very different from that which they subsequently took . . . every one of the hypotheses that I came to accept had long been the subject of fretful speculation, a kind of turbulence of the mind – nothing arose genuinely *de novo* in my mind and I think it hardly conceivable that it should have done so.

Peter Medawar[2]

The above examples all from more practical scientific ends of the spectrum of creativity, yet each person freely admits to creativity arising rather than creativity being sought out.

Becoming more creative is a matter of attitude, of need, and of perseverance with the risky process of breaking and reframing the very frames which have provided so much of our intellectual and emotional security. If such events are to be encouraged, a vital comfort must be introduced to compensate for the change. This is the responsibility of management.

Managing Creative People Better

Those who are talented at managing others are almost invariably different, attitudinally, temperamentally and developmentally, from those who 'create'. But there are some managers who are better able to manage this creativity than others. They are the in-betweeners. Douglas Stevenson is one of a few people who have successfully managed people who have been master innovators in electronics.

As a senior manager at ITT, he experienced the relative failure of William Shockley to repeat the successes of his tenure at Bell Laboratories where the transistor was born. Stevenson believed that the structure that Bell imposed was a necessary part of creative venture. Released from its boundaries at ITT, Shockley's potential for egotism exploded to a degree that left him without further creative potential. His genius disappeared in an ego which became 'the size of Everest'. Charles Sandbanks was also at ITT. According to Stevenson, he arrived at original ideas like people with green fingers grow plants. Charles Koco was another to come within his influence, as, later, was Iann Barron of Inmos.

Douglas Stevenson was an exceptionally successful student as a child. However, he left school in Edinburgh at the age of fifteen, in the early stages of the Second World War, and acquired most of his technical and managerial education later than most. He joined ITT at the age of thirty, and was Vice-President ITT Europe and Vice-President ITT Inc., responsible for that company's component and semi-conductor operations, for most of the 1970s. Stevenson's recipe for getting the best out of his more creative engineers was to listen, to show them that he cared about what they had to say at the time that they had to say it, and not to prove impatient when they struggled to finish. He is adaptable, and tolerant of eccentricity where it does not interfere with real progress. Of some of the creative people he managed, he observed:

He was status conscious, you had to flatter him in a low-key way.

The company made the mistake of giving him too much space. If he was compressed and held down hard, he would produce, but where he was not under cost or time pressures, his genius became unbalanced. Once we had lost control, we never could get it back.

I couldn't stand the bastard, he was treacherous, and wanted my job so much, he'd try anything. At meetings, where people didn't agree with him, he would lose his head, bang the table, and then get up and go home. But he was a top scientist, a brilliant lecturer, and had gathered around him an incredibly bright group of brilliant thinkers. He was one I could not handle.

Stevenson is himself innovative and has personally registered three patents. But his forte is looking at the big picture, understanding the points of weakness and the deficiencies, and putting them right. He recognizes that all creative people love flattery. They enjoy being invited to explain their latest idea. He challenges them, but adopts the posture that 'they are putting me through an educational experience'. He learned his lessons through his own experiences. He had good models, benefiting from the symbiosis of himself as the young, eager technologist with an older mentor guiding him through the organizational maze and, in return, getting the benefit of his freshness and animation.

Jean-Louis Gassée is a French mathematician. When he was Apple's general manager in France, he made that country the most successful for Apple computers in the world. His reward was to be offered the post of head of R & D in the US Silicon Valley headquarters. Jean-Louis, like Douglas Stevenson, is bright and creative, but he too turned his attention to managing the productive output of others. There the comparison ends. Jean-Louis is the intellectual, abstract, noisily unconventional manager of the creative engineer. Some of his theoretical positions include what he calls his 'quantum view of leadership'. He explains:

Leadership is a dynamic operating between two poles:

the leader as magnet: his followers are brought into an effective configuration by the forces he creates around him.

the leader as non-magnet: the lines of force flow through him. He is then himself magnetized by these forces.

A good leader moves between these two forms. But he must often work hard at becoming de-magnetized.

Sometimes a creative team will hire their leader.

I will listen to creative people, but not endlessly, or with infinite patience. If they intrude on my time, I tell them – come back another time.

You have to be nurturing but demanding – they have to become demanding *for themselves* and of themselves.

As a manager, you have to feel the urge to accomplish yourself – for many years I did not think of myself as creative. I also thought I could not write. I now see myself as a late bloomer.

Most engineering teams are a motley crowd – they always include nerds. I like nerds – they feed me. The nerds work harder than the others, like rats. When it works, when a team delivers, it is a thing of great beauty.

Gassée is fascinated by the Japanese, he is trying to learn the language, as well as origami and other cultural crafts. He says of them: 'Homogeneity is both their strength and their weakness. They work very hard, but fortunately, they are discovering the pleasure principle – we can now corrupt them. We ship them made-for-TV-movies, McDonald's, and Pierre Cardin.'

Like Steve Jobs before him, Gassée left Apple to set up his own company, B Labs Inc. 'I am no longer a corporate jerk,' he told *International Management* (December 1990), echoing many before and, no doubt, many more to come. He has seen large, and he prefers small. He intends to hire some engineers who understand marketeers, and some marketeers who understand engineers. At Apple he wanted engineers who could write, who would recognize what the customer would buy, and how they would use it, who would feel what the user felt, and come up with the things that he would buy. This was the Jobs philosophy at Apple, in the beginning.

Winston Fletcher interviewed a number or people who were managers and leaders of 'creative business'. These were businesses whose perceived product was creativity. They were mostly media folk. In his book *Creative People*, the childlike nature of the 'creative' (the word advertising agencies use collectively for their productive children) constantly emerges.

Wally Olins was one of the people Fletcher talked to. Wally runs a very successful corporate image company: Wolff-Olins. He is a stern-looking man, with a quick, sharp tongue, firm views and something of a chip on his shoulder. The world still sees him as the uncreative one of the original partnership. Michael Wolff left it a few years ago. Those who know them saw Wolff as the one with all the ideas. Olins was the rainmaker. Fletcher quotes Olins as follows:

> The most irritating aspects of working with creative people are their arrogance, their egotism and their total self-centredness, their feeling that the world has to revolve around them, that time doesn't exist, that time is their property: their complete selfishness in relation to other human beings. That is the worst conceivable aspect of working with creative people, that they are babyish and selfish. They are not all like that, only a small minority are like that, and if anybody behaves to them as they behave to other people they are bitterly resentful.
> If they are young and immature emotionally, which they frequently are, and if they become successful very quickly, the pitiful remnants of any self-discipline that may have been drilled into them at school or at home disappear totally and they become completely unmanageable.[3]

Fletcher also highlights the second feature about 'creatives' in such organizations: how often their managers feel the need to comment on their likeability. For example, Paul Hamlyn noted: 'Creative people are certainly more difficult, sometimes more difficult in unpleasant ways. Some of the big, best-selling authors are pretty obnoxious. As people. But you put up with them.'[4]

Michael Grade goes a step further, and provides one of the central answers to the question of how they should be managed: 'If they've got talent, I don't have to like them. I have to like their talent. I've worked with a lot of creative people I couldn't stand. They wouldn't know I couldn't stand them. They never know that.'[5] Mr Grade seems to underestimate the sensitivity of these people, as well as the power of non-verbal communication. But the sentiment is right. Creative people care about being liked. Showing them that they are not liked creates severe barriers. But most managers care about being liked too. Most people care about being liked.

Liking a person, or not, should not be an important aspect of any manager's response. But the power of 'people who are like me' to be directly interpreted as 'people who are the best for our organization' is enormous. Its converse: 'If I do not like them as people, it cannot be good for me to have to work with them', is a fundamental error of any manager in a creative field.

The main elements in bringing out the best of creative talent in subordinates is shown diagrammatically in figure 11.2. The manager, having recognized the talent for what it is, and not having mistaken a simple eccentric for a putative genius, needs to provide for effective challenge, leadership (mentoring), mediation (between the organization and the creative process), and patience. If any one of these is missing, the creative potential is substantially reduced.

Figure 11.2 Managing Genius

The Creative Team

Much research and observation over the years has shown that productively innovative research teams have managers and superiors who are collaborative, consultative and supportive. They set boundaries, but do not thereafter interfere except as facilitators. The evidence to date suggests that these teams should not be seen as permanent. The most creative output comes before the team starts to get used to each other; before standards begin to become set and rigid, and cohesion begins to dominate over output; before the self-similar nature of people in mature groups begins to impose its own will. Any group of people who have to work together need one member who will always challenge existing orders, whatever they may be.

Belbin[6] gave the name 'Plants' to the people who naturally played this essential role. He showed clearly over years of research that without such a role being taken (or, in the right circumstances, that of its outward counterpoint, the 'Resource Investigator'), groups can be effective, but cannot sustain originality of output. The role of the manager in respect of a subordinate playing such a part is clearly to control his licence. Two Plants in one group can be disruptive. Even where circumstances determine that creativity is good, this does not mean that more creativity is always going to be even better.

Alan Chalmers of EMI Lighting emphasizes the need to keep people moving. 'Every now and then I go and rattle the bars – if they don't respond, then I start to worry . . . ' 'I have to encourage people to talk to each other, to revisit the purpose of their projects – it's so easy to lose our sense of direction . . . ' 'I keep the organization flexible, move people around, it's a fine judgement whether I move them so fast that they do not get a chance to make a contribution, or so slow that they get bored or stale.'

Clearly the best attribute for managing creativity in people is to pick the right people in the first place. Most organizations take relatively few pains over the process of getting the mix of people right. They choose managers most often on the basis of their records in similar jobs or in subordinate jobs. Then they leave these managers either the task of choosing those who will join their team, or give them no choice at all except the power of veto.

Alan Chalmers, like Gassée and Angus Ogilvy and many others has strong views of the kinds of people he would look for in a creative team: 'What I need is people who can cut across a specialism, the prizes now are for the people who manage the interfaces. I like people who can think with their hands.' It is actually not difficult to spot a confirmed and ably creative person. The difficult part is creating the environment in which the most beneficial advantage can be made of him.

Organizing for Creative Professionals

Joseph Raelin has articulated many of the issues surrounding the management of modern scientists, and professionals in general, in his book *The Clash of Cultures*.[7] He lists the polarizing values that split the organization's representatives, namely its managers, from the professionals they supervise. The polarization comes about from the problems of:

- overspecialization
- autonomy
- supervision
- formalization
- ethics

In each of these areas the managers of professionals and the managed professionals tend to take up opposing viewpoints. These need to be understood from both sides if they are not to prevail over productive good sense.

In the case of overspecialization, there is often a conflict between managers wishing to compartmentalize professions, so that in each discipline they perform standard tasks in their special cells, and professionals seeking to conduct their lives in terms which reflect 'putting my knowledge to use in full' rather than in consideration of what the organization wants of them. The action of many organizations in placing their professionals in geographically isolated pockets does not help to mediate this division.

Creativity comes from testing, bending and crossing boundaries. So both the managers and the professionals are contributing to a diminution of creativity by their respective natural behaviours. If creativity is sought, then professionals must be engaged in understanding each others' specific and unique strengths. They must also seek to grasp this fundamental of the organization's business: open, positive, extensive communications are imperative. Mentors are vital. People must be identified as responsible for ensuring that boundaries are made fluid.

Autonomy is something all professionals seek. Given their heads, professionals will always seek to do their thing in their own way. Managers, however, do have a tendency to interfere with what their subordinates are doing, day-to-day, rather than concentrate on presenting and ordering the objectives, purposes, conventions and values of their organization.

The introduction of dual careers is one of the solutions designed to resolve the issue of autonomy. The accomplished professional is offered an alternative career where his autonomy is maintained and his standing as a professional remains unimpaired by his not becoming a manager and thereby taking up the administrative responsibilities required by the role. Many organizations practise dual ladder career structures. Many more, which do not offer the alternative, frustrate their most creative people by offering no choice to their ambition. Dual ladders are not without their difficulties, however. The crucial issue is one of selection. There are some professionals who simply cannot adjust to management, and who therefore tend to end up on the professional career ladder more by default than by a reasoned assessment of their ability.

There will always be those who see management as their perfectly natural vocational progression as almost invariably, the organization will show its preference for those who are its managers. This favouritism must draw into those ranks many professionals who would be better advised to resist. Raelin saw three potential disasters here. First, there are the professionals who go into managing to replace a progressively unrewarding professional life: to escape. Second, there are those who move to management as a way of staying with their current employer and advancing, rather than making the more appropriate choice of staying with their profession and taking trouble to seek a new employer. Third, there are those who fear that their professional skills are becoming obsolete, and who wish to avoid the threat of the younger professional finding them out. If the management career is seen as an opportunity for failing scientists, or the professional career ladder as a place to park inadequately managerially skilled professionals, then the organization will fail.

Managers are often tempted to employ too close a supervision of scientists. In addition they tend to impose too much formalization. In their turn, scientists resist this through their insistence on outside performance standards. This contest of wills is often overcome by the use of peer reviews. In these, the guidance and assessment of the performance of professionals are provided by a group of scientific equals, at least some of which are from outside the organization concerned.

Matrix management, project assignments, involvement in department decision-making, all help to integrate the active professional into the organization's issues. Despite such attempts at integrating their efforts, binding their loyalty and committing their minds, the most creative individuals will always tend to look for opportunities to be free to be creative again on their own terms. If the organization does not offer them these challenges, then it is likely that they will look for them elsewhere. No amount of manipulation of career structure to hold their interest in non-creative organizational settings will succeed.

The differences of ethics should diminish over the years. Businesses are becoming more obliged to consider their public image, their response to prospective legislation, and their needs to retain key staff. However, despite this change in attitude, the management of creativity remains a polarizing issue which does not ever go away.

Why does the Management of Creative People go Wrong?

In all researches into creative people, the conflict between the child and the grown-up consistently emerges. The child is the innovator, but also the rebel. The parent is the controller, the nourisher, but also the orthodox, the conventional. It would help all managers of creative people to study Transactional Analysis (TA), which codifies and articulates the nature of relationships in ways which show great insight into the organization of genius.

Eric Berne wrote the first paper on Transactional Analysis in 1957. He died in 1970. Between these two dates, he wrote eight books, including, in 1964, his bestseller *Games People Play!*.[8] This book recommended a worldwide exploitation of TA as a model for exploration of personality, personal development, psychopathology, and, above all, communication. Berne intended TA as a means by which lay people, untrained in medicine or psychoanalysis, could learn to recognize the more significant aspects of human living.

During the 1980s interest in TA declined. It suffered from overexposure, and the strong association with the 'touchy-feely' school of management development. In managing creative people, however, it remains a singularly effective instrument for explaining, exploring and sustaining a high quality of professional insight.

The central theme of TA is its representation of the human decision-making process as containing three major elements: Parent, Adult and Child. Experiments have shown very clearly how little is truly forgotten. It is a small assumption to make that if things are not forgotten, then, if only by accident, they can still affect current behaviour. Berne's proposition was that we have within us, in various ways and proportions, the residue of all of our prior experiences as we mature from baby to adulthood, and that these add up to our complex and unique feelings, beliefs and understandings as adults. Thus, in each of us there is a sizeable something of the person we were at zero, five, ten, twenty, etc.

Behaviour and values and memories from each of these prior conditions continue to influence how we are at subsequent stages in our life. The Child is more likely to be strong on the feelings of the past, the feelings of insecurity, but also of guiltless pleasures; the sensation of over-dependence, but also the pure pleasure of discovery; the fascination of intuitive conclusions, of very rapid learning, of gradual mastery of an area of endeavour, of quick and rewarding achievement. Within our Child is the behaviour we learned to follow as we reacted to the world of adults around us, the earliest behaviour that became automatic for us.

This could include beliefs about what is clean and what dirty, particular ways of eating at the table, and attitudes towards authority. It could also include the behaviour that worked for us as children in getting away with selfish ends, such as sulking, dumb insolence, crying or running away. This is what Berne called the Adapted Child. Most of us bring a substantial part of this behaviour into the adult world, where it can still be adaptive, saving us the effort of having to think things through from scratch. However, it may be non-adaptive, where it is seen by others as so inappropriate in an adult person that it does not achieve the ends it accomplished when perpetrated as a child.

We all meet people as we grow up who communicate their personalities to us in ways we feel we need to copy, to match. They are our role models, people we feel that to imitate will lead us to a successful outcome in our dealings with the world. Berne called these images our Parent, and divided them into our nurturing Parent and our controlling Parent. Most of the messages carried by these models are our cultural inheritance. They are the repeating behaviours and beliefs that create the national, regional, class and religious cultural differences that both unite and divide the human race. Parent behaviours emerge in women when they have to deal with children. They repeat their own mothers' patterns, even using the same words, expressions and intonations. These Parent patterns also manifest themselves where people sense their own power and position. Parents are not creative. They are the defenders of the paradigm. They use words like 'ought' and 'must'. They try to help others. They bind families, talk about 'us', and our duties.

Our Adult is the here and now, the conscious decision-making in real time. In Adult we seek to manage the day-to-day. We question, we calculate, we assess probabilities. It is our operational computer. It solves our problems minute by minute.

Each of us grows up under a unique set of circumstances and influences. The nature and quality of our early life, and the impact on us of its range will determine not only the shape, content and texture of our Parent, Adult and Child, but also their relative power. It is very likely that more creative people will give a greater prominence to their Child than to their Parent. A person with a prominent Child but little evidence of Parent would find living and working with others quite difficult. He would have no rules to look to, no ethical or interpretive framework in which to make judgements. Intuition will dominate his thinking processes. He could even make up his own logic, and have problems communicating with others. Such a condition could well be brought about by certain conditions of childhood.

From the experiences of renowned geniuses, the detached father, the solitary childhood, the self-assertive mother could leave the patterns of the past overly laden with Child behaviour and experiences and Child motivation and satisfaction. Another person could have found childhood a forgettable experience, but have taken on board some very powerful Parent processing. Such a person is unlikely to find fun, but to concentrate his energies on the serious issues of planning, controlling and processing the daily life of self and others.

This is the personification of many traditional organizations. With or without such people as Jobs or Branson in an organization's history, it is possible that it will behave, and be seen by employees, as exclusively a Parent. The basic trauma of the creative individual working within the orthodox organization can be explained in such a way by Transactional Analysis. The conflict between the professional and the managerial culture is well described with the language of TA.

Where creativity is often trapped is where there is no interpretive, supporting intermediary between the individual Child and the collective Parent. So how does knowing this help to manage creative people better? First, in recognizing that the qualities of child*like* are not the same as child*ish*. The Child in us is not pretending to be a Child, or acting in a pretentious way, it is us, acting in the way we did as children, but using the data substrate of our world of today. As has been said elsewhere in more general terms, the solution, the means of reaching and profiting from the creative Child, is to offer patronage, the nurturing Parent, and not to patronize. In fact, this is the nanny, the paid parent, the supportive developer, distant and constraining, demanding and caring but not encompassing or pre-emptive.

Second, it is helpful to learn the nature of Berne's games because these are often practised, and to the third degree, between people who operate in and around the more creative playgrounds of modern business life. Games are played by people who have an intention to win, even if it means destroying in the process, but who achieve this within the normal boundaries of social intercourse.

Organizations have to provide the human bridges. The overly controlling, Parent-dominated manager cannot easily manage the Childlike creative prodigy. There are too few points of contact, far too many pits of potential misunderstanding. Put two such people together in an organization, and they will destroy each other. A well publicized example of a whole company being bounced about by such forces was the Apple computer company in the early eighties.

Invented in 1976 by 'two scruffy kids, college dropouts, true sons of Silicon Valley', as they are always called, Apple grew from a rudimentary computer manufacturer, based in Steve Jobs' father's garage, to a billion-dollar corporation employing 5000 people, within a period of eight years. Its engineering pioneer was Steve Wozniack, who, to all intents and purposes, played little part in the organization after a plane crash in early 1981 put him into hospital and gave him temporary amnesia.

In 1983 Apple, in common with a number of other high-profile, hi-tech Californian, companies hired a consumer heavyweight for the top management position. In Apple's case it was to be John Sculley, recruited at great expense from Pepsi. As Frank Rose put it in *West of Eden*: 'Sculley's consumer marketing skills didn't matter to Apple as much as his Wharton M.B.A. and his solid corporate background. He was like one of those heavy oil paintings on the walls (of Wall Street brokerage houses). He could make the Street feel safe.'[9]

The hiring of Sculley shows that the problems facing innovative companies are the same as those which face innovative people, departments, or business units in organizations. The questions of confidence, of safety, and of predictability always light up where the commercial issues become sufficiently prominent to ignite them. This can happen because the innovators increase their relative stature in the business world. Their eccentricity ceases to be gnome-like. They become ogre-sized. Also, it happens because the commercial environment seeks to impose a more rigorous control. Periodically the business cycle swings from a preference for risk to one concerned for cost containment. In 1983 the change in the mood of the country was very much away from risk. Jobs took on aspects of an ogre.

Rose's research shows that initially Sculley and Jobs got on very well, indeed intimately well, together for a time, but that when it came to the crunch, the fight for position which took place was almost identical to that in the prologue. Jobs did not believe that Sculley had the charisma or the feel for leadership that would be necessary to take Apple through one of its many business crises. He said so. He said so to quite a few people. Sculley's response was to hand the decision back to the senior people in Apple, who, naturally enough, went for security rather than adventure. So Jobs was driven into a non-job, and subsequently left. The separation was contentious, and, to some extent, litigious. Advisors were drawn into the argument. Passions were roused. Regrets were manifest, but the deed was done. The form and process is so much like a divorce.

Comments about Steve Jobs as a person showed the familiar characteristics of the unorganizable genius. Frank Rose wrote:

> There was a great deal of the child in Steve – the wondering child, the impatient child, the self-indulgent child, the feral child – and to reap the benefits of one, it was necessary to put up with all the others. Right now, [1984] it was the self-indulgent child that was showing itself, which meant that life would be very difficult for everyone around him.[10]

And elsewhere he added: 'They [senior management] summarized the situation briskly: If Jobs threw Sculley out, it would look like the inmates had taken over the system; if Sculley threw Jobs out, it would look like he'd extinguished the eternal flame.'[11]

Such crises are always settled dramatically. The immature behaviour perceived of the creative individual repeats itself everywhere these matters are discussed. The 'Parent' in the organization always feels fully justified in disciplining the Child, even where he is a major shareholder or he is the most famous and productive research scientist in the world.

The people who are seen as the better front-line managers of the creative process, people like Stevenson and Gassée and Michael Grade, are people who are not threatened by creativity because they are themselves creative. They enjoy it around them, and they benefit from it without feeling the pangs of envy, insecurity, inferiority and anger suffered by the less creative. They are the Adults with more than a touch of Child themselves.

Conclusion

For all the success that managers of creative people might achieve through understanding better the essence of the potential relationship between the more creative subordinate and the less creative boss, without a fiercely supportive chief executive very little improvement in innovative output can be sustained. The organization's culture must reward and encourage behaviour which challenges it, which burns with the desire for change. There must be sponsors who provide microclimates that nurture and nourish creative beginnings. Executives and professionals need to be trained in how to improve their own creative potential: the more they feel that their potential is being enhanced, the less threatened they will be by the assertiveness of gifted subordinates.

The bigger organization must find ways of ordering an informal network of champions, sponsors and innovators, ensuring that people of the appropriate profile of talent and interest are both selected and warranted. The whole organization needs to pulse with the expectation of change, the challenge of the status quo, and the determination to succeed at pace. This is the creative culture, where failures are celebrated because from failure everyone learns.

Organizations do not have to be small to be innovative. In fact, if the more innovative units are quarantined, the chances of there being a successful transfer of their innovative output to mainstream business is small. The steeper the cultural gradient between units, the stiffer the resistance to creative transfer. The vital ingredient is to recognize and manage the mixture, and to accept that the greater the size, the more homogenous the product, and the more mature the market, the greater are the number of mechanisms needed to ensure that creativity makes its headway, and the greater the effort everywhere required to overcome intrinsic and inevitable organizational inertia.

The organization must therefore structure itself in a way that enables the small, flexible teams of innovators, including their one or two Plants or Resource Investigators, led by their creative 'but not *so* creative' mentor-managers, to act through a level of sponsors, or manager-innovators, who can interpret the needs of the organization as well as they can the opportunities presented by the innovators. It is often the latter connective tissue which goes missing, and loses us all so much of what we need.

It becomes more and more clear that adaptive innovation depends not so much upon the individual genius, or prodigy, or even mildly creative individual within the organization, but on the organization itself. Creativity is neither good nor bad, but in our monstrously changing world, adaption is innovation is survival, and our creativity has to be put to use if our innovation is to give us a competitive advantage.

Clearly the day of the large homogenous organization has gone. It cannot move with sufficient speed to adapt. Rosabeth Moss Kanter concluded her book *When Giants Learn to Dance* with a chapter called 'Beyond the Cowboy and the Corprocrat: A Call to Action,' in which she writes:

> For corporations to get in shape for Olympic Competition then, they must evolve flatter, more focused organizations, stressing synergies; entrepreneurial enclaves pushing newstream businesses for the future; and strategic alliances or stakeholder partnerships stretching capacity by combining the strength of several organizations. Together these strategies constitute the strategic, business action agenda.[12]

But, as she herself points out, there is a palpable tension still between people in the 'newstream' and the 'mainstream' where they are in the same organization.

> In many ways, the existence of newstreams flowing alongside the mainstream business loosens traditional hierarchical authority, undermines respect for bureaucracy, weakens corporate identification in favour of project identification, and teaches people they can rely on themselves, thereby reducing their dependency on the corporation to give them a career.[13]

This is a division between the Child and the Parent. Eric Berne would predict much noise, and frequent games-playing, in those places where the innovators and the perpetuators (for want of a better word) are kept apart in discrete sub-sets of the same organization.

The solution appears to be to have the organization divide itself into autonomous sub-units, each contracted to provide services preferentially to the others, but each organized in a way which maximizes the relevance of their own individual purpose, structure and culture to their own members. Each of the organizational units can be effectively focused, but can also adapt its own time-scale to its reward system and its function. Each can make its own alliances. Binding these units would be a complex exercise in cross-ownership and cross-contracting. Intra-organizational career ladders can disappear altogether from such a scene, but they are casualties of most competitive environments. Corporations seeking to provide effective general management from amongst their own ranks must make a special, deliberate effort to achieve this. Otherwise, it will not happen.

The challenge is to make it work. The individual manager and professional are threatened now in ways which have not been the experience of recent generations. The comfort of a career is now an illusion. In the West, we cannot compete with the advantages of organizational commitment inherent in the Japanese culture. We cannot any longer rely solely on brilliant, arcane, solo individuals. What we need is to understand and reach for the flexible ground between the two. But time is running out.

Notes

1 George Orwell, *Selected Writings* (Heinemann Educational, London, 1958), pp. 315–16.
2 Peter Medawar, *The Threat and The Glory: Reflections on Science and Scientists* (Oxford University Press, Oxford, 1990), p. 86.
3 Winston Fletcher, *Creative People: How to Manage Them and Maximize Their Creativity* (Hutchinson Business Books, London, 1988), p. 134.
4 Ibid., p. 32.
5 See note 4 above.
6 R. M. Belbin, *Management Teams: Why They Succeed or Fail* (Heinemann, London 1981).
7 Joseph A. Raelin, *The Clash of Cultures: Managers and Professionals* (Harvard Business School Press, Boston, 1985).
8 Eric Berne, *Games People Play: Psychology of Human Relationships* (Grove Press, New York, 1964).
9 Frank Rose, *West of Eden* (Century Hutchinson, London, 1989), p. 82.
10 Ibid., p. 165.
11 Ibid., p. 277.
12 Rosabeth Moss Kanter, *When Giants Learn to Dance* (Simon & Schuster, London, 1989), p. 344.
13 Ibid., p. xx.

Corporate Culture and
Creative Potential

James: I don't think it's going to work.
Mark: Well, why don't we try the other option?
James: No I wouldn't do that. It smacks too much of
desperation to try things on the off-chance.

Creativity is a complex subject. Innovation is a difficult objective. In common with many seemingly insurmountable problems, the temptation is to give up, and look elsewhere for more tractable propositions. Surveys of UK and US industrialists have consistently shown over the past few years that when it comes to the tough decisions about innovation, this is what they do. It has been so much quicker and simpler to invest money in the 1980s than to earn it. For some countries, all of the creative endeavour has focused on novel financial instruments, new ways of making money turn over. This bubble has now burst, and international banking, or those parts of it that survive, will have to turn elsewhere to find the next target for exploitation, probably a mixture of the ex-Communist states and Green issues.

Meanwhile, competitive positions are becoming well-established, and the consequences are being well documented as well as frequently publicized. A few examples of the press commentary over the past two years show that there is little disagreement as to the focus of concern.

In 1975, 65% of new patents in America were for the inventions of Americans, 9% were for the work of Japanese inventors, 8.5% Germans and 7.5% British and French inventors combined. In the following decades, America's share fell by ten percentage points, to less than 55%. West Germany's share rose a bit, Britain's dropped a bit, and the French stayed much the same. Japan's inventors now own more new patents in America than those from Britain, Germany and France.

The Economist, 20 May 1989

Reasons offered for this shift include that it is a consequence of increased prosperity, and that there is a natural and inevitable change in the national priorities which drive innovation. The number of scientists and engineers per 10,000 people had risen steadily in Japan since the early 1960s. In America this proportion peaked in 1969. By 1986, Japan had a higher proportion of its population engaged in R & D than did the US.

A CBI conference on 14 September 1989 boasted a good attendance and some impressive speakers, but its message was bleakly put by Mary Fagan reporting in *The Independent*:

A survey of the heads of research in 92 private and 73 public organizations shows that Britain is seen as the worst of all major countries at taking innovation seriously and much worse than Europe, the Far East and North America at producing well-trained and motivated staff. In spite of the British belief that they were great innovators, three-quarters of those questioned said the education system failed miserably to encourage innovative thinking. What there was got nowhere in the end, because there was hardly any long-term financing in the UK geared to exploiting new technological ideas.

Gross research and development expenditure in the UK, including civil and military R & D, has remained about the same as a percentage of Gross Domestic Product from 1976–1987 (writes the Organization for Economic Cooperation and Development), although it rose in the middle of these years to the same level as that of France (which has risen) but well below Germany and Japan (2.3 per cent compared to 2.9 per cent).

The Annual Review of Government-funded R & D for 1990 also supports this trend. It reported that in the late 1980s British industry was patenting fewer inventions than the late 1960s, while Japan increased its patented innovations more than eleven-fold. Government funding for civil R & D is in decline, in absolute terms and as a proportion of national wealth.

Research and Development is ready to follow behind manufacturing in migrating to other countries who do it better. *The New York Times* ran an article on 27 February 1989 under the headline: 'Exporting R & D operations could hurt US Economy'. Its author, Louis Uchitelle, began:

> There is no mistaking the trend: US corporations increasingly are doing their research outside the United States . . . In the past two years, for example, IBM, Eastman Kodak, W. R. Grace, Merck & Co and Upjohn Co have opened research laboratories in Japan. Amoco Oil Co. pays scientists at the University of Eindhoven in the Netherlands to seek breakthrough technology for oil refining. Air Products and Chemicals Inc. will spend $14 million this year on research conducted overseas – 20% of its research budget. Five years ago, not a cent went abroad.

The trend for large mature companies to look towards a global market place, spurred on by the management gurus of the 1990s, will clearly encourage the migration of the resources, and opportunities to create, to places where these companies ajudge that the reward will be the greatest. This is in addition to the merging of the R & D interests of two or more organizations. This provides yet more evidence of the move towards packaging and the confining of creativity to specific loci of organization functioning, and points to a serious decline both of innovation itself, and of concern for the decline of research and development everywhere in the UK and USA.

The consequences are clearly drawn by Sheridan Tatsuno in his book *Created in Japan*:

> Despite these many challenges, we are likely to see Japan becoming more creative in the 1990s . . . Frustrated with cultural barriers and slow progress in the Japanese market, many Western companies will seek quick profits elsewhere . . . Meanwhile Japan will be strengthening its scientific infrastructure. Japanese corporations will be forced to modify their management policies to accommodate the growing numbers of working women, independent-minded young people, aging managers, and returnees from abroad.
>
> New technologies will come pouring out of the new corporate laboratories and software development centres scattered throughout Japan . . . Japanese companies have already passed us by in opto-electronics, high-definition television, memory chips, robotics, factory

automation, and computerised language translation. They are now making a bid for superiority in supercomputers, nano-mechanism technology, medical electronics, marine development, optical communication, and automotive electronics. 'Created in Japan' may soon replace 'Made in Japan', as a symbol of industrial intelligence.[1]

Creating the Creative Culture

Changing the creativity of a company or a country implies severely changing its culture. What people do without thinking, the direction they would choose to go in the absence of being told, this is the culture that they respond to. Increasing the emphasis on creativity must mean changing the culture to one which more substantially supports the behaviour that creates.

Geert Hofstede defined culture as the collective programming of mind that enables one group of people to be distinguished from another. Edgar Schein defined it as the pattern of basic assumptions that a given group has invented, discovered, or developed in learning to cope with its problems of external adaption and internal integration. Culture differs between organizations in respect of the values, models and expectations that employees have, supported by their recognition of heroes, by rituals, by practices and by ceremonies. Corporate culture is modifiable and its modification is a perfectly legitimate management process. 3M have a very well-defined culture, the nature of which would appear to fall comfortably in line with the corporate purpose. It needs to be shaken up now and then to keep it animated, and it clearly suffers from the relaxations and the tensions of business cycles. But, nevertheless, the 3M culture seems a successful outcome of much consistent strategic thinking.

Johnson & Johnson is an old-established pharmaceutical company that adheres strongly to the notion of autonomous production units combined and coordinated by a single very strong and repeatedly reinforced culture. Comparing the J & J 'Credo' as published in 1948 and as reissued in 1988, there is very little difference. In both are the statements: 'We must experiment with new ideas' and 'Mistakes are paid for'. Each leads with the same declaration: 'We believe that our first responsibility is to the doctors, nurses, and patients, to mothers and all those who use our products . . . Everything we do must be of high quality.'

Such a culture as one that sustains such continuity over forty years would be very hard to change, but, since the Credo also contains the time-honoured phrase: 'Each person must be considered as an individual', it would not be one that many creative people would want to seek to change. People who join J & J stay for many years. Many stay for a lifetime. Leaving the company after a few years is seen as a form of desertion. Such a culture supports creativity in as much as it provides security of tenure. But it will also smother, and the richer, more assertively individualistic creative people will often leave before they feel compromised.

Some Models of Culture

There have been many attempts to depict corporate culture. Few of them have been very helpful in contrasting one culture with another, because the descriptive concepts used have tended to define only the unique characteristics of one organization rather than its relative position.

While it is possible to look at a company like 3M, or Johnson & Johnson, and say that it must be a creative organization both because it performs in terms of new products, and because it says so loudly, this does not help to define how much potential for creativity exists, or should exist, in Company X.

Organization culture has been described in terms of predominant structural patterns. Charles Handy caught up a typology in his book *The Gods of Management*.[2] He wrote of the 'Club' culture, which he named after the god Zeus, the 'Role' after Apollo, the 'Task' after Athena, and the 'Existential' after Dionysus. The club culture is a spider's-web, run by the spider through the formal and informal network. There is one boss, and everyone knows who he is. Entrepreneurs favour clubs, feel good about being Zeus in their own heaven. They give up their power very reluctantly. Power motivation is very evident in such organizations, and power is often also used as a definition of the primary cultural value.

The role culture of Apollo is the rational bureaucracy. This is the stable state organization, where each member knows his current place, and his future place. Order, dependency and tradition appear prominently in such an organization. It is a thing of beauty, but unfortunately in these turbulent times, no longer a joy for ever.

The task culture is about achievement. It is the network. The goddess, Athena, is she of youth and energy and creative intent. This organization is loosely knit, but knows its way.

The existential is not an organization at all, so much as a collection of individuals, sharing resources. Dionysus was the god of wine. Visually, the existential is presented as a star cluster, like the partners in The Firm. They do their own thing in their own way, surrounded by paid administrative angels, and potential partners straining to join in the wine and the song.

David McClelland[3] modelled motivation in three parts. Some use his model to define organization cultures in terms of power, achievement and affiliation. The problem of these models is that they tend to oversimplify. Of the Handy models, clearly only Apollo could be accused of being non-creative. The creativity of a Zeus culture depends on the qualities of the resident chief. The other two cultures do not lead us automatically to assume that they are more or less good for corporate creativity. One is more collective, the other more individualistic.

Certainly the theory does not help to identify the sure route to a more creative culture in the organization searching for such an end.

Terence Deal and Allen Kennedy[4] explored the components of corporate culture through its values, heroes, rituals, ceremonies and communication networks. In examining companies in America, they concluded that there were two primary factors which determined corporate culture: the level of risk that was entailed in an organization's activities, and the speed at which it could get feedback on how successful its strategies had been in the market place. From these influences, they also established four types of culture, which they called:

The tough-guy, macho culture
The work-hard, play-hard culture
The bet-your-company culture
The process culture

The first is of the individualistic, masculine, entrepreneurial competitive world exemplified by advertising and contracting organizations. It has similarities to Zeus. The second comes into play where risk is low and feedback fast. The heroes are the workers and it is addictively short term. No creativity here. The third is high-risk, slow feedback. It has to take the long-term view, to back its research, support development, but to recognize, like most of the big pharmaceuticals, that patience and a level head are required when gambling the company's future on a may-be product. The process culture comes from low feedback, low risk. It is the same as Apollo. Clearly any company can be a mix of all four, hopefully matching each organizational unit culture with its specific environmental circumstances.

The essence of a good model is that it is usable without being simplistic. It is never truly representative, but it does give sufficient variety to be realistic, and it must offer both an effective diagnosis and a range of remedial entry points. The models of Handy and others do not yield enough fruit to enable the organization to securely plot a path from the non-creative to one inducing more creativity. They are too simple to be usable. One of the most elaborate yet practical models so far devised also owes its origin to Geert Hofstede.

The Hofstede Model

Having done earlier work in international culture (see chapter 9), and refined the description of national differences under five dimensions, Hofstede and his team looked into company culture, using a mixture of qualitative and quantitative approaches. The team examined twenty organizational units of a very wide variety in Holland and Denmark. Their investigation took several years, and was undertaken in the style that a social anthropologist would employ in approaching an unknown tribe – curious, exploratory, but severely non-judgemental. From this work emerged six further dimensions[5]

1 Motivation	Process-oriented (Activities)	– Results-oriented (Outputs)
2 Relationship	Job-oriented (job)	– Employee-oriented (person)
3 Identity	Parochial (Corporate)	– Professional
4 Communication	Open	– Closed
5 Control	Tight	– Loose
6 Conduct	Normative (Conventional)	– Pragmatic

Each of these cultural dimensions would predict to some degree the creativity inherent in the organization.

The tables on the following pages show real data from two different units of the same organization, which bears a familiar household name. RND is a research and development facility, PDQ is the production plant. The processes and techniques which have been brought together to provide this data are proprietary and known as DOCSA (Diagnosis of Organizational Culture for Strategic Application).[6]

As part of DOCSA, a 150-item questionnaire is issued to the employees of an organization unit. The questions are about culture and work values. The results are analysed in three groups: management, professionals and staff. The definitions of these groups are a combination of educational and organizational. The division is made on the assumption (often shown) that the three groups do have quite different perceptions of the company and of the nature of their commitment to it. The dimension scores for each level are compared to data-base averages.

The dimensions as listed are not in order of their importance to creativity in organizations. Some of the names of the Dimensions have been changed from the Holstede originals.

Motivation: Activities vs. Outputs

For the Motivation dimension, the organization which was very activities-oriented would have such characteristics as these:

> Avoids risks, formal, restrictive, concerned for rules, values modesty, data-based and analytical, conflict-concealing, reliable, rooted in past procedures, accepting of authority, especially hierarchical.

Such a culture would be perfectly appropriate in most parts of a successful large mature retailing establishment, where performance is determined by highly organized buying and selling, and where a particular style has been evolved to give that retailer a distinctive image and competitive advantage. This is the image of IBM that Apple portrayed in 1982: traditional, old, conformist, grey-suited and dull, in contrast to Apple which was young, responsive, exciting and creative. Such a culture would also be appropriate to a highly sensitive chemical manufacturing operation, or some departments of State, where the rules are vitally important to sustain personal and public safety.

The highly outputs-oriented organization would be more likely to be:

Pioneering, direct, challenging, informal, flexible, tolerant of mistakes and deviance, intuitive, valuing accomplishment, conflict-confronting.

Clearly there are more opportunities in such a culture for the creative individual to make a mark, more especially in the Anglo-Saxon or Nordic type of environment, or others where individualism predominates nationally.

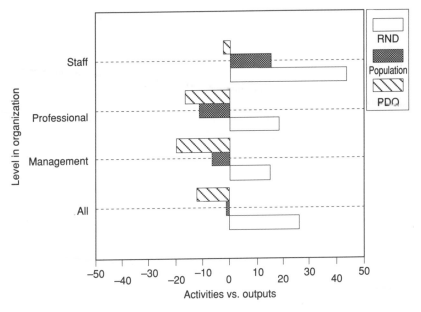

Figure 12.1   Activities vs. Output.

The DOCSA data shows RND to have a distinct outputs orientation. This culture encourages effort, energy and the single-minded pursuit of difficult goals. It contrasts markedly with its manufacturing cousin, where the emphasis is on adherence to clearly established norms and procedures. Efficiency is the order of the day.

Neither culture is right nor wrong, but each is uniquely adapted to its function. RND's professionals and managers display strong concern for results, a concern that is not only shared but surpassed by that of the other staff. Culture can be used by creative organizations to yield a competitive edge, but at the cost of a smooth, predictable, error-free performance.

Identity: Corporate vs. Professional

The Corporate versus Professional dimension is probably the second most important distinguishing cultural dimension between the creative and the non-creative organization. Identity controls the psychological alignment on the part of the employee with his employer. A Corporate culture is tribal, it is the family, the coherent, close-knit group focus, where people derive significant aspects of their personal identity from their membership. It is the culture that creates the specific response to the question, 'What do you do?' with, for example, 'I'm an IBM-er' or 'I'm a civil servant' or 'I'm with Coca-Cola' rather than 'I'm a salesman' or 'I'm a pharmacist' or 'I'm working in market research'.

Corporate organizations concern themselves with uniformity just as activities-oriented companies do, and could well be high on that dimension, but for different reasons. When hiring, such organizations consider many aspects of a person's background which are to do with whether he is 'one of us'; they encourage a merging at the boundaries of work and non-work. Spouses are expected to conform as well as employees. Rivalry between departments is not seen as dysfunctional. Newcomers are tyros, irrespective of their other qualities. They have to go through the rituals, and pass the test of entry before they are given their rights of office. Holstede's original name, Parochial, implies that such organizations are founded and grown in one location. The new appellation, Corporate, is perhaps more appropriate to today's modern world, where an insistence on one corporate culture is frequently cited as a strategic objective.

Corporate is very much the nature of the company that dominates one locality. Steel-works and mining companies are Corporate. Breweries used to be, and local authorities. Kodak, in Harrow, Middlesex, for three generations, became so before growth in the UK required the expansion to Hemel Hempstead and beyond. These organizations tend to be stable and complex. They are very frustrating to the creative, impatient professional, who often finds them patronizing and inhibiting. On the other hand, when such an organization is seen as highly successful, especially offering work facilities that are unsurpassed elsewhere, the creative professional can find a good home. IBM and Hewlett-Packard are Corporate companies which have managed this trade-off in the past with consummate skill. Yet close examination of the productivity of such companies in research often reveals a contribution per professional below that of smaller, more mobile groups, especially when the reputations and status of the individuals are taken into account. IBM are suffering now from being beaten to the market by many much smaller fry.

The organization at the extreme of the Professional end of the scale exhibits a much stronger identity with the profession of the leading groups. It is more informal, since there are fewer rules about the kind of person employed, as against his qualifications to perform. The climate is more individualistic, more forward-looking, but less internally competitive, less political. Professionals need to share if they are to reap the benefits of the organization, therefore they meet each other more often, in pursuit of information as well as projects, and are much more aware of competitive forces. It usually takes very little time for a newcomer to be accepted. This is because there are few rituals attached to such a relatively unimportant act. Also judgements of personal worth are made on relatively narrow bands, such as of technical competence alone.

RND is Professional at all levels, with managers and professionals almost entirely so. They are all more interested in the substance of what they do than where they do it. They all participate in a knowledge workers' culture. It is the strength and consistency of the RND profile that sets it apart from its production counterpart. Expertise is the only currency that carries any real interest.

A generally non-creative organization could have units within it which would be more distinctively Professional while their prevailing culture was highly Corporate. However, the overriding need of such an organization is to sustain its policies and support a performance which has the vital comfort of predictability. So the Professionally oriented unit in such a company would need to have some strong insulation.

The Corporate organization will demand a commitment from its

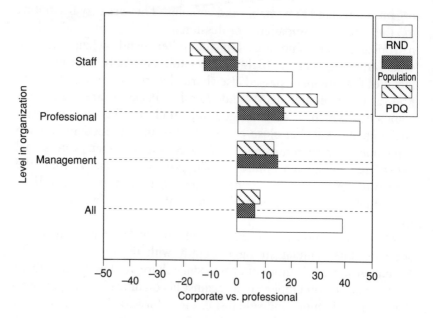

Figure 12.2   Corporate vs. Professional

membership that would exclude the maverick professional from entry. It will offer a career structure in exchange for this commitment to stay with it. Length of service will be honoured and rewarded. Status will be respected. This is an organization built to extract the most out of its market and economic strength and position.

Relationship: Job Orientation vs. Person Orientation

Each of the other dimensions can reflect differences in the creative potential of the organization in ways which depend very much upon its circumstances. The dimension which contrasts Job orientation with Person orientation is not dissimilar as a scale to Blake and Mouton's concept of task-versus-people orientation, as it describes management style. It defines how the company and the individual see their relationship one with the other. The task-driven manager, the autocrat, assumes that the company lives because of his performance.

In a very people-driven organization, such a person would be most unhappy. It is possible to be a 9 : 9 management style, but it is difficult to imagine a 9 : 9 organization, unless it has neither external nor internal competition. Task orientation by its nature tends to be drawn into the short term rather than the long term. Where this works against the underlying need of the creative process, then it could well inhibit creativity. On the other hand, deadlines, under the right circumstances, can be a powerful driver to creative output, as in newspaper journalism and advertising art and copywriting.

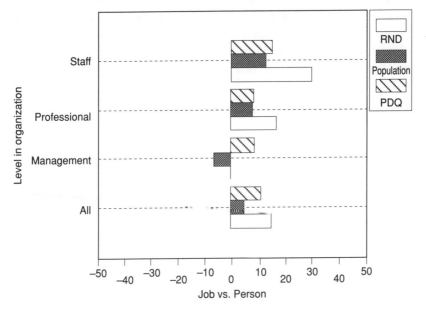

Figure 12.3   Job vs. Person

In table 12.3, both RND and PDQ display slight person orientation. This is more pronounced in RND, particularly at the staff level. Person oriented cultures tend to value training as a reward or incentive. In their Job oriented counterparts, training is usually seen as a remedial exigency. The Person culture is more sensitive and adaptable to the individual needs and capacities of its members. There is an emphasis on the care and nurturing of individual talent, creative or otherwise. Decision-making is groupy and consultative. Control is exercised by ensuring that the environment is conducive to this. None the less it says more about the style of the organization than it does about the quantity and quality of its creative outputs.

The drive to create is already in creative people. Their need to be carefully and tenderly considered as people by the organization is perhaps less important to them. For most of their day-to-day work, it is the strong concern for performance and for output that animates their intrinsic motivation. A consistently true need of all creative people is for peer support, recognition and acceptance. The broader organizational role is secondary to them. Provided it does not actively work against a Person orientation, this dimension should need relatively little attention. However, an excessive concentration on financial rewards, time-limited contracts, or systems of payment that discriminate against the creative individual can all add up to problems by emphasizing employee orientation in a very negative sense.

Communication: Open vs. Closed

The climate of communication can be characterized as Open or Closed. The position on this scale of a company culture can have a considerable impact on creativity. Its full impact depends on the other circumstances prevailing. In most commercial research establishments there has to be a degree of secrecy, simply because of the risk of industrial espionage. However, if research scientists are to test their competence and their contemporaneity, they must expose their thinking to the world of their peers. The scientific world is global. Thus, if the best scientists are to be retained in the commercial world, there is a need to have an open culture.

Government laboratories tend to attract and retain some of the more gifted, but at the same time more socially poorly equipped, professionals. The more typically social, expressive individual often finds these secret, closed establishments to contain and care for some exceedingly strange folk.

In brief, the most Open corporate culture would be:

easy to join from the outside, and to learn about once inside, accepting of eccentricity, and informal in interpersonal interaction.

Conversely, the most Closed corporate culture would be:

difficult to join, only particular kinds of people being accepted into membership, intolerant of dissension, cool and formal and inward-looking.

Organizations of all kinds tend to move from Open to Closed as they mature. In research establishments this maturation process can lead to arteriosclerosis. The ruling group, perhaps increasingly insecure in the belief it has in its scientific competence, creates bureaucracies, walls, and traditions which make their early permeability more and more solidly concrete.

Both RND and PDQ display a general tendency towards the Closed. In places it is even exaggerated, professionals and managers succumbing to the lure of the relative anonymity and camouflage that Closedness bestows. For some research establishments, keeping a low profile can represent an adaptive advantage.

Creative output cannot emerge from a Closed culture. In such an environment, creativity will have a severely limited and restricted life.

Control: Tight vs. Loose

The dimension of Control contrasts Tight and Loose. This dimension probably represents the least well understood aspect of creative corporate culture. The Tight organization is:

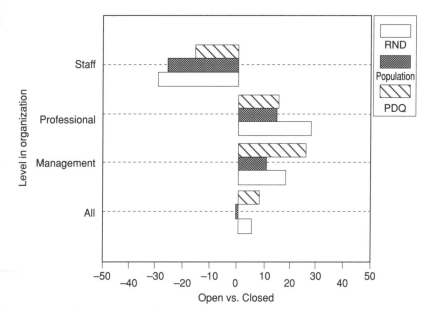

Figure 12.4   Open vs. Closed

Cost conscious; insists on punctuality; has detailed rules, clearly recognized and implemented; is serious about itself; is careful about dealings between people, mediating conflict rather than confronting it, and it values precision and expertise.

The Loose organization, in contrast, is:

relaxed about most things including costs, time, deadlines and rules; everyone does his own thing; dress is informal; people joke about the organization, which is willing and able to have people confront it whenever they choose.

The common error is to assume that the Loose organization is the more creatively productive under all conditions. This again is based on the public images of the design studios, the advertising agency and media operations. The assumption of the creative person as a bohemian, who acknowledges no rules, and who needs total freedom to create, is not one which holds up under close inspection.

The Tight organization is found in many Japanese and German research and development institutions, which are as productive of

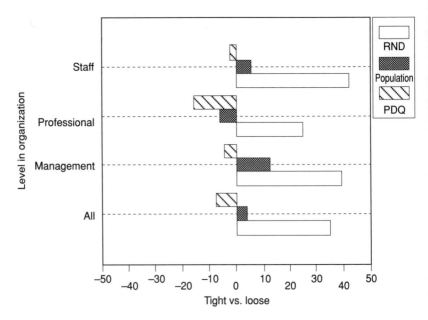

Figure 12.5 Tight vs. Loose

novelty as any. It is found in some advertising agencies. It is found in most creative scientific and engineering subcontractors. Looseness can be a creative liability.

The contrast between the Tight and the Loose in this company is certainly a striking feature of its corporate culture. Many battles are fought between the Tight headquarters unit and the Loose RND. To the HQ, RND as a unit verges on the anarchic and irresponsible. To RND, HQ appears boorish and petty.

Conduct: Conventional vs. Pragmatic

The way in which employees conduct themselves especially in relations with the outside world, is a vital dimension in articulating corporate culture. Hofstede gave the terms Normative and Pragmatic to this aspect of culture. Here the style, maturity, technology and positioning of the organization can have a considerable impact on what is likely to be most creatively productive.

The Normative or Conventional organization exports its values. It preserves its rules independently of the market needs and customer pressures. It tends towards hierarchy and autocracy, simply because the rules are unshakeable. It has high ethical standards and considers that these should prevail irrespective of the results.

In contrast, the Pragmatic organization takes on the coloration of its customers. Its pragmatism is all about results – results, moreover, which are expressed wholly in the terms of its market place. It is constantly aware of competition, will cut corners whenever this will give it the edge, and sees itself above all as genuinely caring for the consumer of its products and services. It customizes.

The question that should be asked of each of these is, 'Would you short-cut where it comes to personal safety?' Most chemist's-shop customers, who are to accept a clinical prescription to alleviate an unpleasant symptom, would probably prefer the research that led up to the formulation of this product to have been undertaken within a Conventional organization. This is probably one reason why market shares of blue chip companies are not quickly eroded by price-cutting, low-overhead competitors. In some countries, Conventional research organizations, or Conventional creative organizations, are more the rule than the exception. The creativity which is delivered

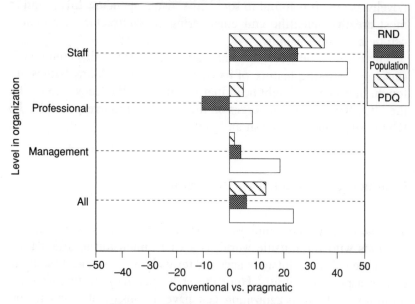

Figure 12.6   Conventional vs. Pragmatic

may not be so wild, or as much of a breakthrough as the Pragmatic organization might produce, but it has the value that it can be trusted to work.

The organization of which RND and PDQ are a part is in the white goods business. Keeping close to the customer is a core concern, the more so for RND. The appreciation of customers' needs drives many aspects of the product development process. Great energies are committed to finding new ways to satisfy their aesthetic and functional needs. This is creativity at the Corporate edge, characterized by a consistent desire to modify, adapt and improve; ahead of the competition.

The Mix of Cultures

Most organizations are differentiated. They have sub-units which have specialized functions. These functions are made more, or less, effective depending upon the culture they have created, or have had put upon them. If the prevailing culture of a large organization is heavily Conventional, then its market should be a strong oligarchy where it can command secure and substantial market loyalty. Alternatively it should be a regulatory body. In today's world, it would otherwise not last long. Furthermore, such a prevailing culture across the whole organization would intimidate the experimentalists, even where they need to be encouraged to break out of the mould. The example of the Ford Sierra, discussed in chapter 8, was an illustration of this.

There are subordinate units of the organization where, if it is to make the best of its human resources, the culture needs to vary from whatever the prevailing superordinate culture-profile might be. This provokes three questions: how can culture be measured; how can it be changed; and how can the interfaces between opposing cultures be managed successfully?

Measuring culture is a matter of assessing the relative occurrence of practices and beliefs within the population along the dimensions used. It can be done through using questionnaires, but there is a need for a comparison database if sense is to be made of the results. In measuring culture, it is not only important not to judge the results too soon. Where it comes to values, it is better not to judge at all. When asked, people will only offer their true prevailing views if they believe that these will be received with genuine interest. There are no good or bad cultures, only more or less appropriate ones. Appropriateness is determined by where and how the organization sees itself going: first it must determine its purpose and direction, and only then can it clarify the effective style of its getting there.

There needs to be a decision, or a consensus, on both these issues, depending upon the current condition of the organization, before the appropriate culture can be designated. This process needs to take place not only for the organization as a whole, but also for each of its major subordinate units. The case studies that have been used to illustrate cultural variations are taken from real examples, but they are composites and do not represent any existing or past organization.

Making Corporate Culture More Creative

Changing organizational culture is always a difficult process. Before any attempts at change are made, it is important to decide on the following:

- The urgency of the need to change.

- The extent to which the need to change is apparent, in its direction and urgency, to all concerned.
- The amount of change that is required.
- The dimension(s) along which change is required as a priority.
- The distance from the existing value of that dimension the change needs to reach.

The detailed mechanisms for change are the subject of other texts not this, but, among the particular concerns in reaching for a more creative culture, the following are the most important:

1 Define the targets sought within the dimension of Motivation and Identity. What behaviours are to be changed, by how much, and to what end? Culture-change is extremely haphazard without concrete measures of the starting and target characteristics.

In creativogenic units of an organization, there would be a clear need for an Outputs oriented culture. Motives must be driven by results, not by activities. These are some of the features that should be sought:

- people talking always about the future;
- ad hoc, unplanned meetings;
- characteristically challenging leadership;
- pioneers and achievers being celebrated;
- no status symbols;
- chances taken, and mistakes made, provide opportunities for learning not for punishment.

The signs that would preferable not to see:

- everyone has to be a team player;
- people expected to live the values of the company;
- belief expressed that 'our strength is in our reputation';
- celebration of long-service;
- worship of the founder, unless he is still the creative genius of the company;
- the trappings of office.

2 Clarify the reward systems, financial and non-financial, and calibrate where they reinforce the existing practices. What changes can be made? Creative people respond to equity but not to incentives. They are not motivated by focusing their attention

on the extrinsic reward but they very quickly rebel where they believe that their rewards do not match their worth.

3 Examine the prevailing behaviour of senior staff, the role models, the heroes, the people of the past and present who are seen as the ones who were successful. What are their characteristics? Are there new or potential heroes which more closely represent the ideas and values of the new culture? How can they be made to take the place of the old?

4 Explore the rituals, the routine acceptances of behaviour that mark important events. Which events have the greatest symbolism? How can these be changed? The creativogenic culture needs to be open. This means that: keeping everyone in the picture is more important than keeping confidences; that there should be few profit centres, not many; that the rewards should go to generalists rather than specialists, and that wild parties and open doors are more in evidence than not.

James MacGregor Burns[7] distinguished between transformational leaders and transactional leaders. The transformational leader is the one who will redefine organizational objectives, who will rebuild according to new challenges, who will have people follow him into the unknown. Some managers cannot handle things staying the same. When there is a genuine need for stability, such people can be dangerous. They will change that which is better left alone. Steve Jobs is transformational, so is John Sculley.

More prevalent are the transactional leaders, who set priorities, then allocate and manage resources efficiently and effectively according to the existing order. Transactional leaders tend to be famous only within their own organization. In the West, they are getting rarer by the week. For the time being, in Eastern Europe, they have nearly disappeared. Any culture change needs transformational leaders.

William Bridges deals very sensitively with the issues of organizational culture change in *Surviving Corporate Transition*. Among his recommendations are:

• Recognize the stress of transition. It is not possible to go from one stable culture to another without going through a passage of enormous turbulence between them.

- Give structure to that transition. Set up symbols, milestones, and points of reference, so that threatened employees feel that they are being given navigational help.
- Consider and design both interim benefits and rewards structures and the ultimate compensation. At each stage match the rewards appropriately to the required behaviour.
- Explain, communicate and train – not focused, skill-based training, but training in what will be, training that helps orientation.
- Give people the time and help to reframe, to rework their priorities, re-establish their own needs; identify how these can be successfully shaped within a potentially threatening new environment.
- Find a vision of the future, animate it, orchestrate it, and rehearse and present it, over and over again.
- Bring together project teams to communicate, to help in the transition. Bring people together from all parts of the organization. Ask that they take responsibility for honest communication.
- Acknowledge that most change creates loss for someone. That loss is real, and it consequently has to be managed. The management resources provided to manage it should not be stinted.

These are a number of suggestions for action. It may well be that the only way to change the culture in the time-frame required is to replace the prime influencers, the leading management group, with people of a fundamentally different persuasion.

Wherever culture change is implemented, people will become nervous and concerned for their futures. It is vitally important to put in place interim structures, to directly address the issues of change, and to substitute activity for anxiety, control for a general sense of powerlessness.

Under conditions of great change, where employed people are driven to defensiveness and concern for their personal futures, creativity can be assumed to be lost. Creativity delivers change, but its perpetrators do not always thrive on the consequences of those changes.

Tom Peters provided a 560-page recipe for changing corporate culture. He called it *Thriving on Chaos*.[8] Fast-paced innovation is a core need for the survival of corporations in the new millennium. His rules included:

- Invest in applications, in small market areas.
- Encourage pilot schemes, act small, learn to stop quickly.
- Go for team-driven development and flatter organizations.
- Forget not-invented-here, analyse the competition, use their ideas as if they were your own – called 'creative swiping' (Drucker termed this 'creative imitation').
- Listen to the market, organize informal communication networks.
- Support 'determined beyond reason' champions (each day, find an opportunity to support at least one in some way).
- Symbolize innovativeness in everyday affairs.
- Support failures, reward defiance, batter down obstacles.
- Set measurable and measured goals for innovation.
- Make innovation a way of life for everyone, make it for the long term.

Some of these rules are very individualistic (in the Hofstede sense), some very Japanese. Most of them will be resisted somewhere by people in a mature organization, especially a large one.

Conclusion

The creative organization is always facing the impossible: the dilemma of maintaining its flexibility, offering creative people easy entry, and, for the most part, equally easy exit, yet at the same time trying to hold on to them, gain their commitment, and retain their value. It has to manage the paradoxical consequences of its hard-won success.

Apple is the classic case of an organization which started out small, adventurous, creative, won a market, and became so successful that it got to be big, conservative and Conventional, requiring it to employ numbers of people who had nothing in common with its originators. GE has been given much publicity in its attempts to break out of the big company mould and tap its employees' creativity through 'work-outs'. The work-out takes a group of fifty people from all ranks in a GE site company, gives them a three-day opportunity to attack problems that they have, and then the senior managers are asked to help resolve them. The concept of the work-out is an attempt to break out of the corporate corset. It works because Jack Welch, the chief executive officer, keeps pressing for it.

Creative people are non-conformists. Most organizations cannot survive without a degree of conformity. Most creative people need access to more resources than they can reach or acquire on their own. The deal they do with big companies is often purely instrumental. If they could do without those resources, they would.

Alan Kantrow's *The Constraints of Corporate Tradition* serves as a warning on corporate culture.

> We often underestimate, and underestimate badly, how gradual things are, preferring to think about them as if they represented simply points in time. Processes of slow, adaptive change are all about us. In the corporate world, for example, decisions do not get made or implemented all of a sudden. They have a certain duration . . . Even if a CEO pounds a fist upon the table in memorable fashion and says, 'Let's do it now!' that timber-rattling order does not emerge from a vacuum. All was not dark and void a day or a week or a month before. More likely than not, parts of what become an idea or a decision churn around in solution for some length of time before getting precipitated out in the form of a hard crystal of fact.[9]

For the organization seeking to find the touchstone, the following extract from an editorial by Ted Levitt in *Harvard Business Review* (Reprinted by permission of *Harvard Business Review*. Excerpt from 'From the Editor: The Innovating Organization' by Theodore Levitt (January–February 1988). Copyright © 1987 by the President and Fellows of Harvard College; all rights reserved.) should help to clarify the issue:

> Nobody who leads or manages knowingly resists self-examination and adaption. But to keep the barriers low takes effort. It requires open advocacy and demonstrable receptiveness to innovation. The history of long-surviving and thriving enterprises is a history of innovation, mostly by their forcing changes on others and on themselves. Sometimes these occur suddenly and painfully. Mostly they happen gradually, continuously, even imperceptibly. What's key, especially in the complex organization where work is deeply regularized, is leadership that insists on constant, open self examination of everything, on demonstrable receptiveness to change, and on the budgetary encouragement of innovation. It seeks out, encourages, and supports intelligent, experienced people who have the will, energy, and courage to make changes they think make sense.

A non-creative organization could have units within it which would be more Professional than Corporate in their prevailing culture. There is a need in any complex social order to include units which are high in innovation and others which resist rapid change amongst their own people.

The greatest need for the successful modern organization is that it can accept that it needs different sub-cultures and that it spends the time and resources required to keep these cultures interfacing successfully. This requires that those at the interface accept the differences between the cultures, and respect them. To do this, they must have insight into the origins and value of these differences. Then they can make them work. There must be no value judgements, except of effectiveness. A totally and exclusively innovative culture will fall apart, just as an unconstrained creative entrepreneur will bankrupt his company. The need is for a mixture of excellence, not a single answer. This may be one vision for all, but there cannot be just one set of values.

Notes

1 Sheridan M. Tatusno, *Created in Japan: From Imitators to World-Class Innovators* (Ballinger Publishing Co., USA, 1990), p. 267.
2 Charles Handy, *Gods of Management: The Changing World of Organizations* (Souvenir Press, London, 1978).
3 David McClelland, *The Achieving Society* (Van Nostrand, New York, 1963).
4 Terence Deal and Allen Kennedy, *Corporate Cultures: The Rites and Rituals of Corporate Life* (Addison-Wesley, USA, 1982).
5 Geert Hofstede, *Cultures and Organizations: Software of the Mind* (McGraw-Hill, UK, 1991).
6 DOCSA is a proprietory culture-change programme. DOCSA Ltd., 99 Gray's Inn Road, London WC1X 8UT, 071 414 0256.
7 James Macgregor Burns, *Leadership* (Harper & Row, New York, 1978).
8 Thomas J. Peters, *Thriving on Chaos: Handbook for a Management Revolution* (Macmillan, London, 1988).
9 Alan M. Kantrow, *The Constraints of Corporate Tradition* (Harper & Row, New York, 1987), p. xx.

Epilogue

Let us learn to dream, gentlemen, and then perhaps we can find the truth.

Friedrich Kekulé

The chairman of MEI was a wise man. He thought long and hard about the real issues confronting him. He talked to his friends, consulted his colleagues, both scientific and non-scientific. His primary task was to ensure the continued prosperity of the company. He knew that this could only take place if the company were both seen as an environment which attracted top quality creative people, and in reality supported them in their innovative endeavours. As a corporation, it did not have the massive resources of the bigger groups, or the Japanese, or the newly assertive Koreans. It could only survive if it was strikingly innovative. The first conclusion that he came to was that the organization could not afford to lose either of its two luminaries, either in body or in spirit. He must find a way not only to keep both, but to keep each in a way which magnified the company's yield from their services.

He talked to each of them, in turn, off the record, away from the trappings of status and office. First, he heard from Nardelli. He learned that Dr Nardelli had never intended that Count del Ponte Vecchio should have large amounts of management authority or responsibility. It is a misfortune of fame, that in order to offer a famous man a place within an organization, a location within the hierarchy must be found which matches the public face with an appropriate corporate position.

This means a location which, in the nature of things, demands a much greater number of 'subordinates' than often makes sense for the individual. Nardelli never thought that the count would take up the greater role. It never crossed his mind that the count would choose to manage. Everyone knew he could not manage people and could not care less about such a disability. Del Ponte Vecchio had the power to do what he chose. He could set up his own group. He could give his creative powers full reign to make what he could of a free and supportive opportunity. He could leave the rest for the professionals to get on with. Unfortunately, there was this antipathy between the men. Clearly the count did not fully see the merit of his 'superior', either in technical or in organizational terms, so he took him on in both. As time passed, so animosity increased, conflict grew, more people joined either the count or Nardelli in the fight, and more time and energy was spent both in guerilla warfare and in redrawing battle lines than in getting on with the job. It had to stop soon, but how?

Dr Nardelli was very attached to his role in the company, and felt he was doing well. Perhaps the productive output of his own small research group was not as good as it might be, but there was no doubt there were some brilliant people in the R & D function as a whole, and it was only a matter of time before breakthroughs would occur. Dr Nardelli was not complacent. He recognized that the conflict between him and the count was not the only problem around. But he knew that if it could be resolved, there was much to look forward to.

Count del Ponte Vecchio, in his turn complained that he had thought long and hard over his own career about how industrial research should be organized. Development was a very distinctly different activity and function. He had the experience of academic and commercial research, and had proven to himself what could be done. While he was the organizational subordinate, in practical terms, he was confident he had much more to offer. If only he was listened to, rather than threatened and ignored, he would offer it.

No, he had not understood that he should have formed his small group and left the management to others. He was full of energy and ideas. He had joined the company believing that they wanted those ideas in full measure, not just confined to a small university-style laboratory. He had been there, and found it very constraining. He wanted to test his ideas early, to see if they worked in the right environment. He wanted to take chances in the market place, like the Japanese do, to push prototypes out, to get quickly into commercial play. If they failed the test, then he would learn much from that failure. If they succeeded, he would be that much further ahead of the game.

The count felt that the company's position had always been conservative. It looked for reasons for not pushing products to market, being overly worried about reputation and convention. It put sales engineers in charge of technical trials, not scientists. How can any researchers get a true study of the receptivity and shortcomings of any prototype when salesmen, not scientists, are in charge of the evaluation? Such an evaluation is a matter for science. Research is a matter for scientists. We have to have the best from each discipline, he continued, and keep them in contact with the best of their discipline. We have to give them the best resources, otherwise we will not succeed. Development is about cash and management. Research is about commitment, focus, intelligence, and the wisdom to know when to go and when to stop. It needs small teams of creative people, who can drive large supporting teams of professionals, experts who effectively make their contributions as subcontractors. We need materials, scientists, electronics wizards, nuclear physicists, practical mathematicians. We need them to be trusted by us, and by each other, to drive new ideas into places of market verification, then to quickly pass them on to the development teams. Throughout all stages, we need people who are prepared to dream dreams without coming to depend on their continuance.

All this seemed to the chairman to be eminently sensible. Clearly it was possible to see the count's single-minded and pugnacious enthusiasm as egotistical, arrogant, irascible and self-serving. Yet even if it was all of these things, it was still worth ten times more to the company than five polite, altruistic, docile, decent chaps without an original idea in their heads. There seemed no real basis of animosity between the two men other than that which had been generated by too much, too public, conflict.

The first course of action became very obvious to Rossi. He did not know how good either Nardello or del Ponte Vecchio were as engineers, scientists, as managers or as businessmen. He had only gossip and hearsay to work from. His gut feeling told him that the count was the one he should back if push came to shove, but how could he judge? He needed an intermediary who would help him sort out which work was good, and which was not so good. He, the chairman, had to take on the role of champion, to demonstrate the company's long-term backing of its research and development effort. It was too important to be left to the R & D director alone.

Fortunately, there are people around whose objectivity, public recognition and critical scientific capacity are both high and equal. Rossi found one, Professor Carlo Benetti, from the same region as the count, but not known to him, at least not as far as anyone could tell. He offered him the role of scientific advisor to the board, a non-executive director position which was quickly accepted. Carlo Benetti was a modest man, but there was no doubting his honesty, his energy, or his reputation. This position was the first he had undertaken in the commercial world. Most of his work had been in universities and with the Defence Ministry research establishments. He was used to keeping highly political secrets.

The chairman's next step was to introduce Carlo to his board and take the time to consider MEI's whole business and scientific strategy for the next five years in parallel. The chairman sought much preparation for this venture, requiring each division to have senior managers meet, discuss and conclude their submissions as to scenarios, missions, plans and opportunities.

When the board met, it became clear that opportunities for R & D well exceeded the capability of the company to back them, as is always the case. However, projections showed that development, as defined by the count, well outpriced any research. Development work included a very large proportion of effort supporting existing products and manufacturing processes. This was mixed up with those resources which intermingled original with research, and with market testing. It was all very confused.

Quickly the board reached a conclusion. Creativity was not just about new products or research, or development, it was about managing a high-technology business as a whole. R & D division was broken up. The three different product divisions were each allocated a budget appropriate to their proportion of the R & D allocation, and helped to decide afresh how this should be spent.

Company-wide technical development was set up as an independent organization, an Associazione In Partecipazione, with shareholding offered to its staff, and launched as a business venture in its own right. MEI retained a minority shareholding. MEI was encouraged to contract non-dedicated, development work to this company, but not to be confined to it as a sole source. The cost-discipline on this potentially very uncontrollable aspect was therefore given its checks and balances. In any event, there are enough contract houses in Italy to fulfil most, if not all, MEI needs. This is a competitive market.

As to Nardelli and Count del Ponte Vecchio, each was asked to prepare a case for his own research company, identify its organizational and cost structure, its forward plan, and its constitution. They were required to consider the resources for only long-term research ventures. They must demonstrate that there was some relevance (not necessarily even very much) to MEI's long-term business aims. In particular they had to prove that they had the champions in place to make it happen for them. These forecasts were prepared in detail and put to Rossi, his finance director, and Carlo Benetti. They adopted a generous position in terms of allocation of funds.

Nardelli retained his position on the board as R & D director, with a focus on ensuring that interfaces between research and development worked effectively. The count was encouraged to set up his research unit as a Società a Responsabilità Limitata. He was able and willing to contract research both to MEI and elsewhere. He would offer research using funding sourced from within his internal budget. In this way MEI manages to have its cake and eat it too. Count Guiseppe del Ponte Vecchio gets his freedom, can create his own innovative culture and purpose, and finds no frustration to his ventures other than their proven eventual utility. Once the count's base was fixed and his interests secured, the chairman felt certain that he could ask more and more of him as an advisor on the research of others, on competitors and on possible licensors.

This left Rossi to turn his attention to the company's main concern. World-wide competition had eroded the relative standard of MEI products. The directors had become complacent because of the historically high earnings and relaxed market conditions. He needed to make people alive to the threat from the East. He embarked upon the far more arduous task of turning the whole company into a research and development establishment. He insisted that each product division set up supplier and consumer panels, where regular assessments were made by purchasers (internal and external) on the quality and competence of the supply. All potential new products were given the fastest possible airing and the highest priority. He encouraged the development teams in each division to work even more closely with the mainstream business to ensure that all status quo was tested for the value it added to the business. He put himself about, forever asking the question, 'What have you done today that gives us a better tomorrow?' He encouraged the organization to set up quality circles, offered rewards and recognition for the stars of innovation in the company.

He found a whole new source of satisfaction in his job, advancing across the company a new concept of user-dominated innovation.

Index

natural selection 142, 159
Nayak, P. R. 16, 17, 103
Netherlands 114–16, 166, 174, 235, 239
  Confucian Dynamism 177
  modesty 175
  New Scientist xxii
  New York Times, The 235
Newton, Sir Isaac 81, 125, 142
Nixdorf 111
Nobel Prizes 86, 94, 96, 123, 180
non-innovating companies 114
Norman, Donald 50
Norway 174
Nouvelle Revue Française 97
novelty xvii, 137, 150, 160, 207
  bounded 189
  changing lives through 124
  established as orthodoxy 158

obedience 13
objectives 19, 102
Ochse, Rhona xxi, 136, 189
Ogilvy, Angus 222
Ogilvy, David 57
Ogilvy & Mather xxiii 44
Oldfield, Mike 62
oligopoly 118
Olins, Wally xxii, 56, 220
  see also Wolff-Olins
Olivier, Laurence, Lord 138
Omni (magazine) 22, 155, 216
openness 13, 106
Oppenheimer, Robert 85–6
opportunism 79
opportunity 149, 154, 199, 208, 213
  restriction of 179
order 12
Organization for Economic Cooperation and
  Development 234
organizations 20, 56, 158–9
  creative 98–119
  innovative, opposing values in 12–16
  non-creative 117
originality 12, 30, 160–1, 204, 222
Orwell, George 212
Osborn, Alex 192, 200
overspecialization 223
Ovshinsky, S. R. 150
Owen, Maurice 113
ownership 69, 70, 114

PD (power-distance) 168–70, 171, 176
pain 202, 205
Pakistan 177
Panama 169
Parikh, Jagdish viii

Paris 95
Parker-Follet, Mary ix
partnership 73
passion xvii, *xviii*, 19, 205
Pasteur, Louis 141
patents 74, 103, 206, 218
  applications 178
patience *221*
patrons 47
Patterson, Neil 43
peer groups 49, 175, 212, 224
  evaluation 20
  reviews 110, 224
Pentagram 41
People's Express 63
Pepsi 228
perceived value 47
perception 167, 168
perfectionism 212, 213
performance 20, 113
  competitive 154
  standards 224
perseverance 14
persistence 130, 141, 175, 176
personal development 225
personal stability 176
personalities 225, 226
personality tests 54, 128, 203
Peters, Michael 41
Peters, Thomas J. vii, viii, 101, 254
Philippines 169, 174
Picasso, Pablo 200
Pickering, George 126
Pilkington Micro-electronics 28, 29
Pinchot III, Gifford 151
Planck, Max 138
planning flexibility 93
Plato 85, 179
Plessey 28
Poincaré, J. H. 134
Polynesia 65
Porsche 37
Portugal 169, 170, 173
Post-it 103, 104
potential 138
Powell, Nik 67–8
precision 12
predictability 12
preparation 133–4
presentation 29
Priestley, Joseph 178
primal virtues vii
Prince, G. M. 124, 195
problem domains 133, 134
problem-solving 36, 147, 191, 196
procedures and processes 102
prodigies 148, 163

Developmental Management

The following titles have now been published in this exciting and innovative series:

Ronnie Lessem: *Developmental Management* 0 631 16844 3 ☐
Charles Hampden-Turner: *Charting the Corporate Mind** 0 631 17735 3 ☐
Yoneji Masuda: *Managing in the Information Society* 0 631 17575 X ☐
Ivan Alexander: *Foundations of Business* 0 631 17718 3 ☐
Henry Ford: *Ford on Management** 0 631 17061 8 ☐
Bernard Lievegoed: *Managing the Developing Organization* 0 631 17025 1 ☐
Jerry Rhodes:*Conceptual Toolmaking* 0 631 17489 3 ☐
Jagdish Parikh: *Managing Your Self* 0 631 17764 7 ☐
John Davis: *Greening Business* 0 631 17202 5 ☐
Ronnie Lessem: *Total Quality Learning* 0 631 16828 1 ☐
Pauline Graham: *Integrative Management* 0 631 17391 9 ☐
Alain Minc: *The Great European Illusion* 0 631 17695 0 ☐
Albert Koopman: *Transcultural Management* 0 631 17804 X ☐
Elliott Jaques: *Executive Leadership* 1 55786 257 5 ☐
Koji Kobayashi: *The Rise of NEC* 1 55786 277 X ☐

* Not available in the USA   All titles are £18.95 each

You can order through your local bookseller or, in case of difficulty, direct from the publisher using this order form. Please indicate the quantity of books you require in the boxes above and complete the details form below. NB. The publisher would be willing to negotiate a discount for orders of more than 20 copies of one title.

Payment
Please add £2.50 to payment to cover p&p.

☐ Please charge my Mastercard/Visa/American Express account
   card number ☐☐☐☐☐☐☐☐☐☐☐☐☐☐☐☐

Expiry date _____

Signature _____
         (credit card orders must be signed to be valid)

☐ I enclose a cheque for £_____ made payable to **Marston Book Services Ltd**

(PLEASE PRINT)
Name _____

Address _____

_____ Postcode _____

Tel No _____

Signature _____ Date _____

Please return the completed form with remittance to:
Department DM, Basil Blackwell Ltd
108 Cowley Road, Oxford OX4 1JF, UK
or telephone your credit card order on 0865 791155.

Goods will be despatched within 14 days of receipt of order. Data supplied may be used to inform you about other Basil Blackwell publications in relevant fields.
Registered in England No. 180277 Basil Blackwell Ltd.